EDUCATIONAL
PSYCHOLOGY
CASEWORK

of related interest

Frameworks for Practice in Educational Psychology
A Textbook for Trainees and Practitioners
Edited by Barbara Kelly, Lisa Woolfson and James Boyle
Foreword by Sue Morris
ISBN 978 1 84310 600 5

How to Help Children and Young People with Complex Behavioural Difficulties
A Guide for Practitioners Working in Educational Settings
Ted Cole and Barbara Knowles
Foreword by Joan Pritchard
ISBN 978 1 84905 049 4

Addressing the Unproductive Classroom Behaviours of Students with Special Needs
Steve Chinn
ISBN 978 1 84905 050 0

Helping Kids and Teens with ADHD in Schools
A Workbook for Classroom Support and Managing Transitions
Joanne Steer and Kate Horstmann
Illustrated by Jason Edwards
ISBN 978 1 84310 663 0

Making the Move
A Guide for Schools and Parents on the Transfer of Pupils with Autism Spectrum Disorders (ASDs) from Primary to Secondary School
K.I. Al-Ghani and Lynda Kenward
Illustrated by Haitham Al-Ghani
ISBN 978 1 84310 934 1

Promoting Emotional Education
Engaging Children and Young People with Social, Emotional and Behavioural Difficulties
Edited by Carmel Cefai and Paul Cooper
ISBN 978 1 84310 996 9
Innovative Learning for All series

EDUCATIONAL PSYCHOLOGY CASEWORK

A PRACTICE GUIDE

SECOND EDITION

RICK BEAVER

Jessica Kingsley *Publishers*
London and Philadelphia

Table 2.1 on p.28 is adapted by permission of Mark Friedman.

First published in 1996 by Jessica Kingsley Publishers.
This second edition published in 2011
by Jessica Kingsley Publishers
116 Pentonville Road
London N1 9JB, UK
and
400 Market Street, Suite 400
Philadelphia, PA 19106, USA

www.jkp.com

Copyright © Rick Beaver 1996, 2011

Library of Congress Cataloging in Publication Data
Beaver, Rick.
  Educational psychology casework : a practice guide / Rick Beaver.
    p. cm.
  Includes bibliographical references and index.
  ISBN 978-1-84905-173-6 (alk. paper)
  1. Educational psychology--Great Britain. 2. Educational psychology-
-Great Britain--Case studies. 3. Child psychology--Great Britain. 4.
Child psychology--Great Britain--Case studies. 5. Interviewing--Great
Britain. 6. Interviewing--Great Britain--Case studies. I. Title.
  LB1051.B294 2011
  371.40941--dc22
                          2010043269

British Library Cataloguing in Publication Data
A CIP catalogue record for this book is available from the British Library

ISBN 978 1 84905 173 6

Printed and bound in Great Britain

Acknowledgements

I would like to thank Sue Bromage who shared the original idea of writing this book, and with whom many of the interviewing techniques were written.

I wish to gratefully acknowledge the professional inspiration and guidance of Tom Ravenette, from whom the ideas of professional educational psychology practice in this book derive, as do many of the interview techniques described. I also thank Tom for his valuable thoughts and comments on early drafts.

I would like to further acknowledge and thank all those colleagues from Newham Educational Psychology Service, Newham Child and Family Consultation Service, North West Kent Area Educational Psychology Service and Redbridge Educational Psychology Service who have also been so influential in the development of the ideas put forward in the book. I am paticularly grateful to, and thank, my colleagues in Somerset who over the last ten years have been inspirational in developing our service and helped me develop as a psychologist. I hope the model of practice described in this second edition benefits from a greater overall coherence and rationale than the previous edition, which is a reflection of the Somerset Service.

Contents

List of Figures and Tables

Preface

This book is intended as an introduction to some basic skills for educational psychologists, and others, who are involved in working directly with individual children and young people, in order to understand them better and promote change on their behalf. The models are presented to give an outline of both the theoretical background and guidance on how this translates into practical work.

The theoretical perspectives particularly arise from Personal Construct Psychology (PCP), Neuro-linguistic Programming (NLP), and family therapy, which complement the solution-oriented approaches which are now prevelant in educational psychology practice, and from experience have proved useful in bringing about change. It is not, however, intended as a reference text in respect of these models. Suggestions for further reading are included in the References section.

The ideas presented in this book are not original and have developed over time through work with numerous colleagues. The style of professional practice described is derived from the adopted practice of the educational psychologists in areas where I have worked where it is found as intrinsically rewarding, enabling change and generally valued by both the education authority, schools, parents and children.

However, the major ideas behind the practice, and much of the material presented, derives from the work of Tom Ravenette, who had been for at least two decades the Principal Educational Psychologist in the London Borough of Newham. It was his orientation to psychological practice, and his clear approaches to the work of psychologists, which provided a coherent, distinct and rational role for the psychologist. This allows a creative and constructive use of psychological skills and understanding, to make the work both exciting and meaningful. Although Tom died some years before the publication of this second edition, it is a tribute to his far-sighted view of educational psychology practice that these approaches continue to provide a firm foundation for current psychological practice.

This strategic contribution, however, was minimal in comparison to Tom's contributions to psychological casework practice. A well-known figure in the world of PCP, he had developed the means for the application of PCP to work with children. Several of these techniques are presented in this text; they show the application of PCP in a form which is accessible to children and young people. As interview techniques they also make PCP more accessible to the practising psychologist.

The techniques are not static procedures, but offer the foundations to develop creatively the application of theory into the practical interview situation, and perhaps for this reason they have not become published interview proformas.

Tom's assertion is that the question is the essential tool of the practising psychologist, but not just as a means to gather information; the question potentially shares a hypothesis and offers an intervention, enabling the client to explore more thoroughly their own personal meanings and sense of self. The techniques are ways of putting questions; the skill of the psychologist is to ask the question which will direct the client's exploration of their model of the world, and offer more constructive understandings. Perhaps the techniques are best seen as helping us, the psychologists, to ask more useful questions. The significance of the question as an exploratory tool for both psychologist and client is underlined by major sections of the text detailing questions derived from the theoretical models.

Although many of these interview methods are based on the application of PCP, Tom used a wide range of theoretical frameworks to provide an understanding of the children and young people he worked with. The crucial issue is always the exploration of the 'sense of self', that is, the child's understanding of the world in which they live and themselves within that world. This 'personal meaning' provides the sense and understanding of why behaviours (in the widest sense) occur, or not. The option of change can be offered through presentation of alternative understandings, or the offer of alternative 'personal meanings', to provide new perspectives of the world and the 'sense of self'. An interview offers the opportunity to provide the possibility of profound change. For the young person our meeting should be the point in time where change can begin: we are always seeking out a difference that can make a difference.

Of the other key influences brought into the text the most notable are NLP and systemic family therapy. NLP is a framework originally put together in the mid-1970s by Richard Bandler and John Grinder, and since developed extensively. There is an easy compatibility of NLP and PCP both sharing significant concepts of personal meaning, sense of self and a model of the world, and offering a solution-focused orientation. The two models are complementary, and the intention in the text has been to present the models as a coherent whole, although indicating from where various aspects have been derived, to aid further reading.

Family therapy models provide a systemic and contextual framework to the casework perspective. Children do not operate in isolation within the world, and an appreciation of their context including a systemic perspective is crucial to complement individual-based frameworks if we are to make a difference.

CHAPTER 1

Introduction: A Role for Educational Psychologists

The role of educational psychologists and the service we offer continues to come under scrutiny as does the rest of the education service through various initiatives from central government. We continue to need to demonstrate the effectiveness of the service we deliver in achieving positive outcomes for children and young people, and also ensure we are cost-effective intervention agents.

Since the first edition of this text there has been a widespread increase in the degree to which Special Educational Needs (SEN) resources have been delegated to schools without recourse to extensive assessment by psychologists. For psychologists working in Local Authorities (LA) which have adopted these models, and removed the traditional role of the psychologist as a gateway to resources, it has provided the opportunity to develop creative intervention-focused educational psychology approaches at both organisational and casework levels.

This text aims to present a framework for the psychologist's casework practice, which, while by no means original, presents as a basis for an effective educational psychology service which has an impact through achieving positive outcomes for children and young people.

We start from a view that psychologists are involved in enhancing children's achievement and well-being, as opposed to identifying deficits, or problems, in functioning. The concept of special educational needs can too readily provide the implication of a child or young person with a deficit, or difficulty, as opposed to an education system with a problem to solve. There are the same arguments around issues of disability. The most productive problem to focus on is what the system of influential adults within the child's world (this includes school staff, parents and others) can do to enable the child to make most effective use of the time they spend in education to develop and fully participate in society. The five outcomes from *Every Child Matters* (Department for Education and Skills 2003) provided a helpful framework to define the overall focus of our work, and while this model may have a limited lifespan, there is an overarching responsibility for all those working with children and young people to promote their safety, well-being and achievement.

It is proposed we accept the assumption that the system of influential adults has the resources to promote positive changes on the child's behalf. Despite the views of many (teachers, parents and psychologists), change does not always require more in terms of resources. It does frequently require new approaches and strategies to enhance the child's educational and developmental opportunities. It may be that alternative strategies and opportunities have resource implications. At times a plea for additional resources can be an alternative to accepting the challenge to create real change within the system. Indeed, seeking to identify the special educational need can be a vehicle for ensuring the problem is firmly located within the child or young person, rather than the system, and serves to allow the system around the child to remain unchanged, rather than recognise the need for the system to change.

The role of the psychologist therefore, far from identifying the child's special educational needs, should be aimed at identifying potential initiatives for change in the system. Psychological skills may be required more in terms of an ability to create change in the attitudes and behaviours of the adults than in devising detailed interventions for the child. The goal is to attempt to change the functioning of the system around the child in order to enable the child to change.

The psychologist is in a unique position to work with the immediate system around the child. By virtue of not being a full member of that system, the psychologist is able to have a 'meta' perspective, and is in a prime position to look at the wider system around the child, including the school, family and any other key individuals and influences. Our ability to take this wider perspective is particularly pertinent as our profession engages in a broader role with parents, schools and other services for children through which we can influence a wider spectrum of the child or young person's world.

This systemic perspective has a social constructionist approach, and incorporates the concept of circular causality as opposed to linear causality. This distinction is helpful in adopting an 'intervention opportunities' framework of practice in contrast to a 'child deficit' model. Circular causality does not presume to define the 'cause' of a difficulty within a particular individual, but acknowledges it as part of the functioning of the system as a whole.

There are two elements to the psychologist's role:

1. There are the psychological *skills* which enable the successful engagement with children, young people and adults, and also

promote effective relationships between them. Broadly these are rapport skills.

2. There is the psychological *knowledge* which provides a basis for making sense of situations and developing interventions, and an understanding of processes which promote change.

Rapport skills

Rapport skills are the essential part of any psychologist's ability to work with children and adults to create change. Where rapport is well developed, people will work well together, share objectives and attain solutions. Probably more than any conceptual framework for change work, rapport is the most influential factor in achieving a satisfactory solution or outcome to our work.

Many authors have linked the success of therapeutic intervention to the relationship between therapist and client (e.g. Strupp, Fox and Lessler 1969). Our own intuitive knowledge would indicate that, where there is a positive relationship between the child/young person, parents and school, problems are less frequent, and where issues arise solutions can be more readily found and achieved.

The research detailed in Appendix 3 provides some evidence of the link between school/parent contact and behaviour change in students in Key Stage 3. However, while these changes in behaviour seemed to be most strongly related to the school involving parents, parental involvement did not necessarily lead to change, nor did it always result in change for the better. Improvements in behaviour appeared to have an association with particular meetings where parents and school began to appreciate each other's point of view, potentially reflecting a developing positive relationship between school and parents. In contrast, where behaviour deteriorated, there was much less prior involvement between school and parents, and possibly a poorer quality of contact and relationship.

Chapter 3 will consider the skills necessary for the development of good levels of rapport.

The change process

Overview: Plan–Do–Review

The framework for the change process is presented in three parts: Plan–Do–Review (PDR). This is not dissimilar to change models in many forms of professional practice. Critically there needs to be a strong emphasis on defining the intended outcomes of any work.

The three elements of the process are described below.

PLAN

Planning involves an initial stage of sharing information and developing hypotheses about the nature, or dimensions, of a problem/issue which will underpin any intervention plan. This requires discussion between the psychologist and the person/people bringing the concern and able to facilitate change. It will involve exploring the issues and drawing up the intervention plan, and crucially includes agreeing the intended specific outcomes for the intervention.

The outcome is what we are seeking to achieve through the intervention. Gaining a shared agreement about what the specific outcome of the piece of work is across all participants is a significant step to creating change, and at times will be the most significant step in the change process.

This process should apply whether the focus of the work is individual casework or more organisational. The outcome, agreed by all the participants, not only provides a shared focus for the action plan, but also provides the basis for evaluating the effectiveness or impact of our work and the intervention.

In casework this planning needs to be done in partnership with those who know the pupil and are likely to have the greatest impact on the child's world. This will particularly include teachers and parents, and as we move to be more fully integrated with other children's services, there is the potential to include a range of other professionals.

Planning may require additional information and perspectives to be sought and may involve the psychologist in:

- discussions with a broader group of teachers and parents

- discussions with external professionals

- observations of the child/groups of children

- individual meetings with the child and/or parents.

The work at this stage is targeted to the development of an intervention plan based on clear hypotheses and may also, through developing hypotheses, refine the detail of the outcome.

DO

Having agreed the intervention plan, those key individuals participating will need to be clear about their roles in implementing the plan. This should be done over an agreed period of time up to a review date. The intervention plan is likely to involve both parents, school and possibly other professionals, and may involve the psychologist directly.

REVIEW

The review is essential to determine if the intervention plan is supporting change towards the previously determined intended specific outcomes. The degree to which the intended specific outcome is achieved can be used as a basis for determining the impact of the work.

Agreeing specific outcomes in planning, and reviewing progress to the outcome, provides validation of the process, hypotheses, intervention plans and the basis of our professional contribution.

We also recognise the crucial role of review in ensuring a commitment to participation and implementation of the intervention plan.

The role of the psychologist

Within this process the psychologist does not have total control of the planning or ongoing intervention, and in this respect the effectiveness of the intervention in achieving the specific outcomes is not the sole responsibility of the psychologist. However, the psychologist's input is significant in providing a psychological knowledge base to support the development of hypotheses and intervention plans. The psychologist leads, and will have a significant degree of control of the process, and through interpersonal skills and an understanding of negotiation, communication and interpersonal dynamics has a responsibility for supporting the positive participation of participants. To this extent the psychologist does carry a significant responsibility for the effectiveness of the intervention in achieving the outcomes.

Details: The problem solving and intervention process

The PDR process incorporates a number of key principles which are summarised below:

- identify the key people who need to be involved

- share responsibility for the solution to the problem

- be clear about what the solution is (what we are trying to achieve)

- focus on the Plan to achieve the solution

- clarify who will Do what

- agree timescales and Review.

We can extend the detail of the simple PDR process in change work through incorporating a problem solving and intervention model.

The model can be described by the flow chart in Figure 1.1. At each stage of the process information may be obtained which feeds back to refine the development of the earlier stages. The whole of the flow chart, from information gathering to review, represents the PDR process which in itself is cyclical as the reviews inform future planning.

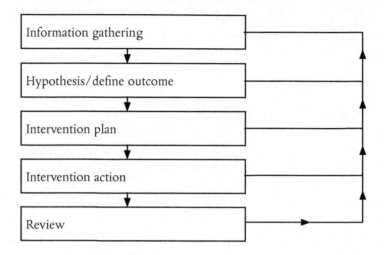

Figure 1.1 Problem solving and intervention model

The elements of planning: Information gathering, hypothesising and defining outcomes

Any information we have about a situation immediately provides the basis for a simple hypothesis, and an understanding of the dimensions of the problem. This emerging hypothesis helps identify what further information is needed, namely what further questions to ask, and what should be the focus of our outcome or what we are seeking to achieve.

Initial issues may be:

- what the problem is
- where it happens/doesn't happen
- who is concerned/not concerned
- what the secondary gains of the current situation for different participants are (which leads to the problem being maintained)
- what the consequences will be if the problem continues.

In gathering information about the concerns, we are attempting to gain some understanding of what underpins those concerns. The particular theoretical models the psychologist adopts provide the framework for understanding the information offered and for generating hypotheses, which in turn inform what further information may be usefully sought. The process is cyclical.

In solution-focused approaches, the emphasis will be more on gathering information to explore the detail of the potential solution, rather than protracted investigations of the problem. This reflects a greater concentration on defining and specifying the outcome. It is important to remember that the principal purpose of the involvement is to develop an intervention, and not necessarily a detailed analysis of the problem.

The psychologist, at a consultative level, not only brings particular psychological perspectives and hypotheses to the system, but also provides direction to look for solutions and interventions rather than a protracted analysis of the nature and degree of difficulty. In this respect hypotheses will reflect the problem and hypothetical solutions.

Where it is difficult to generate hypotheses, this is likely to reflect a need for more information.

The psychologist may have hypotheses about the functioning of the system which it is useful to share, or alternatively, through taking a meta-perspective to the system, they may have hypotheses about the system that they would wish to think carefully about before sharing directly with the members of the system.

Hypothesising and information gathering is a cyclical process which will progress into a developing intervention. The stages are not discrete. The process of information gathering and hypothesising is in itself an intervention. It is important to acknowledge that the way information is collected and any hypotheses presented will be oriented to promoting the potential for change in an appropriate direction.

To quote Dr A.T. Ravenette (e.g. Ravenette 1980), the chief tool of the psychologist is the question, and each question is a potential intervention. Particular attention needs to be paid to the form in which it is asked. Later chapters in the text outline theoretical models which are particularly strong in generating questions.

In establishing any working hypotheses with the system it is important to also gain agreement on the intended outcome to be achieved. This may be reflected in the initial concern, but may be refined through further information gathered, and the development of the hypothesis. The agreement of all participants to the intended outcome is a crucial step in ensuring that there is commitment from all participants, which will be necessary if they are to implement interventions.

Intervention

Interventions may be developed in several ways depending on the theoretical model used. Interventions may have an individual orientation or a systemic orientation, but always need to be solution oriented. That is, the intervention needs to be directed to achieving an outcome which will be a form of resolution to the concerns.

The psychologist needs to have hypotheses to inform ideas for interventions. Interventions based on systemic hypotheses may not always have the full detail of the hypothesis disclosed to the system, particularly if this is likely to create, or exacerbate, existing conflicts or disagreements.

An intervention needs to be agreed by all those who are going to be asked to contribute to it, and ideally should not require a commitment from any member of the system who is not present to give that commitment.

Realistic and 'do-able' interventions need to be proposed as these will be achievable, and also recognised as achievable. It is important to establish ways in which the success of an intervention can be demonstrated. The agreed outcome will provide the foundation for this.

This part of the process is probably that which offers the psychologist the greatest opportunity for creativity. The success of an intervention is predicated, in the first instance, on its being carried out. The psychologist's ability to develop rapport with the system will be a major factor, as well as the match of the intervention to the expressed concerns, and agreed outcome, identified by the members of the system. Clearly where interventions can be developed by the members of the system this will be the most valuable way of ensuring a commitment to carry out the intervention.

These key aspects, namely agreement, commitment and acceptance of a shared responsibility by the members of the system, underpin the ability to move from the intervention plan to the intervention action or implementation.

Review

The effectiveness of interventions needs to be reviewed. The review is a source of information which may suggest that further information needs to be sought, alternative hypotheses considered and further interventions suggested. It also gives the opportunity to celebrate success.

The period up to the review will need to be determined by the needs of the case, the confidence of individuals within the system of each other, and the intervention. The review process provides the basis for the psychologist's ongoing involvement with the case, and the basis by which to maintain the impetus of the intervention.

The agreement to a review is singly the most important driver in ensuring the commitment of the individuals involved in the intervention to carry it out. Adults with the best intention will carry out an intervention for a period of time. However, without the opportunity for review, which implies a commitment to the intervention for a fixed period of time only, it is unlikely that the intervention will be sustained.

In this respect the review is fundamentally a key element of the intervention process.

Effectiveness and impact

The impact of our involvement is defined through our work with the children and young people, and the system of the key adults around them, in reducing concerns through achieving the agreed intended outcomes. The review stage of the process provides the opportunity to do this where those in the system can reflect on the degree to which the intended outcomes have been achieved. While the degree to which this outcome is achieved provides the performance measure for determining the impact of our involvement, it is important that this measurement process arises from the work, or enhances the effectiveness of the practice itself. We should not allow the process of measuring performance to interfere with or confuse the change process.

Individual child interviews

Within this framework of practice the individual interview of a child with the psychologist has a foundation. The interview is frequently seen as information gathering, but also offers the opportunity to develop a rapport with the child (who is not often given the opportunity to share adult concerns in an open and blame-free way). There should also be the opportunity to help the child identify opportunities for change themselves, as every element of the involvement is an opportunity to promote change.

Child-initiated changes frequently occur and, when these are recognised by the adults in the system, they can be a powerful introduction to lasting change.

In general, interviewing is an attempt to gain information about how the child makes sense of themselves in relation to their world as they perceive it. From an educational point of view in particular, one may be interested in gaining insights into how a child makes sense of, and uses, information presented in a number of forms. This may appear to parallel a testing and deficit model, but there is a difference in approach. Instead of trying to identify cognitive deficits, more helpful approaches focus on:

- identifying the cognitive strategies a child uses, or attempts to use, in making sense of, and learning from, the different forms of material presented or the tasks given (e.g. NLP)

- identifying aspects of the child's approach to the learning paradigm and ways of mediating which are successful in supporting the child's learning (e.g. dynamic assessment).

The psychologist can be effective in helping to devise new strategies with the child and engaging those in the wider system to help the child. Even such intra-child-focused interventions can promote change in the wider system, as it is members of the system who will be involved in helping the child utilise these strategies.

The systemic perspective is particularly appropriate for psychologists working with a consultative model. Concerns expressed to the psychologist need to be viewed in terms of identifying the possibilities for intervention within the system. It may be necessary, if change within the system does not alleviate the concerns, to widen the system to include others in the discussion (parents, school, other professionals, other family members, etc.).

Individual interviews of children by psychologists may be useful where there is a perceived gap in the information available to those in the discussion, and it is felt that the required information could be gained through this course of action. An interview may also be helpful where it is felt that this will contribute significantly to the intervention. Psychologists need to plan their interview in advance to ensure that it will focus on what they hope to accomplish from the interview, and how this will effectively progress the casework.

The consultation model provides the basis for the psychologist to operate as an ongoing caseworker working towards change, rather than an identifier of needs. Indeed 'need' in this context is essentially the fact that someone in the system has a concern.

There is, of course, an end point other than the successful alleviation of all concerns. Unfortunately there are cases where despite best efforts change does not occur. This is when the system around the child has done all it can, or at least it is acknowledged by all that the system is unable to do more to promote change. At this point a radical change for the child may be the most appropriate step; this may involve a change in educational provision, referral to a more intensive provision, fostering, or accommodation by the local authority. This could be considered a failure of the casework of the psychologist (and others), in that they have been unable to fulfil their roles as caseworkers in promoting change on the child's behalf. This comment is not intended as a criticism of the casework, but is intended to highlight that achieving these outcomes is not a successful *psychological* intervention.

Resource-based changes may be based on no new information being available and consequently provide little qualitative difference in terms of new interventions. To this extent these interventions may well provide 'more of the same' and may unfortunately represent endeavours to cope with the problem rather than finding an opportunity to alleviate it.

Although it is often the case that more resources are needed to facilitate an intervention, it is important that it is the intervention that drives the requirement for resources and not merely information or hypotheses about the perceived difficulty.

The following chapters

The next chapter (Chapter 2) considers some of the issues around how we understand the purpose of our work, how we are able to demonstrate and reflect on our effectiveness and the impact we make on behalf of children and young people.

The text is then set out to consider the elements of the framework set out above. This includes: the development of skills for rapport building based on non-verbal and verbal elements of communication; models for gathering information and generating hypotheses based on systemic and individual-oriented approaches; and interventions.

In addition to a number of case examples to illustrate particular points, two fuller case examples are given (Chapters 13 and 14), to outline how interview approaches used together can provide information to help develop hypotheses and intervention plans.

The elements are not mutually exclusive, and a rigid separation is not attempted as it is particularly important to emphasise that information gathering, hypothesising and intervention are continually intertwined. It is hoped the text emphasises the spirit that every moment is an opportunity to make a difference.

CHAPTER 2

Measuring the Impact of Educational Psychology Service Practice

Most Educational Psychology Services (EPSs) adopt a consultative style of delivery and there is a professional consensus favouring consultative approaches and evidence-based practice to inform the methodology of our professional input. However, while agreed or evidenced methodology informs our approaches, it does not demonstrate the impact of our work or our professional effectiveness. It is important that we establish performance measures which enable us to monitor the effectiveness and impact of our contribution.

Service evaluation has traditionally used a number of approaches, the general thrust of which has included combinations of the following:

- service and LA contextual information (how many psychologists, pupils, statements, etc.)

- activity measures (time spent on different activities)

- hard data (SATs, exclusions, attendance, etc., timeliness of statutory advice)

- qualitative evaluations (questionnaires and interviews with service users).

The first two are not measures of impact on outcome. The third, hard data, represent some potential measures; however, the impact of our work on broad local authority-focused outcomes is likely to be distant and provides poor sensitivity as a measure of the impact of the service. Qualitative evaluations can often reflect how our client groups feel about the way our service is delivered rather than providing a measure of the impact it has on outcomes. Evaluations of this sort often reflect the level of rapport, mutual understanding and agreement the recipient has about the methodology of the service delivery.

Friedman (2005) provides a framework for our thinking about accountability. He acknowledges the frequent confusion in the use of terms and suggests clarification is necessary. The following are based on his approach.

- **Population outcome**

  This is a condition of well-being which is sought for children, families, etc. This is regardless of whether anyone receives a service or not. The five outcomes from *Every Child Matters* (Department for Education and Skills 2003) are of this form.

- **Indicator**

  This is a measure that helps quantify the achievement of a population outcome. For example, the number of children on the child protection register is an indicator of the outcome 'Staying Safe'.

- **Strategy**

  This is an action plan that is intended to lead to achieving particular outcomes. Consultation working or adopting an evidence-based practice are strategies aimed at achieving particular outcomes.

- **Performance measures**

  This is a measure of how well a service or action programme makes improvements for clients. This is the key measure of impact or effectiveness of the service and needs to be based on the degree to which the service makes an impact on the *specific outcomes* it seeks to achieve.

Friedman makes the distinction between 'ends' and 'means'. Population outcomes and indicators are about 'ends'. Strategy and performance measures are about the 'means' to achieve these. He also distinguishes between population accountability and service accountability. Population accountability refers to population outcomes as defined above, such as those from *Every Child Matters*. Service accountability reflects the contribution made by a service to population outcomes by achieving specific outcomes.

Friedman proposes a model of performance measures based on the intersection of quality and quantity vs. effort and effect. These are outlined in Table 2.1.

Table 2.1 Model of performance measures

	Quantity	Quality
Effort	*What we do* Number of customers served Number of activities	*How well did we do it?* Percentage of customers served well Percentage of activities performed well
Effect	*How many are better off?* Number with improvements in: • skills • attitudes • behaviour • circumstances	*How much better off?* Percentage improvement in: • skills • attitudes • behaviour • circumstances

Source: Adapted from the work of Mark Friedman in the book *Trying Hard is not Good Enough* (Friedman 2005).

Friedman indicates that not all of these performance measures are of equal importance. The more pertinent are the 'Effect' measures (those which tell us whether our clients' lives are better – lower half) and 'How well did we do it?' (those which tell whether our service and its related functions have been done well – upper right quadrant). The latter may include measures such as:

- timeliness
- accessibility
- cultural competence
- turnover/staff morale.

The more important 'Effect' measures he proposes are:

- Did client skills improve?
- Did client attitude change for the better?
- Did client behaviour change for the better?
- Is the client's life circumstance changed for the better?

Client here may be taken to refer to any group or individual on whose behalf a piece of work is done; however, the important link is that the specific outcome is supporting a population outcome. In this way the measure based on a specific outcome could link directly to the five population outcomes set in *Every Child Matters*, or any other overriding population outcomes which are set as the context and agenda. The link between the specific outcome and the population outcome provides the validity for the service engaging in the piece of work.

We can use the achievement of specific outcomes as the basis for performance measures for our own personal work as psychologists and the measure of service impact. The standard will be relative, that is, in relation to our own history (where our previous performance provides our baseline). Our challenge then is to seek to improve our performance against that baseline. Having a baseline of performance measured against specific outcomes gives us a very clear focus for reviewing and improving our performance and practice.

In order to be sensitive to the impact of our input, the evaluation needs to be close to the focus of our work and intrinsic to the model of service delivery.

The PDR model with a specific outcome negotiated and agreed with our partners in the system (child/young person, school staff, parents, other agencies) gives us a focus for a performance measure in terms of the degree to which the specific outcome is achieved. This provides an index of the impact of our involvement.

Friedman acknowledges that, for services or agencies working with children and families, service delivery is crucially linked with partners, and a significant question for us to ask in terms of our service delivery is how we can engage our partners to support the impact of our service delivery. In Chapter 1 we noted that the psychologist brings both psychological knowledge and skills to the situations in which they work. The ability to use psychological skills to engage all the partners in the system to work together effectively is a part of our role. While the effectiveness of the involvement in attaining the agreed specific outcome is the responsibility of all the participants, the psychologist does have a significant role in creating the circumstances where the participants will engage effectively. As such the effectiveness of the partnership in attaining the specific outcome through the PDR process is a good indicator of the impact of psychology service delivery.

In November 2009, an event for Principal Educational Psychologists to focus on the development of performance measures for EPSs attracted 160 delegates, representing one of the largest gatherings of Principal Educational Psychologists nationally and demonstrating how crucial this issue is for our services and profession. The imperative to show the value of the contribution of psychology is widely recognised in an increasingly challenging environment where demonstrating the positive impact on outcomes is expected. As a profession with a significant methodological and research bias, this should be intrinsic to our work. However, to be part of our everyday work, it is important that measurement of impact is simple, and intrinsic to the work, and does not become the end in itself.

The Audit Commission was represented at the conference and suggested the following points in relation to measuring impacts:

- It does not need to be rocket science.

- It does not require primary research.

- It does not have to be perfect.

- It should be applicable to indirect and direct work.

- It should be more widely applicable than just EPSs.

Essentially these parameters warn against our approaches being too sophisticated or over-elaborate.

As indicated above, the PDR problem solving approach, with its focus on setting intended outcomes in the early planning stage and reviewing against those outcomes at the review stage, provides a structure and foundation for measuring impact of service delivery across all pieces of change-focused casework, and other types of work where as good practice we adopt the same framework.

There are a number of models for evaluation of impact based on PDR using defined specific outcomes in the planning stage to indicate progress at the subsequent review as the performance measure of the impact of service delivery. The models described below are all founded on the PDR process.

The models

Goal Attainment Scaling

Goal Attainment Scaling (GAS) was developed by Kiresuk and Sherman (1968), with a focus on the evaluation of mental health services. It has been promoted as a model in educational psychology by a number of practitioners including Imich and Roberts (1990) and Baxter and Frederickson (2005).

In the plan stage of the PDR cycle, outcomes are defined from the areas of concern. It is suggested that there should be up to three areas of focus. These are operationalised as goals and a baseline descriptor is taken with a form of quantitative measure. This quantitative measure is then used to define an expected level of progress which could be expected by the time of the review. At the review stage this expected level of progress is used as the standard against which to define the actual progress at the review stage where the level of progress can be defined as:

+2: much better than expected level of progress

+1: better than expected level of progress

0: expected level of progress

−1: less than expected level of progress

−2: much less than expected level of progress.

This is done for each level of progress. The conversion of the progress into numeric values allows the collection and collation of data to give performance measures for the service.

Examples of the expected levels of progress descriptors are given below to show how the model can be adopted to reflect progress in learning and behavioural and emotional issues (examples from a very helpful briefing by Mallon 2006).

PRODUCTION OF WORK
With no more than two prompts:

−2: produces less than 30 per cent of expected work

−1: produces 30 to 60 per cent of expected work

0: produces over 60 to 75 per cent of expected work

1: produces over 75 to 90 per cent of expected work

2: produces over 90 per cent of expected work.

IMPROVE PLAYGROUND BEHAVIOUR

−2: excluded from school at lunchtime

−1: reported incidents on 3 or more out of 5 days

0: reported incidents less than 3 out of 5 days

1: reported incidents in less than 2 out of 10 days

2: reported incidents of less than 2 per month.

RAISING SELF-ESTEEM
When asked about self:

−2: identifies 0 positive things

−1: identifies 1 or 2 positive things

0: identifies 3–5 positive things

1: identifies 6–8 positive things

2: identifies 10 or more positive things.

Mallon also provides a more sophisticated approach to using the model which reflects the greater complexity of psychologists' work. One example is given below.

Case example

A pupil isolated in the playground does not have the skills to approach others or join in games (he has previously been diagnosed with autism). The focus or specific outcome for the intervention is for him to become more engaged with others in the playground, and the current baseline descriptor is that the pupil does not show, or is unable to use, any of the skills that are part of interacting with peers socially or in the playground.

The levels of the goals in this example might be:

+2: he will be observed as being a leader for games or as a child who starts up games

+1: he will be playing with others five times per week

0: he will be involved in playing with others on the playground three or more times per week

−1: he will only play with others sporadically (one or two times per week)

−2: he remains isolated in the playground.

ISSUES

As with all models based on the achievement of specific outcomes, defining the goals and descriptors of the expected outcomes is key to the validity of the model. Three points for consideration are:

- The ambition of the partnership working on the intervention will influence the degree of challenge in setting the goals and the descriptors of expected outcomes.

- Judgements in determining whether goals have been achieved will be dependent on the precision of definition in setting them at the planning stage.

- In choosing up to three goals, it is likely that these are not mutually exclusive and there is the potential for significant overlap.

The final concern which many authors in this area raise is that the model can be time-consuming, adding to existing practice.

Target Monitoring and Evaluation

In considering how to use GAS effectively in the PDR practice of psychologists, Dunsmuir *et al.* (2009) identified some of the issues above and sought to refine the model to make it more applicable in practice while retaining the rigour of the evaluation. They referred to this as Target Monitoring and Evaluation (TME). This retains many features of GAS particularly referencing progress to better than expected, expected or worse than expected. However, whereas GAS uses the five-point scale (-2 to $+2$ with predetermined descriptors), the TME model uses a 10-point scale similar to a scaling line in a solution-focused approach.

As with GAS, it is recommended that up to three targets are agreed with the participants involved, and these should be linked directly to the intervention plan.

For each of the targets a descriptor of the current or baseline level is defined, which provides a clear, unambiguous description of the current situation. This can relate to learning, behavioural or emotional targets. This baseline level is identified and marked on the 10-point scale.

At the same time the expected outcome of the intervention (as anticipated at the time of review) is similarly defined in a clear, unambiguous description. This expected outcome level is also identified and marked on the 10-point scale by the participants in the intervention. Logically this will be higher than the baseline level.

At the review, the post-intervention situation is described by the participants in similarly clear, unambiguous terms and used to form a judgement of where this should be represented on the 10-point scale.

On the scale the post-intervention level can be compared directly with the expected level. Where the post-intervention level is higher than the expected level, progress has been better than expected, and if lower progress is below that expected. In summary the possibilities for outcomes are:

1. Worst progress (post-intervention outcome score is below baseline).

2. No progress (post-intervention outcome is at same level as baseline).

3. Some progress (post-intervention outcome is rated less than expected level but above baseline).

4. Expected level of progress (post-intervention outcome matches expected level).

5. Better than expected progress (post-intervention outcome exceeds expected level)

This 1–5 coding of individual interventions provides quantifiable data which can be collected and collated to give performance measures for the service.

The model is easier to use than the GAS model, and also has close parallels to the scaling line in solution-focused approaches. It could therefore provide a positive practice approach to the PDR process.

Work status codes

This model is based on PDR with the inherent expectation that intended outcomes are agreed in the planning phase, and this forms the basis for review. At the review stage the partnership of participants determines how well the intervention has worked to achieve the outcome, and a key feature of this is the decision about how, or if, the work needs to be taken forward in another PDR cycle. The work status model collects this information as a simple record which can be used for evaluation.

This model has been used by Somerset EPS over a number of years for many aspects of service delivery including individual-focused casework. It uses a number of codes for recording the status of work at any particular point in the PDR cycle. The codes at review are defined to give an indication of the effectiveness of interventions in achieving the specific outcomes through defining the next phase of work as agreed with the psychologist and other participants.

The codes are recorded as part of a wider work recording system on the Education Management System database which records visits and work carried out by the service. The codes cover all stages of the PDR cycle; those used at the review stage are given below.

Review codes – performance measures

SI *Significant improvement* has been achieved – i.e. the identified concern or problem had been addressed, the desired outcome achieved and no further action is required at this stage.

IM *Improvements* but continued involvement by others required. Improvements have been achieved but continued monitoring or actions are required to maintain progress – i.e. the action plan seems to be effective, but needs to continue in its present form to ensure progress. This can be managed by school/parents/others without further involvement of the psychologist at this stage.

ICA *Improvements and continued action* — improvements have been achieved but continued planning, intervention and monitoring is required by the PDR group – i.e. interventions may not have been fully effective in achieving the desired outcome and need to be redesigned, modified or repeated.

NR *No real change* identified at this stage — continued work required.

EC *Escalating concern* — i.e. continued work with a refocus on the problem, outcome, hypothesis or intervention may be required, or the involvement of another agency.

SC *Significant change* in need identified – i.e. the previous action plan is now redundant and a new planning approach is required.

NLN *Intervention no longer needed/*relevant – e.g. child moved away, no longer in placement, etc.

The incorporation of the system within the existing activity recording means there is little additional work for the psychologist. Information can be collected and collated from the education management system to report on service effectiveness.

The annual reporting of performance data is given by the percentages of each coded category at the review stage. A typical example follows.

Case example

The data suggest that in approximately 33 per cent of reviews there has been a successful achievement of outcomes to the extent that the psychologist no longer needs to be involved in that piece of work (SI + IM). This is particularly significant when the context is that there may have been several PDR cycles prior to this successful achievement.

A further 46 per cent of reviews show improvement, but require further continued involvement of the psychologist (ICA).

This indicates that at review improvements are noted in 79 per cent of occasions.

Integrating approaches

Each model above can provide information to report the effectiveness of service delivery. They are all grounded in the PDR cycle, and derive their measure through establishing a shared intended outcome for the work at the early planning stage. The way these outcomes are defined and described is important in setting the standard for the measure of impact at review.

Ideally any approach needs to support or enhance the PDR work rather than create an additional process for measurement of impact. Certainly the TME approach, bringing an overtly solution-focused approach to the adults in the system, will have a strong appeal, but to be effective for measurement of service impact there needs to be universal adoption within a service. While the Somerset model has universal adoption across the service, the impact data are recorded by a proxy indicator.

Kent EPS developed a Target Monitoring and Review (TMR) process which aims to integrate the TME approach within the broader service model of practice: 'Kent Consultative Process – The Practitioner Practice Framework', which is based on the PDR process, and the Problem Analysis Framework (Monsen and Frederickson 2008).

The model emphasises the need to triangulate participant perceptions and behavioural-level indicators to inform judgements over time. The pilot work in Kent also raised the need to train colleagues in undertaking 'critical conversations' to clarify needs and plan coherent interventions based upon an accurate appraisal of presenting information so that a more targeted intervention can be planned and implemented. This is an important step for the service to begin to embed the TMR process within the general psychologist's practice.

This is an area of ongoing work for the profession and it is likely that several services will be trialling approaches over the coming years, adopting and refining processes as they develop.

Situations for use

Each model can readily be seen as applicable to individually pupil-focused work. However, the PDR principle should be applicable to most aspects of psychologists' work including group work, projects and research, set within the school or wider. All these forms of work should have specific outcomes from their initial inception and the impact of involvement can therefore be defined at review.

In addition to reporting on service impact the data can be used to improve practice and reflection personally and with others.

Personal reflection

At a personal practice level impact data can be an effective way of monitoring personal effectiveness as an educational psychologist and the effectiveness of the partnerships which arise in schools, particularly identifying those situations which are more effective than others.

Reflection with partners

Bringing an outcome focus to the work we do with our partners and/or clients also helps them focus on what they are seeking to achieve and provides a greater validity to partnership efforts to promote change.

Clear outcomes provide a vehicle to celebrate success at review and provide a further spur to develop subsequent interventions, and conversely when efforts are not making a difference they help focus on the barriers to change.

The impact data can be used to look at which partnerships seem to work effectively and which less so. For instance, it is easier to approach a school to discuss how effective work is if we have some comparative data on which to base the discussion.

Value in supervision

Impact data can be useful in supervision, reflecting on difficult cases, and processes within school. The data may help supervisors reflect on the different styles and practices of different psychologists that yield quite different levels of impact.

In all the examples above, the performance measurement data in itself does not provide a basis for making value judgements about practice, but can provide data which informs areas for further exploration of practice, including that which is successful and that which is not. In this respect the monitoring of practice through performance measurement provides some basis for our continuous improvements in professional practice. This will have implications for our own work as psychologists, but also can be used to inform school processes and practice.

These approaches may seem to reduce service impact to a numerical percentage and ideally we need to see this in parallel with other indicators including other hard data and qualitative indicators. However, it is important that services are able to present this type of information given the national focus on performance measurement. These models based on PDR using specific outcomes defined by the working partnership and reviewed by the same group are close to direct work and provide a relatively rigorous basis for evaluation which is sensitive to professional practice.

As a model for evidence-based practice, performance measures provide an opportunity for demonstrating the effect of our practice. This is based on each piece of work and can be used to inform future approaches to practice. The importance of the approach is in the constant monitoring of practice and application. There is also an explicit message within services, the profession and externally of the focus on the effectiveness of service delivery through demonstrable impacts.

CHAPTER 3

Rapport Skills

Although there are an enormous number of models and theories which provide frameworks for counselling and therapeutic work, the key factor which determines whether therapeutic goals are achieved is the quality of the relationship between the client and the worker. This suggests the most important element that the psychologist can bring to a situation is not their models for understanding problems and achieving solutions, but their ability to develop a rapport with those they work with. Strupp *et al.* (1969) found that patients' trust in their therapist was the single most important variable in successful work, to the extent that they wrote, 'This faith in the integrity of the therapist may be called the capstone of a successful therapeutic relationship subsuming other characteristics' (p.36).

At a very simple level it would seem quite obvious that no matter how valuable the hypotheses the psychologist's model provides, nor how potentially effective their proposed intervention strategies, if they are unable to develop the degree of rapport in their relationship with the client, these insights and suggestions will not be heard, or acted upon, and consequently will have little influence.

In all work with people, respect is generally shown by not presuming to attempt work without first establishing their desire for change. However, when work occurs within psychology services for statutory agencies, the perceived client is rarely the actual commissioner of the work. This is particularly the case for school-based work where schools generally define the client, and also define the desired direction for change.

Although to some extent it may be possible to re-define the client as the school in such circumstances, psychologists frequently find themselves working with a client who does not own the initial concern. In these circumstances the ability to establish rapport is a crucial element to successful work.

In any casework setting there can be a large number of individuals within the system who could be identified as the client or clients. It is important that in developing rapport with any one individual this does not compromise relationships with other members of the system. Enhancing the relationship with one member of the system must not be at the expense of the respect and relationship with another member. To promote really effective change possibilities, we need to create a working partnership including the young person, and the key people in the system, generally their teachers and parents.

The psychologist has several potential opportunities for engaging members of the system into a partnership, and it is important in doing this that they adopt and develop appropriate relationships with members of the system to maximise the possibilities of promoting change.

Key elements in creating such a partnership are neutrality (the basis of our relative relationship with all the partners), recognition of the young person's locus of control, and rapport skills.

Neutrality

In taking a lead in promoting change it is important to acknowledge that there is a problem, that the various people in the situation are uncomfortable with the current situation, although possibly to varying degrees. However, our stance should be that we do not take sides with any party against the others in exploring the nature of the problem and do not seek to attribute blame to individuals as the source of the problem. (There may well be exceptions to this – around child protection issues, for instance.)

In maintaining a neutral position it is important to avoid being judgemental, positively or negatively, about the validity of contributions of those involved, but seek to understand how they are making sense of what is happening.

Family system models offer neutrality as the appropriate professional orientation to work with systems. Neutrality in this sense implies that the psychologist remains neutral with respect to individual members of the system so that no allegiances are formed with individuals or sub-groups within the system which supports one part of the system at the expense of the other.

Adopting an orientation of neutrality helps the psychologist's perspective to remain 'meta' to the system, that is, the psychologist keeps an overview of the functioning of the system and does not become a part of it. This keeps the perspective of the system as external, rather than internal. Clearly if the psychologist were to fully accept the perspective of any individual within the system as the definition of the functioning of the system this would not be a meta perspective. Neither would it be a useful perspective, in terms of developing new ideas about the functioning of the system, as it would lead to the same stuck position experienced by that individual in the system.

A perspective of the system that is internal will not provide a full perspective of its functioning, as the perspective gained is dependent on the position it is taken from.

The notion of neutrality links with the principle of circular causality which recognises that 'blame' for a particular behaviour cannot usefully be attributed as the total responsibility of any one member. Instead circular causality acknowledges that the behaviours of individuals within the system be seen as an integral part of the functioning of the system as a whole. As such it would be inappropriate to provide support to any part of, or individual within, the system at the expense of another, as this would represent an acceptance of the perspective of the system from that individual's standpoint, which would tend to linear causality.

However, having made the point that the orientation of neutrality is the most appropriate stance for the psychologist, this is not to suggest that the psychologist should be cold and aloof. On the contrary, there is a need to develop a good close working relationship with all members of the system with whom there is direct contact, and also to respect the integrity of those in the system who are not available for direct work. It is most unlikely that any constructive work is likely to be achieved without this.

To be therapeutically neutral the psychologist must develop positive relationships with all the individual members of the system with whom there is direct contact, but offer no preference or unilateral support for one part of the system.

Support should be offered to the system as a whole with the purpose of facilitating its change. Developing a rapport with each member of the system, and establishing a trust and respect for all, provides a good model for those in the system and promotes the principle of co-operatively working together to enable the system to take responsibility for addressing the concerns.

Locus of control

Locus of control refers to the level of personal control the individual has in a particular situation. This is relevant in thinking about the degree to which the child/young person can take responsibility for change, and the extent to which the system around the child (the key adults) needs to take that responsibility.

For younger children, the system is predominantly defined by the key adults in the child's life. The adults define what is wrong and right, what should or should not be done, and to a significant degree what can and cannot be done. The child's sense of identity, values and beliefs are also closely defined by the key adults in their world.

The young child has less personal locus of control and, in terms of responsibility for change, adults need to see themselves as the key players. While the child should be an active participant in voicing and understanding the concerns, defining the sought-for outcome, and developing the interventions, the adults need to take responsibility for initiation and maintenance of the process. The implication is for greater systemic work, that is, changing the way the system works around the child.

Older children and young people can be seen as having a greater personal locus of control, and while this may enable a greater level of personal responsibility to be given to the young person, it needs to be paralleled with a greater engagement with them in defining the problem, and the problem solving process. However, there also needs to be recognition that aspects of the world about them could be a force to promote change, a barrier to change, or represent inertia to change.

For older young people there is a wider system likely to be defined by a broader group of influences, media, peers and a range of adults beyond parents and teachers. The world itself can be harder to engage in the change process and this provides a practical reason for a greater focus on individual work. Nevertheless it will be important to ensure that the key players in the system are engaged as a force promoting change and supporting the intervention.

Rapport and interpersonal communications

Interacting with people with whom we have a good relationship, whom we know and feel comfortable with, is easy; we get on well, tend to find areas of agreement, appreciate each other's point of view, and our work goes smoothly. Most of us find this reasonably easy most of the time, and we can quickly develop working relationships with people.

Workers in the field of NLP, have looked in detail at how good relationships evolve, in order to understand how rapport develops so that we can model the process and enhance our effectiveness in forming good relationships. These skills become of particular use when working with people we may otherwise find difficult to get on with, when we find significant areas of disagreement, and when we have limited opportunities to develop a good relationship. In an interview, be it with an individual, or group, there is only a limited time to develop a relationship of trust, so the skills to enhance the speedy development of rapport become particularly valuable.

Effective relationship building is often considered to require 'warmth', 'empathy' and 'genuineness', following Rogerian-based approaches (e.g. Rogers 1965) which emphasise positive affirmation. Though these are useful principles, if we are to be skilled in developing relationships quickly, we need to explore the specific details of rapport skills.

The underlying processes can be identified and broken down into behavioural skills which can be learned. As with most skills, however, they require practice to be used effectively and elegantly.

Rapport starts with what in NLP is called Internal Subjective Experience, that is, our understanding of the world and everything in it, including ourselves, is built on our individually constructed internal model of the world. This model is subjective, based on the experiences we have encountered in life, and represents all the rules and understandings we have inferred about the way the world works. These rules are the model by which we make sense of our world and the people in it, including ourselves.

Clearly we will all have different models of the world as we have all had different life experiences. Our model of the world (sometimes also called map of the world) will include all our beliefs, values and sense of personal identity, in addition to our understanding of how things (and people) work and behave. For each of us the world is only what we understand it to be.

We can never actually experience another person's model of the world, or have another person experience our model of the world (we might at times think we do, but this is an illusion as we are not able to mind-read). In communication, however, we do attempt to share with another the content of our model of the world. Within the communication process there are several points where information is lost through interpretation, or misinterpretation.

In attempting to communicate about our model of the world we have to put our internal subjective experience into a communicable form, language, gestures, vocalisations, etc. The recipient of the communication has to interpret these behavioural and language-based communications within the context of their own model of the world to infer the meaning of the communication.

When considered as a two-way process over time, it is almost surprising that effective communication ever occurs. It may well be that communication does seem to occur effectively not just because our models of the world are similar, but because the forms of communication we are able to use are so vague and imprecise in content that we are able to make a satisfactory interpretation of the communication in the context of our own model of the world, which we are happy to accept as the intended meaning of the communication. However, this may be quite different from the actual intended meaning behind the communication. In this way we seem to be able to go through our interactions quite satisfactorily with possibly only the vaguest shared understanding of what we each really mean.

Given that we all operate out of our models of the world, then all our communication will be a reflection of our model of the world. Our communication can be considered to be the entirety of our behaviour; that will include what we say and how we say it, in addition to how we stand or sit, the gestures we use, etc.

Mehrabian (1972) conducted studies to determine the relative importance attributed to the elements of communication, finding:

- verbal content (words) accounted for 7 per cent

- vocal influence (tone, tempo, volume) accounted for 38 percent

- non-verbal influence (distance, gestures, posture, etc.) accounted for 55 per cent.

The study indicates the powerful influence of the non-language aspects of communication in an interaction. The generalisation of the results from the original paradigm has been criticised, and one would certainly expect that the relative importance of the language content would be greater in a lecture than a conversation, for instance. Nevertheless, the study does show the potential importance of the non-language elements in effective communication. There is a value in being able to communicate effectively both non-verbally as well as with spoken language.

In developing rapport our aim is to use our communication skills effectively to communicate a sharing of our models of the world. With people we get on well with, we are easily able to communicate at some level that we share an understanding about the world.

The three elements of rapport are that we *recognise* that a person has their own model of the world (which will not be the same as our own); we provide *reassurance* that it is safe for them to demonstrate their model of the world, and disclose aspects of it in the interaction; and finally that their model of the world will be *respected.*

Rapport is essentially a congruent communication from one person to another that they appreciate the other's situation and thoughts, and understand their point of view. This is communicated both verbally and non-verbally, and there must be congruence in these elements of the communication.

This communication, that there is a matching of models of the world, has to be done despite the imprecision in the communication system referred to earlier. We can never know the content of another's model of the world; however, given that their behaviour in the form of communication reflects their model of the world, we can demonstrate the shared perceptions of the world through matching elements of their communication directly.

This matching of communication is particularly effective in relation to the non-language elements of behaviour, as these tend to be less in conscious awareness than the language elements.

Pacing and leading are the key concepts for a systematic means of building rapport. Pacing is the process of matching, over time; that is, communicating the recognition and respect for the other person and their model of the world. By giving a subtle match of their communications verbally, and particularly non-verbally, this message of commonality, or appreciation of the other's model of the world, is conveyed.

Although the concept of matching is one which seems to suggest the action of one person on another, an interaction is a two-way process. Matching in this way will occur in both directions between the people involved in the interaction. One person is not likely to gain a rapport with another person where it is not reciprocated. Pacing is a two-way process. As one person follows the other's behaviour in matching, the other will be effectively leading the process. Who is pacing and who leading will change backwards and forwards through the interaction. In the interaction there is mutuality; one does not control the other. Another way of viewing it is that in order to lead the other into a new direction one has to give up control of the situation by pacing to begin with, so control is only gained by giving up control. Control, therefore, is not a key element; the value of developing these interaction skills is in becoming more aware of one's own behaviour, the behaviour of others, and the interdependence of this in the developing interaction.

Pacing and leading occur naturally in any arena where people interact. A good example is watching a group of people chatting over a drink. In getting on well together they tend to adopt very similar postures, gestures and other external behaviours; notice when one of them takes a drink the others will follow the lead, all taking a drink at the same time.

Pacing behaviour over a period of time can establish a level of rapport so that with a change in behaviour it is possible to change from being the follower to the leader. The other person will be inclined to follow this new behaviour as an extension of the ongoing interaction. This is called leading. With the development of rapport through pacing all elements of the communication, it is possible to lead the other person into new behaviours, perceptions, understandings and ideas, the process operating not just at a behavioural level but in more cognitive and affective areas as well. Pacing and leading can be seen as the essential feature of such techniques as reframing where the reframe is likely to be accepted if it is initially paced into the other person's model of the world before the lead into the reframe is offered.

The skills of pacing and leading, as all skills, are developed through practice. Practice and observation can provide interesting experiences and will enable very professionally skilled communication. An essential element of matching communications is that the match needs to be kept at a largely unconscious level. When pacing becomes conscious and obvious, as is the case with mirroring, then this will serve to break rapport.

A series of exercises are given in the appendices which can be used to develop rapport skills, particularly non-verbally. These have been developed by various NLP practitioners and trainers (e.g. Robbie 1987). To develop skills in pacing and leading, the exercises in the appendices emphasise the need to develop flexibility in our own behaviour in order to match the behaviour of others, and our sensory acuity in order to detect the subtle changes and behavioural patterns others characteristically use.

An example of the value of rapport skills in working with clients as a psychologist is given below. This example is included because, although many examples of the effects of rapport skills can be felt to have been valuable in working with clients, and many examples of pacing and leading can be given, this casework example represented a piece of change work which, at least initially, was based purely on developing a good level of rapport through pacing and leading.

Case example: Nora

Nora, a girl of Asian origin, speaks Urdu as a first language. She would speak this at home, particularly with her mother. She would speak English with her peers at school, but not to her teachers. Nora's father had expressed concern to the school that she would rarely speak to adults outside the family home, even relatives with whom she was very familiar. Although concerns about Nora's reluctance to speak had been noted since nursery school, she had made reasonable progress academically. Both the father and school were mystified at Nora's reluctance to talk.

It was agreed Nora would be seen once individually by the educational psychologist before suggesting a more family-based approach.

Initially in interview Nora appeared nervous and gave little more than nods and shakes of the head. However, by matching the postures, gestures, breathing and tone and tempo of her brief utterances, rapport was developed. After 20 minutes with gradual leading in rapport, Nora was happy to tell the story of a book she had recently read. She further became involved in a discussion of how adults, particularly the head teacher, would be interested in listening to what children had to say. By the end of an hour the head teacher had been invited into the room and had become involved in the discussion. Nora finally agreed to finish reading her current reading book and tell the story to the head teacher.

Pacing and leading is a major theme of NLP; it is the primary skill to learn and forms the basis for rapport building, a necessity for all interpersonal work. At a more fundamental level it is the major prerequisite to all the methods which are considered in this text. The focus is an appreciation and respect for the other's model of the world. It is necessary to meet the other person at their model of the world before it is possible to offer them an alternative view which they will be able to use or appreciate.

A number of the intervention techniques considered later, such as reframing, use of stories and metaphor, will have a clear principle of pacing and leading underpinning their effective use.

Matching and mirroring

Matching is very different from mirroring. The latter is a direct copy of the other's behaviour, as would be given by a mirror. If mirroring were used this would be likely to cause offence (in effect breaking rapport), as it is very apparent what is being done, which is not experienced as respectful. Attempt mirroring with a friend and it soon becomes apparent that it is quite hard to sustain the interaction. Usually this results in a breakdown into laughter. If the same were attempted with an unfamiliar acquaintance the consequences may be more serious, and aggressive!

There are a number of ways of providing a match to behaviours which avoid mirroring; this may be using similar behaviours or communications, but with a time delay, or in a minimised form. For instance, if someone is using bold hand and arm gestures, these may be matched using small movements of the fingers which convey the same pattern of movement.

In another approach the pattern of behaviour can be matched but in a quite different form, for instance matching breathing with the rhythm of your voice is a powerful match for rapport in Ericksonian hypnotic techniques (e.g. Bandler and Grinder 1975).

An example of this was related by a colleague who, while attending a lecture by quite an eminent psychologist, was practising matching skills. Through the talk the lecturer paced from one side of the stage to the other. This offered my colleague an opportunity for matching by swaying gently from left to right in his seat as the lecturer walked from left to right across the stage. After a period of matching in this way my colleague suddenly stopped in mid-sway and reversed direction. The lecturer promptly made an about turn in the middle of his walk from one end of the stage to the other. This happened three or four times before my colleague became a little embarrassed and decided to start paying a bit more attention to the content of the talk.

Paying attention to the subtle behaviours of others, practising matching and developing these skills can be both informative and at times surprising. It is, of course, important to be respectful of others and if the signs are that the other person is aware of something going on then this is an indication that the matching is not subtle enough.

Gaining the balance between effective matching and yet not being overt is an area for practice and development.

Leading

The process described in the previous example is that of leading. This is where rapport has been gained to such an extent through matching that the other person will now match when you change your behaviour.

Observing non-verbal behaviour in meetings is useful. A group of people meeting round a table will often have very similar postures as they are all engaged in the discussion. If, for instance, each person is sitting leaning against the table, and one of the group sits back, the entire group follow almost like a domino chain. Similarly one person can bring them all back to the sitting forward position. Observation of the interactions of others and oneself in such situations can provide good learning experiences.

Essentially leading is making some form of behavioural shift once in rapport, after pacing. If the other person follows the lead then it can be inferred that a level of rapport has been developed. Leading occurs when the other person has a sufficient sense of rapport that they will pace, or match, the lead which has been given. In this sense leading can also be used to gain feedback about the level of rapport that has been achieved. If a lead is not followed then there is the possibility that rapport has not been established sufficiently and more pacing is required, or alternatively the lead represented too great a discrepant shift from the model of the world being paced.

Pacing and leading can be considered a basic principle in all communication from non-verbal behaviours, through language patterns to ideas, understanding and self-identity. This represents and demands a high level of respect for the other person, both for themselves, their model of the world and their identity within it.

Congruity and incongruity

We have noted that there are numerous channels of communication. Often messages given are not congruent, that is, the same in each channel. For instance, the verbal message may be 'yes' but the non-verbal message may be 'no'. In order to develop rapport it is important that all channels give a congruent communication in providing a match, otherwise the communication will appear insincere.

Clearly when the communication from the other person appears incongruous it will be difficult to pace this satisfactorily. There are a number of strategies for dealing with this, as to address it directly may not necessarily be the most useful. Some examples of these are given in the appendices.

CHAPTER 4

Problems and Solutions

While it is important to explore the dimensions of a problem (an exploration of what makes it a problem and for whom), it is not necessary to search the past for a cause of the problem, nor indeed is it necessary to understand the cause of the problem to find a solution. Within the world of child development and psychology it may not be feasible to identify a precise cause to a problem. Where attempts to do this are tried, it can often result in an identified cause which is not within our scope to make a difference, and as such can be a hindrance to finding solutions rather than an aid.

Attempting to define the problem through identifying a cause, or who/what is to blame, as an agreed perspective for all participants in the system can be difficult to achieve. Alternatively aiming for a shared perspective of recognition of the current state and developing a shared perspective for an agreed outcome, which can be the basis for exploration and developing a solution, is the more helpful focus.

It is useful to explore how different participants (child, parents, teachers, etc.) may perceive the problem, and how it is a problem for them. This is important in establishing rapport as it is meeting each participant at their model of the world. It also offers the opportunity to identify how potential solutions can help resolve different facets of the problem for each of the participants.

The different participants may each have a different way of understanding the cause of the problem and attributing responsibility or blame, but as previously noted, exploring these aspects is likely to be unproductive and unnecessary. It can also hinder the process, as there are likely to be significant disagreements on these issues, and they are not necessary to work towards defining the solution.

The key principle is that it is not necessary to search for a cause, or have an understanding of the cause, of a problem in order to achieve a satisfactory resolution or outcome.

To give an over-simplistic example, if a young person complained that Mr Smith (a teacher) was picking on him, a non-neutral response would be to say, 'Mr Smith is a very fair teacher, who has high standards and works hard to get the best out of pupils, so he does expect a lot of work and attention in lessons.' Though positively connoting Mr Smith's approach, it effectively denies and dismisses the young person's view, and, by implicitly defining Mr Smith's behaviour as reasonable, defines the young person as the problem – which is unlikely to engage them in a process to help resolve the problem.

A more neutral approach would acknowledge the young person's perspective (though not necessarily agreeing with it), and explore the issue. This exploration could take many directions. It could focus on the detail of the problem, or explore potential opportunities for solutions. This may then challenge the young person's conclusions and generalisations about the situation.

The difference in approach is characterised by the contrast in questions. Some question forms seek to identify the cause of the problem; some explore the detail of the presenting problem; while others explore potential areas of solution.

Approaches

In relation to the example above, these approaches are outlined by the questions below.

Questions which seek to identify the cause of the problem

How does Mr Smith pick on you?

How come Mr Smith chooses you to pick on?

Why does Mr Smith pick on you?

Does Mr Smith pick on other pupils?

What do you do which makes Mr Smith angry with you?

Questions to explore the detail of the problem

What does Mr Smith do when you think he is picking on you?

When does he do it?

What do you do when you think Mr Smith is picking on you?

What's important to you in the way that Mr Smith behaves that makes it feel like he is picking on you?

How come it's important to you to behave in the way you do when you think Mr Smith is picking on you?

What do other people think when Mr Smith does that?

Questions to explore solutions

>Are there any times when Mr Smith doesn't pick on you?
>
>When Mr Smith doesn't pick on you how do you speak to each other?
>
>What would be different if you didn't feel like Mr Smith was picking on you?
>
>>What would Mr Smith be doing differently?
>>
>>What would you be doing differently?
>>
>>What would other people be doing differently?
>
>How would you know if Mr Smith wasn't picking on you?

The questions demonstrate the difference between accepting and seeking a cause of the problem, exploring the problem, and exploring the solution. While not denying or dismissing the young person's point of view, the questions to explore details of the problem and solutions seek to explore and expand the young person's perspective, potentially identifying underlying issues, as opposed to causes. These types of question promote a greater sense of partnership in exploring the issues, maintain neutrality and recognise the balance in locus of control between a personal responsibility and the impact of the context of the world around the young person.

Exploring the solution

Frequently when there is a problem, participants have little idea of what it is they are seeking to achieve as a solution. A solution is not the absence of a problem; it needs to be defined so that there can be a (shared) perception of what is to be achieved as a positive outcome.

To achieve change we need to identify the desired state, solution or outcome. In our role in supporting the change process we want to arrive at an agreement amongst the key participants about the form of outcome we are seeking to achieve. This in itself can be a highly significant step towards achieving the solution.

In exploring and developing solutions, we work on the assumption that there are exceptions to the problem state, that people have resources and competencies which will help achieve the outcomes, and that small changes can generalise to larger changes, as a virtuous spiral.

Acknowledging and exploring exceptions

It would be rare to find that any particular problem occurs all the time in every situation. There will be times when it does not occur. These are the exceptions. In some ways the times when the problem does not exist are those times when a solution or satisfactory outcome already occurs. We need to know more about how this happens.

In exploring the exceptions we want to identify the contexts, surrounding events and how people are interacting and feeling when the problem is not occurring.

Questions to elicit exception

Can you tell me about a time when [the problem] does not happen?

When does the problem not happen so much?

At what times does the problem not bother you so much?

When are things going well?

Questions which focus on the details can also be helpful

When does Johnny talk politely?

When does he get on with his work?

When does he pay attention?

When do you feel positive in his company?

What is the closest you have come to feeling calm when working with him?

Can you tell me about the times when John manages to stay in lessons?

What sort of strategies have you used which saw even some small sign of success?

Can you tell me about a time when you have got on with Mr Smith?

Can you tell me about a time when you did get your homework in on time?

Can you tell me about a time when you felt angry but controlled yourself?

Exploring the difference between the problem state and the exception can give useful information

> What is different about this example and the times which lead to trouble?
>
> How come it's different then?
>
> What do you do that is different?
>
> How come you did that?
>
> Who would notice that things were different?
>
> Who would notice that you were trying to make things different?
>
> How would you know that other people had noticed a difference?

These types of question provide a lot of opportunity for exploring the issues surrounding a problem from the basis of seeking the solution. They can identify opportunities for change, and will also highlight barriers to the solution (but this is not the same as exploring the source of the problem).

Finding and exploring competencies and resources to solve difficulties

Often people assume they are not able to resolve a problem, or find a solution, because they assume they do not have the personal resources to achieve it. They attribute the failure to resolve the issues as due to their own shortcomings.

In general people can find personal resources to resolve problems in their lives, provided they are committed to the solution, and are prepared to put their efforts to it. However, they may not recognise the personal qualities that will help them attain the goals they seek, within the particular area of the problem. They may have significant and useful personal resources which are apparent in other aspects of their life.

Young people who struggle with the academic curriculum in school easily take on an academic self-perception as unable, lacking the skills and competencies to learn. However, in other areas of their life they may be able to show high-level skills and competencies. This might be a mechanical understanding and skill in working with tools and machinery; skills in games which require a good conceptual understanding and thoughtfulness to play tactically; and physical activities, dancing, gym, etc. which require practice and concentration.

Exploring, or highlighting, the skill areas where they are competent and confident, and relating this to the area where the problem needs to be solved, can be empowering and help create a sense of personal resource to have an impact on the problem.

This is not just an issue of academic skills as in the example, but can be considered in relation to social skills and confidence in situations, managing emotions and behaviour, etc.

Personal resources may be identified through looking at behaviours, skills, qualities and attitudes apparent in situations where the problem does not exist, that is, exceptions as described above.

Compliments can be a powerful vehicle for recognising or highlighting the person's skills, attitudes, positive identity, etc. For those who experience problems, or are at the centre of problem issues, genuine, credible compliments can be rare, and when received can have a profound effect. However, it must be stressed that the compliment is given genuinely and needs to be credible in terms of the young person's sense of the world and their sense of self. These are the principles of rapport discussed previously.

Identifying resources in people is a question of positively connoting their personal qualities and making the connection for them from one area of their life to another, so that these qualities can be brought to bear on the problem situation.

Small changes generalise to significant change

The experience of a small change by both the individual and the system is important in creating the sense of change as a realistic possibility. A small change presents the real possibility of a virtuous spiral of change arising through the system's recognition and reward of the small change leading to further changes. The key is that when the individual makes the small change, or effort to change, the system not only supports this, but is prepared to look for and able to see the change, to recognise and reward it.

The psychologist is in a powerful position having access to the child or young person and the main elements of the system in which they live, particularly the school and family. Co-ordinating the individual effort to change and the response of the system to recognise and support that change is a powerful approach to promote successful intervention.

CHAPTER 5

Hypothesising and Information Gathering

General points and basic axioms

Our understanding of the system in which a child lives, or the model of the world which a child has, is at the level of hypothesis, and cannot be assumed to be truth. Indeed a number of different hypotheses could be generated in relation to a system and any particular presenting behaviour.

In psychology, however, we need to acknowledge that we do not know the answers, or have the truth. There are no single truths in an interaction, as the understandings which are held can only be based on the perceptions of the individuals involved. It is only possible to provide hypotheses, to give a sense to a situation, or issue. There is no sense in which a hypothesis can be deemed to be correct. Indeed the issue is not particularly relevant; the important issue is whether the hypothesis has been successful in arriving at a satisfactory intervention, that is, one that is effective in promoting a change in the child's (and adult's) behaviour. The success does not have any bearing on whether our hypothesis is correct or not, merely that it has been useful.

Hypothesising is the way a psychologist tries to make sense out of the information that is available about a child and the system in which it operates.

The basis for formulating hypotheses available to a psychologist is provided through the theoretical frameworks and psychological models which help them make sense of the situations, systems and presenting concerns they are asked to work with. The greater breadth of theoretical models that a psychologist is familiar with, the greater will be the range of possible hypotheses. A wider range of hypotheses will offer greater opportunities for intervention. Clearly there could be a number of hypotheses for a particular case.

There may be hypotheses that a psychologist may not wish to share with the members of the system, and others which they may willingly share.

Particular hypotheses about how the child and system are functioning will serve to inform the direction for change, and the basis for devising interventions. Hypotheses also provide a basis for deciding what further information could be usefully collected to refine the hypothesis, seek to confirm its appropriateness, or decide to reject it. Hypotheses are clearly not useful unless they are informative and helpful to the psychologist working with the system, and those in the system.

The following sections and Chapter 6 provide some theoretical frameworks for making sense of information and hypothesis generation in relation to presenting concerns. All psychological models have some validity as frameworks for hypothesis generation, but clearly there is a preference for models which provide an orientation to possibilities for change.

Two useful axioms for hypothesis generation

The first axiom
The first axiom proposed here as a foundation for the work of a psychologist involved in working with people is common to many psychological theories, and represents a central tenet of both PCP and NLP. The axiom is simply that:

> *A person will behave in a way that is in their best interest, given what they know at the time, their understanding of their situation, their model of the world and their view of themselves within that.*

In the interests of brevity of description, the individual's model of the world is always assumed to include their understanding of their world around them and their view of themselves.

This is the axiom which could be seen as separating the professional psychologist from the lay person, in relation to their view of others. There is an acceptance that the client is not damaged, or broken, or behaving irrationally. Indeed it is the assumption that their behaviour is rational that is the basis of the axiom.

People may behave in a way inconsistent with *our* desires, or irrationally in terms of *our* model of the world. Within the axiom this discrepancy between an individual's behaviour, and how we would wish them to behave, is attributed to the discrepancy between that person's model of the world, and our own.

What is in their best interest may not seem apparent to an observer, but reflects the world they understand and how they see their role in it. These views may not be well considered or logically thought out and would not necessarily be easy for the individual to express coherently.

As an axiom of psychological practice, the purpose is to prompt the psychologist to explore the issues as if this were true. The contrary view would presumably suggest that the individual behaved according to some other conditions, or randomly. While this seems unlikely, it is also a situation which offers little opportunity for either understanding or intervention.

The issue is not whether the axiom is correct, but whether the axiom is a useful one to accept as if it were true. For a psychologist working to bring about change this axiom presents as a useful starting point, and basis for their work.

If as psychologists we are involved in a process which offers an individual the option of changing their behaviour, and we accept the axiom that this is dependent upon their model of the world, then our first step in making sense of their behaviour is to explore their model of the world. Having some understanding of the individual's model of the world can give an insight as to how their behaviour makes sense. In this respect it is possible to consider what would have to be different in order to make it possible for change to take place.

THE AXIOM AND THE SYSTEMIC PERSPECTIVE

A systemic perspective of an individual's behaviour implies a perspective which gets away from locating the cause of the behaviour within the individual, but rather sees the behaviour as a necessary part of the functioning of the system in which the individual exists.

This fits with the first axiom. The individual is seen as behaving in a way which is consistent with their model of the world, which parallels the behaviour as functional within the system in which the individual operates. The system in which the individual lives and their model of the world are in parallel. The basic information from which the individual builds their model of the world is from the system in which they live, and how they operate in the system is based on their model of the world. The model of the world is the individual's internalised representation of the system in which they live.

In both these formulations it would not necessarily be assumed that the individual can give a conscious rationale to their behaviour, either in terms of the consistency with their model of the world, or its function within the system in which they operate.

This perspective allows the psychologist to consider how a child's behaviour is functional within the system in which the child lives, and thereby work simultaneously to change the child's model of the world, and the system, the two approaches effectively being synonymous.

Working with a systemic model also allows the psychologist to consider the child's behaviour in a wider perspective, for instance how it reflects some of the underlying attitudes of the members of the system, and how it serves to reflect the relationships between the adult members of the system.

Given that a child's model of the world is based on the functioning of the system in which they operate, their model of the world can be changed through changing the system (or world) in which they live. Psychologists working with children in a school environment, and having the co-operation of parents, have access to the major systems within which the child has to operate. By working to create change in this home/school system it is possible to change the experiences of the child, their model of the world, and through that their behaviour. In this respect there is a synthesis of those perspectives which are intra-child focused and the more systemic approaches.

For psychologists who work in more community situations, this synthesis of perspectives has greater resonance as we can look to create change in a range of settings within the child's world.

A key role for the psychologist is not so much about what to seek to change, but how to present potential interventions in a way that will bring about desired changes within the system from the adults in the system. Eliciting information of the child's model of the world is helpful, but it is important to consider how this information can be used in order to get the desired changes of behaviour within the system.

Intervening in this way is geared to providing the child with experience which creates new perspectives and understandings for them about the way the world is, allowing them to revise their model of the world and begin to behave differently.

Children are often very ready to accept a change to their model of the world, but it is important that the world, or system, does not subsequently invalidate this. The following example demonstrates this.

Case example: Ian

Ian, aged about nine years, attended the Child Guidance Clinic with his mother. One of her complaints was that she had difficulty in getting him to go to bed when she wanted him to. In the discussion Ian indicated that his mother would tell him to go to bed about eight times an evening before she really meant it. She meant it when she got angry, then she would physically carry him up to his bedroom. This created a lot of anger and frustration for both of them. It was suggested to Ian's mother that life would be much easier if she decided she would 'mean' it on the second occasion rather than the eighth.

If Ian did not respond after the second request she would physically take him up to his bed, and this could be done without the degree of anger and frustration that had occurred previously.

The mother agreed eventually, and Ian seemed quite pleased about the idea of knowing what to expect.

At the subsequent meeting two weeks later, it was reported that Ian had consistently gone to bed when asked, since the previous meeting. His mother had not had to ask him more than once.

At the next follow-up meeting Ian's mother noted that he had returned to being difficult to get to bed. On further elaboration it became apparent that one night Ian had not responded to his mother's initial request for him to go to bed and she had not insisted as had been indicated in the initial meeting. Instead she had reverted to making numerous requests, before she became angry and physically took him to bed.

Ian, it would seem, had spent over two weeks operating with the belief that his mother would insist on his bedtime on the second time of telling, and had begun to behave with this as part of his model of the world based on his mother's agreement in the first session that this was what she would do. However, as soon as he discovered this new aspect of his model of the world was not validated by his experience of the system, he reverted to his old model of the world. Interestingly, Ian appeared at least as disappointed as his mother at this failure to change.

Children can quickly adapt their model of the world given small evidence that the world they live in is going to change, but it is important that the change is validated by their experience subsequently. The change in their model of the world needs to be paralleled and thereby validated by the system, and certainly not contradicted by it.

The second axiom

A second axiom is proposed which is intended, not as an absolute, but more as a working principle, which it is useful to adopt until the point is reached at which it can no longer be tenable. This axiom is a presupposition from NLP. The second axiom is that:

People have the necessary internal resources to make changes. This basically takes the assumption that people are not restricted by inherent limitations.

For instance, if I say I am a shy person, this axiom leads to the assumption that I have the resources within me to be something other than a shy person. It is assumed that I can be other than shy in some contexts.

Very simply if asked what qualities or resources I would need in order to be other than shy, I may say confidence, humour and calmness. If I identify aspects of my life where I feel I have each of these qualities, I can begin to think how I would behave in the 'shy' situation if I now acknowledge these resources and review my behaviour accordingly.

A corollary of this, in terms of children's learning, is that children have the necessary ability to learn. Many psychologists may take issue on this point, particularly given psychologists' propensity for attempting to measure children's ability, as a fixed potential.

One could have sympathy with a view that indicates innate or congenital limitations, particularly if thinking of children with severe or profound learning difficulties. However, several models (e.g. Instrumental Enrichment – Feuerstein *et al.* 1980 – and NLP – Dilts *et al.* 1980) present approaches which have supported many psychologists to consider potential in a different light.

Although there is clearly a validity in challenging the axiom at the extremes, the key issue here is that, if psychologists are to work constructively with children in helping them to maximise their educational opportunities, it is hardly useful for them to see their role as identifying limitations in the child's functioning. Most psychologists would probably no longer see their role in these terms, although there continues to be considerable vocabulary in professional circles which implicitly infers limitations through diagnostic terms.

Many of the children psychologists are likely to meet in schools who are failing educationally show competencies in other areas. Instead of contrasting these competencies and the child's educational attainment, the psychologist can help the child acknowledge and value their positive resources, in the form of their beliefs, values and feelings about themselves in those areas where they show competence. These may then be used as internal resources, in terms of self-perceived attributes, in the academic learning situation. Psychologically this would offer them the best opportunity for taking part in academic activities with a view to success.

In Chapter 7, describing logical levels of intervention, consideration is given to issues of environment, behaviour, capability, beliefs, values and identity, in relation to any difficulty and proposed intervention. It can be assumed within the context of this axiom that the individual can have the resources to have a constructive orientation in each of these areas in working to resolve any difficulty. These can frequently be found in other spheres of their lives. Even where an individual cannot find an appropriate orientation in any of these areas from their own experience, it may be sufficient for them to imagine how it would be *if* they had the resource, and explore the beliefs, values, feelings and identity that they would then have. Numerous psychological models and theories give methods for these change processes including PCP, NLP and hypnosis. The case example of Tracey in the use of Self-Description Grids (Chapter 12) gives a useful example of this sort of change work, based on PCP. The 'Swish' Pattern (Chapter 16) is another example from NLP.

Summary

These axioms are presented with the intention of providing a basis for individual work within a systemic perspective. The system needs to acknowledge and validate any change in an individual's model of the world or, at the very least, not provide any contradictory experiences.

Additionally the system needs to be geared to avoiding limiting assumptions about the child's ability to operate in the world, as these will become a part of the child's model of the world and belief about themselves, which in itself will lead to the limitation being realised as a self-fulfilling prophesy. It is important to be aware of what messages the system is giving to the child.

CHAPTER 6

Hypothesising and Information Gathering Based on a Systemic Perspective

Some theoretical points

In this chapter we will explore a number of useful concepts from family therapy models which can be applied to work with the parent/school system.

Circular causality

Circular causality is a principle of systemic thinking which recognises that 'blame' for a particular behaviour or functioning within the system cannot usefully be attributed to any one of the members.

Instead circular causality acknowledges that the behaviours of individuals within the system form an integral part of the functioning of the system as a whole. Therefore, it would be inappropriate to think of providing support to any part of, or individual within, the system at the expense of another.

The 'cause' or functional significance of any behaviour needs to be explored in terms of how it makes sense within or facilitates the functioning of the system, or how the system operates with that behaviour as a feature of its functioning.

Secondary gain

Secondary gain is linked to the principle of circular causality. If a system is functioning so that a particular form of behaviour which is considered a problem is maintained, then there is a secondary gain for the system from the behaviour. This gain is considered secondary as it is probably not readily apparent as a gain. The gain is that other aspects of the system are enabled through the presence of the behaviour.

By way of example, a systemic perspective of a child who will not go to sleep other than in the parents' bed could be providing a functionally significant secondary gain for the family system. One hypothesis is that the behaviour is functional in preventing the parents from having a satisfactory sexual relationship. The secondary gain from the behaviour is in allowing the parents to avoid addressing the difficulties they may have in their sexual relationship, allowing them to avoid addressing wider problems in their relationship. The system has a secondary gain from the 'problem' behaviour, and there is little value in attempts to determine who is at fault (which would be a term only within a linear causality model).

If the child's behaviour were related to the functioning of the wider system in this way, suggested interventions may need to take into account the secondary gain the system derives from the presenting problem, and recognising other potential issues which exist within the system. Otherwise there may be little investment or commitment in promoting change in the child's behaviour if other more potentially destabling issues would be highlighted in the system.

In this sense secondary gains can offer a useful framework for hypothesis generation in considering how the system has prevented the identified symptom from being addressed from within the system, that is, what has prevented the system from managing the difficulty prior to the involvement of an outside agent.

Boundaries

Structural family therapy gives us the notion of boundaries within systems. In a family, for instance, one may expect to find a parental sub-system which effectively represents a boundary between the parents and the children. This boundary is important in preventing the children from becoming enmeshed in the parent relationship or sub-system.

Dysfunctional boundaries may exist within families where there are alliances which prevent the adults agreeing expectations for the children, allowing the children to function without a satisfactory degree of containment. The important issue in these circumstances is to enable the system to re-orient and re-establish the boundaries.

Within a wider context it is reasonable to suppose that there would be appropriate boundaries within the home/school system in which the child lives. If these boundaries are breached, or skewed, then this may allow members of the system (in particular the children) to be subject to pressures which may lead to them behaving in ways which are problematic to the system, but reflect the difficulties within the system. If, for instance, there is not an adult/child boundary that allows adults to negotiate the expectations for children, this can lead the children to experience different and often mutually conflicting expectations from the adults in the system.

The pressures from conflicting demands from different sub-systems can be difficult to acknowledge as they will not necessarily operate in well-articulated behaviours but are probably mediated through the non-verbal behaviours of members of the system.

Viewing the functioning of systems in these terms can be a means to making sense of an expressed concern and providing a direction for intervention. Hypotheses of this sort can be useful for the psychologist, but may be difficult to work with openly in the system. However, as covert hypotheses, from a 'meta' perspective, they can be informative and provide a valuable conceptual tool.

Myths

Myths can be very useful in generating hypotheses from a systemic perspective. They are accepted understandings generally derived from a system's history which provide some shared belief within the system. These may well not be conveyed verbally, or explicitly, between individuals in the system, but serve to create attitudes and beliefs which are passed on through members of the system.

An example myth (dependent on the hypothesis framework chosen) is one frequently commented on in education circles by both professionals and parents alike. Children who have reading difficulties are frequently noted as being from families where there is a history of reading difficulties.

An intra-child hypothesis framework is frequently adopted in interpreting this information, with the implication that there is some hereditary physiological link. While this is a hypothesis, it is inconsistent with the second axiom presented earlier as it enables the system to infer a limitation of the child. It is unlikely to lead to the most useful interventions (because there is little that can be done about a hereditary difficulty, except to bear with it).

A more systemic conceptualisation based on myths could offer an alternative hypothesis. If parents have had difficulty learning to read then they may hold a belief that learning to read is difficult. They may well, quite unintentionally and implicitly rather than explicitly, convey to the child as they begin to attempt to learn to read that this is a very difficult task with which they will have difficulty and little success. Given this perception is held in the system, it will become absorbed into the child's model of the world, which can become a self-fulfilling prophesy.

Myths are essentially beliefs which are held within the system; in some respects they could be considered as representing the system's model of the world. Clearly there are useful and beneficial myths as well as those which are less so.

Myths can also be depicted as the conveyance of beliefs from one generation to another about how the world and the family interact and exist. That includes the assumptions and expectations which are created about how each generation develops: the interactions within and between the generations, and the way members of each generation interact with the outside world. The way in which each generation in the family develops frequently follows patterns based on earlier generations. A very good description of this is given by McGoldrick and Gerson (1985) particularly in looking at multi-generational genograms.

Life events

Life events are the significant changes that happen in the life cycle of the system. They can be represented in a number of ways.

Life events may arise due to the ongoing development of the system over time. For instance, in a family with adolescent children, there will be a pressure on the family system to respond to the inevitable changes in the family structure as the children are growing up and developing towards departing from the immediate nuclear family system.

If the adolescent in the family has a crucial role in maintaining the stability of the system, there may be pressures to maintain the functioning of the system which makes it difficult for that individual to leave the system.

People either joining or leaving the system can create major changes in the functioning of a system, by the demands that arise for the system to re-orient itself.

Life events may have a significant effect on the functioning of the system by virtue of their number. A number of relatively minor changes, which individually the system may have been able to cope with, but arising within a short period of time, could have a cumulative effect which is then difficult for the system to deal with. Such events may be unemployment, house moves, changes of school, illness, change of teacher, class or head teacher, new pressures on the school from local or national initiatives, etc.

Anticipated life events as represented through myths can also be of considerable significance.

Case example: Emily

Emily, a 12-year-old girl, had been referred to the local Child and Family Consultation Service because of the family's difficulty in coping with her behaviour.

Some history of the family indicated that Emily's mother had left home, through going into care, at age 13. Emily's two elder sisters had been taken away from the family system to live with their grandmother around that age. The third daughter, Emily, was beginning to show quite promiscuous behaviour, particularly staying out late at night, and going to parties with much older youngsters.

One hypothesis could be that there is an implicit myth, or expectation, within the system that Emily would leave home as she was coming up to age 13. Such a myth within the system could create a self-fulfilling prophesy.

Gathering information from the system

This section is intended primarily to focus on methods for gaining information from the system about the functioning of the system. Meeting with members of the system does not necessarily presuppose a systemic perspective; indeed there may be a strong focus from members of the system on an intra-child perspective.

The methods outlined below are intended to create a systemic perspective within the system, to highlight the concerning behaviour in terms of the functioning of the system, as well as elicit information about the system. In this respect these methods serve as interventions as well as information gathering processes.

Genograms

Genograms are family trees which most of us will be familiar with. They serve to identify all the people in the family system and provide a focus for exploring how the interrelationships in the family work. They also provide an opportunity to discuss in a systemic perspective some of the issues noted earlier, for instance life events, boundaries, myths, etc.

A common format for genograms is set out in the key in Figure 6.1. Dates of marriages, births, deaths, separations, etc. can be recorded on the diagram.

□ - Male

○ - Female

------ - Permanent bond

- - - - - Short-term liaison

× - Miscarriage or abortion

△ - Baby in utero, or child of unknown gender

M	-	Married
// or D	-	Divorced
/ or S	-	Separated
A	-	Adopted
⊠ or ⊗	-	Died

Figure 6.1 Common symbols for genograms

The genogram is a systematic way of exploring family functioning, and family members frequently become quite enthusiastic about providing the information, rather than seeing the process as intrusive.

Wider aspects of the system can be included in the genogram as necessary. A genogram which includes a number of generations, and elicits information held within the family about the wider family, can be very helpful in understanding family myths, and also piecing together the relevance of significant life events, particularly those which involve the entry and exit of individuals from the system.

Aspects of the wider system outside the family, for instance school or significant others, could also be included to see where the significant points of interaction are, and also provide an understanding of the functioning of the family system within the wider world.

Case example: Kiran

Kiran, an eight-year-old girl, was referred to the Child and Family Consultation Service by her school because she would not talk to any of the children or staff in the school.

All the family attended a number of meetings in the centre. It was quite clear that at home Kiran was quite willing and able to speak to all members of the family. At one point the family even made a tape recording of Kiran speaking at home for the school to hear her voice. This was done secretly with Kiran unaware that the tape recording was being made.

The family had recently moved from a neighbouring area, which had necessitated all the children changing school. The school records were delayed in arriving at the school, but when they did, there was little suggestion of Kiran not speaking.

School records also suggested that just prior to the family's move the mother had been in hospital to have a baby, although there seemed to be some confusion about this. There was also the suggestion that there had been another child in the family who had died very early in life some years ago. In the initial family meeting in the centre the family had given little suggestion of these previous events.

In the light of this information received from the school records it was decided that at the next family meeting it would be appropriate to work through a genogram with the family. The family were keen on the exercise. A simplified version of the genogram (just the nuclear family) is given in Figure 6.2. Although the genogram was done on a blackboard during the meeting, the family copied it down onto paper at the end of the session, so that they could extend it at home, to include photographs of members of the extended family in Bangladesh whom the children had not met.

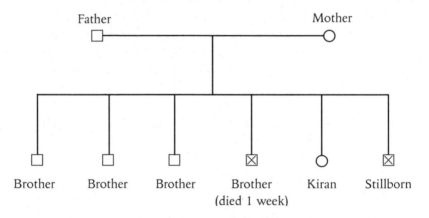

Figure 6.2 Genogram for Kiran's family

All the members of the family who had been alive at the time were aware of the fourth brother who had died one week after birth. The child had been given the appropriate religious funeral rights as he had lived and then died. The experience of this death had been so distressing for the family that they moved house and left the area in which they had lived. In their new home Kiran was born approximately one year later. Some time after this the mother again became pregnant; however, this child was stillborn. At the same time an aunt to the family also gave birth to a child, and was attending the same hospital as the mother. The family were distressed at the stillbirth, and this led to a further move of house and area.

The baby having been stillborn did not, in the parents' view, require the same funeral rights as the one who had lived for a period, and consequently the baby had been given a Christian funeral by the hospital. In the family's distress they did not want to share the grief with Kiran, the youngest child, and consequently led her to believe that the baby her mother had gone into hospital to have was actually the aunt's baby. The stillborn baby had not been spoken about since until this family meeting.

It was suggested that Kiran may well have been confused by the happenings and explanations she had been given, and the subsequent secrecy that surrounded the baby which disappeared. The family had now talked openly about this baby in the meeting, in front of Kiran, so its presence had been acknowledged. They were aware of where the remains of the dead baby were and agreed that they could go, as a family, to visit so that Kiran would be enabled to acknowledge both its presence and absence.

The family did not attend any further appointments, although the father kept in touch by telephone. Some weeks later, in a meeting with the head teacher of the school, it was reported that Kiran was beginning to speak in school.

There are clearly no grounds for saying categorically what Kiran's silence in school related to, although there are a number of hypotheses which can be put forward, based on the information available, and certainly some hypothesis had been behind the intervention task presented to the family in the family meeting. The important result was that Kiran began to speak. The genogram had been a useful tool in enabling the family to talk about issues which they had previously found very difficult to acknowledge. This had been enormously useful in terms of information gathering, and had perhaps formed a part of the process for change.

In school-based work, psychologists will frequently find schools have a considerable knowledge of a child and family when they are raising a concern. This can be sufficient to provide an initial genogram which holds information as a basis for early hypotheses about systemic effects which may impact on the child. The genogram is a particularly useful tool in consultation discussions with schools.

Circular questioning

Circular causality has already been outlined in that the behaviour of any particular individual needs to be related to the functioning of the system in which the individual is operating. In this sense the 'cause', or functional significance, of any behaviour needs to be explored in terms of how it makes sense in, or facilitates, the functioning of the system, or how the system operates around the behaviour.

Circular questions are those questions which seek to explore the significance of a piece of behaviour in the way in which it forms a part of the functioning of the system, and thereby identify forms of interrelationships in the system.

The following is a simple guide to some circular questioning forms.

1. RELATIONSHIP QUESTIONS

(a) Triadic questions: asking one person to comment on the relationship between the other two; for example, 'How do your father and sister get on?'

(b) Questions about the effect of the problem behaviour on relationships in the family; for example, 'What does your mother do when Rachel refuses to eat?' 'Who are brought together or distanced as a result of the problem behaviour?'

(c) Questions about cross-generational triangles; for example, 'When your mother and brother are fighting what does your father do?' 'Which of your children are trying hardest to keep you together as a couple?'

2. RANKING QUESTIONS

(a) 'More or less', 'before or after', 'which parent' and 'which of the children' questions; for example, 'Does the father show more anger when Sean misbehaves or when Lee misbehaves?'

(b) Ranking questions about hypothetical circumstances; for example, 'When all your children have left home who will have the most contact with you?'

3. TIME QUESTIONS

(a) Questions about specific events; for example, 'Did your mother go out more before your father lost his job or after it?' 'Was there more fighting before or after the heart attack last year?'

(b) Questions about the past and the future; for example, 'A year ago did Joe go out more or less than he does now?' 'What will happen in the future if nothing is found which will help the problem?' 'What will happen in the future if there is no longer a problem?'

4. NEW ALTERNATIVE QUESTIONS

For example, 'What help is needed before things will change?' 'What would have to happen before Susan would stop swearing?'

5. ABSENT OR SILENT MEMBERS

For example, 'If your grandmother was here what do you think she would say?' 'If Mary had answered the question I have just asked what do you think she would have said?'

Many of the questions are very clearly based on the hypotheses the psychologist may have of the functioning of the system. The questions and answers serve to confirm hypotheses or provide information to amend them. They also serve by their very form to promote the participants into considering their concerns from a systemic perspective.

It is often quite useful in the initial stages to ask each of the participants for their personal hypotheses about how the problem has arisen, what sustains it, the function it serves, and what they think is needed in order to address it.

Questions that presuppose a systemic perspective can be very powerful in getting members of the system to see the concerns they have from a systemic perspective which in itself can be powerful in enabling them to gain new insights into those concerns and how they may be addressed.

CHAPTER 7

Hypothesising and Information Gathering Based on an Individual Perspective: Some Basic Principles

Although the approaches presented here are based on individual perspectives (the individual's model of the world, and their view of themselves within it), there is a parallel with the system, or world, within which the individual lives. The approaches can serve to generate hypotheses which can then lead to interventions based on systemic principles. Indeed individual perspectives often offer overt hypotheses which may be easily shared with the system, whereas systemic perspectives may often lead to hypotheses about the system which the psychologist may not wish to share openly.

There are many psychological models which offer perspectives of an individual's functioning. The following – logical levels and hierarchy of needs – are presented as two taxonomies, which overlap to an extent, but provide a structure for understanding the different perspectives taken by psychological models, so that different models can be used compatibly, and offer the best resource to the psychologist.

Logical levels

The NLP concept of logical levels provides a useful framework to approach the difficulties a child is experiencing. The levels are a taxonomy of areas to consider in relation to the presenting problem, both in terms of information gathering and generating hypotheses. They form a hierarchy:

- identity
- values
- beliefs
- capability
- behaviour
- environment.

All are aspects of the child (see Figure 7.1).

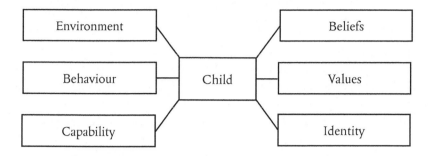

Figure 7.1 Logical levels all apply to the child

Identity

This is the way we see ourselves. Some people who have experienced rejection by key adults/parents and not formed a positive attachment can attribute this to themselves with a consequent negative self-view. If they have not been valued by others they will learn not to see value in themselves. They therefore do not see themselves positively and will distrust adults who try to tell them they are good. Intervention requires the development of a trusting relationship which starts by acknowledging the child's perception and history.

Identity issues are not always a reflection of difficult attachments. Generally it may be helpful to consider identity issues in relation to specific aspects of the child's life, for instance thinking about how they see themselves as a learner, or even more specifically how they see themselves as a learner of maths, literacy or any other subject.

The belief an individual has about their own capability or ability can be very pertinent to their capacity to succeed. Self-beliefs can be related to motivation, as the individual's belief about their ability to succeed will influence their expectation for success and the amount of effort they will put in to attempting to attain a goal.

There is often a common belief that people have talents for particular skills. They are assumed to be born with those talents. Although much of the approach developed here contradicts this view, beliefs of this sort can be particularly damaging to the development of skills if an individual has the belief that they do not have a talent or ability for a particular skill area.

In addition to a general self-concept, many self-concept inventories will look at a range of self-concepts such as:

- social self-concept

- academic self-concept

- home self-concept.

All of these features are part of Identity.

Identity issues are often not about how we see ourselves, but about how we would like to see ourselves, and what we are striving to be. The converse is, of course, also the case in that we often strive to avoid a particular identity. It is where we have these dynamics that our behaviours, attitudes and feelings may be our greatest challenge. Striving to avoid being a bad, incapable, weak, unattractive person can lead to unrealistic self-expectations, denial of any evidence of these qualities and a tenacious grasping for positive qualities which again may be idealised.

Key questions of Identity are:

What sort of a person are you?

What sort of a person are you striving to be?

What sort of a person are you striving not to be?

Values

Values are the things we think are important in the world. For most of us who have had relatively successful educational experiences and benefited from them, educational success is an important value. However, this is not always the case and we will all know many people who have very successful lives without educational success.

Where someone has found education to be a difficult and unrewarding challenge they may diminish the importance of education in order to avoid taking on an important negative self-identity as a learner. In many respects this is a more healthy response rather than taking on the negative self-identity. (See 'Cognitive dissonance' below.)

Key question of Values is:

What is important to you?

Beliefs

With beliefs we are thinking about the beliefs the person has about the way the world works. This could include issues such as:

- The world (or parts of it) is generally benevolent.

- The world (or parts of it) is generally threatening.

- Do you need to aggressively pursue objectives or do successes happen by chance?

- It is easy to get on with people.

- Learning is easy.

- Achieving well in education is the key to a successful life.

For those who have been abused, beliefs may be that the world is unsafe; people cannot be trusted; and it is important to always be in control even if this creates trouble.

The beliefs about the world will link in with our beliefs about how we should behave.

Key questions of Beliefs are:

How does your world work?

What are the rules of your world?

Capability

This is the issue of knowing how to do something, and it is generally an issue of thinking style or strategy. It is about the skills to achieve something or behave in a particular way. It is not about choice of behaviour in relation to beliefs, values and identity.

Key question of Capability is:

How do you go about doing X?

Behaviour

Behaviours are linked to identity, values, beliefs and capability as we have already indicated in our first principle.

In order for a child to adopt a behaviour it will have to be compatible in some way with identity, value and beliefs, as well as within the individual's capability. However, changing behaviour, or adopting new behaviours, is something we frequently ask children to do; compliance will be linked to the degree to which we are able to make the behaviour compatible with the child's identity, values and beliefs.

Key question of Behaviour is:

How does the behaviour make sense in terms of the child's identity, values and beliefs?

Environment

By the environment we are referring to the things that are happening in the system around the child. The impact of the system is in the messages it provides to the child about the way it sees them (identity), the values of the system, how the system works (beliefs), and how to go about doing things (capability). Effectively the model of the world the child develops is the internalisation of the system around them. Their world is based on the experience they have in the system(s) in which they live.

The parallel between the individual's model of the world and the world in which they live, the system, is detailed in Figure 7.2.

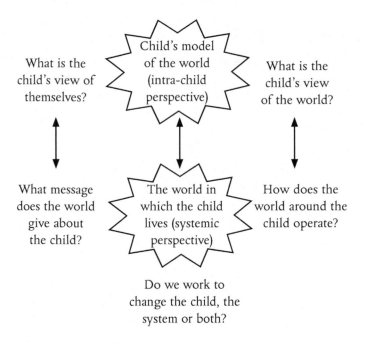

Figure 7.2 Intra-child and systemic perspectives: Parallel models

If we can change aspects of the child's world and the messages the system gives to the child, through working with the most influential people in their system, then we are in a position to help them review, and revise, their model of the world. Clearly this could be positive or detrimental. In our work we would wish to create a more positive and enabling model of the world for the child.

Key questions of Environment are:

What happens within the system around the child?

What values does it promote?

What does it tell the child about themselves?

These six elements provide a framework for an analysis of the key aspects of the child's model of the world which underpins their reactions to the world and their proactive behaviours in interacting with it.

Logical levels provide several potential frameworks for generating hypotheses, which may apply simultaneously, and help to give a perspective which focuses on the whole child. Each of the levels may have an important bearing on a problem. Similarly in devising an intervention it will be beneficial to take into account hypotheses at all levels in developing the intervention. This does not necessarily imply that the intervention needs to be complicated, as most interventions create change at a number of levels, despite often being based on a single hypothesis.

Example

Consider a typical problem which schools often ask psychologists to become involved in, that of a child with a reading difficulty. Each of the levels can be considered in respect of the reading difficulty.

IDENTITY

When the child has begun to view themselves as a non-reader, or even a poor reader, they have attributed their failure in reading to themselves as a part of their self-perception. Change at this level is to ask the child to begin to embark on a process which is, in effect, to change their view of the person they have come to understand themselves to be. Challenging this self-identity will be an important step in attempting to create a successful intervention for change.

VALUES

The child's sense of value about learning to read will be important in developing their motivation to carry out those activities associated with learning to read in a full and positive way. Values may arise from a family's valuing of reading. Some parents who have been successful in life in their own terms without reading can be overt in their sense that reading is not of tremendous importance. Children, however, may come to devalue reading, even in the face of contrary views held by significant others in their world, in order to cope with the dissonance and frustration that would occur should they value reading and yet begin to develop the belief that they are reading failures.

BELIEFS

The beliefs a child has about the task of reading, or learning to read, can have an enormous effect on their ability to learn. Beliefs may simply derive from the child's early experiences with reading which, if negative, may create a sense of reading as a particularly difficult activity or, for example, from a family myth about the difficulties of learning to read, or any other messages the system provides the child. The belief and experience can create a vicious circle of negativism about reading for the child.

As noted earlier, in considering myths within a system in relation to family histories of reading difficulty, a possible hypothesis is that a parent's anxiety about the difficulties of learning to read, from their own experiences, is transmitted to the child by the parent's reaction to the child's attempts in learning to read. This sense of anxiety about reading can then begin to fuel the child's beliefs about the difficulties of reading, and consequently their own likelihood of failure.

CAPABILITY

Does the child have, and use, appropriate strategies in their thinking processes and approach, in order to learn the meanings of letters, words and sentences, and develop appropriate strategies for remembering? For example, some children who have learned to pay exclusive attention to deciphering words by sounding out do not develop other strategies which are important in reading such as word recognition or context cues. This can, on occasion, be rectified by highlighting the value of these additional strategies and giving an initial training in these skills. (For further details see Chapter 17.)

BEHAVIOUR

Even though there may be opportunity in the environment for the child to learn, is the child indulging in behaviours which will promote reading? Does the child take opportunities to practise and develop literacy?

ENVIRONMENT

Important in any reading difficulty is whether the child is exposed to reading material in their environment, for example at home, or if there has been little or no schooling. Is there the opportunity for the child to learn, in terms of appropriate materials, teaching and environments? Feuerstein's concept of cultural deprivation provides a parallel to these issues.

However, the main aspect of the environment is the messages the system around the child gives in relation to each of the logical levels: about their identity as a learner of literacy; how learning literacy is valued; the beliefs about learning literacy; how to go about it in terms of skills and strategies; and how literacy development activity is encouraged and promoted.

Whereas the levels present a useful taxonomy for developing hypotheses about children's difficulties in a number of areas, and informing interventions, they are not mutually exclusive in intervention. For instance, giving a child new strategies in word recognition, which enables them to learn words successfully, may challenge their belief about the difficulty of learning to read. This may allow them to value reading, by removing the dissonance, and enable them to work with their parents and teachers (perhaps involving changes at both the behavioural and environmental levels), in a way which gives added value to their attempts to learn to read, thereby creating a positive value about reading; and finally begin to develop an identity of themselves as a reader.

In devising interventions it is often helpful to consider if all potentially useful changes at each of the levels has been considered.

Although this taxonomy has a focus at an intra-individual level there is also the important systemic thread that runs through the model. The child's orientation at each of the levels is a consequence of the messages they receive about their world and themselves from the system in which they live. This will be the primary determinant in the construction of their model of the world, and their role within it.

Cognitive dissonance: How we manage conflicts of experience and belief, value and identity

Most children entering school are keen to please the key adults in their lives (teachers and parents); they would like to see themselves as learners, will buy into the generally accepted view that learning is valued, and will engage in this process. However, those who are not successful over time become disillusioned with the struggle to achieve.

Where a child has adopted the generally accepted view that educational success is the basis of a successful life (belief), and it is valued as such (values), if they are not able to see themselves as educationally successful (identity), and not developing the skills to succeed (capability), when they try (behaviour), then there is a conflict, or dissonance, in the logical levels and their model of the world.

In order to attempt to resolve this dissonance, they may try to persist with a self-view that they are successful (despite the increasing evidence against this). This approach could lead to conflicts with teachers and peers who keep presenting evidence of failure or lack of achievement.

In time the evidence from the environment makes the persistence with the successful identity implausible. A new identity of being unsuccessful begins to emerge. However, there is then a conflict between the identity (not educationally successful) and the values and beliefs (success is important). In order to resolve this dissonance the child begins to find ways of not adopting beliefs and values which are not dissonant. This internal conflict can easily be acted out in behaviour as they are challenged by, and challenge, the messages from the system.

This is cognitive dissonance, first outlined by Festinger (1957). Dissonance between the logical levels is an uncomfortable position and when it occurs the individual will seek ways of reducing the discomfort or dissonance. Initially the way this might be achieved is to find ways to change or challenge the messages from the environment which create the dissonance, but if this cannot be sustained the alternative would be to adopt different values, beliefs or identity to bring consistency. The most likely way of doing this in our example may be a change of value or belief to one that holds that educational success is unimportant, to match with the identity of being educationally unsuccessful.

Where a child or young person has difficulties academically then helping find positive and compatible self-identity, beliefs and values is important to maintain a positive approach. An example is where schools try to promote a cultural value that effort rather than success is the most important value, which can be compatible with a similar identity.

For many young people developing a valued area in which to have a positive identity can negate the impact of not being able to retain an identity of educational success. Unfortunately, if not available, young people can easily find alternative identities which are valued within various sub-cultures but not valued within the mainstream school culture. This is not unfamiliar to those working in schools. The cognitive dissonance model does give some useful insights into understanding the process the young person goes through and the challenges their experience of the world creates for them.

Hierarchy of needs

A further useful model for making sense of a child's behaviour is to consider how their needs are being met, given that appropriate school-related behaviours will be dependent upon a number of more fundamental needs being met, in order to allow the child to concentrate on the school activity.

One of the best known hierarchies of need available from psychology is that presented by Maslow (1954). Basically he suggests that more primitive needs will take precedence before the higher order ones become significant. Maslow proposes seven levels in the hierarchy.

Maslow's hierarchy of needs

1. *Self-actualisation needs*: to find self-fulfilment and realise one's potential.

2. *Aesthetic needs*: to have symmetry, order and beauty.

3. *Cognitive needs*: to know, understand and explore.

4. *Esteem needs*: to achieve, be competent, gain approval and recognition.

5. *Belongingness and love needs*: to be with others, be accepted and belong.

6. *Safety needs*: to feel secure, safe and out of danger.

7. *Physiological needs*: to satiate hunger, thirst, etc.

A child's motivation for success in school-based activities will derive from the higher order needs, and therefore basic physical and emotional needs have to be addressed before the child can perform in school at a level which would satisfy these higher order needs. For instance, a hungry or emotionally vulnerable child is unlikely to work for success in mathematics, which might satisfy esteem, cognitive, aesthetic or self-actualisation needs. Maslow's needs are, perhaps for us as psychologists, a much more constructive understanding of need than those supposed by the term 'special educational needs'.

The links between the hierarchy of need and the logical levels can be reasonably easily made, which may serve to further refine any hypotheses generated from either framework as a starting point.

Although these taxonomies are based on an intra-child perspective, clearly the influence of the system around the child will be most pertinent in providing the interactions by which change can be brought about. Consideration needs to be given to changing the system which has brought about these environments, behaviours, beliefs, values and identities for the child, and met (or not) the child's needs at various levels.

The theoretical perspectives outlined in subsequent chapters are presented to explore the identity, values, beliefs and strategies of logical levels. The behavioural and environmental levels have not been emphasised as it is assumed that readers will have a good grasp of behavioural principles, and that in considering the psychologist's role in the education system teachers have expertise in these areas.

CHAPTER 8

Beliefs, Values and Identity: Personal Construct Psychology

PCP was developed and described by George Kelly in 1955 (Kelly 1955). It is not intended to go deeply into the theory here, except to provide a basic understanding as it is the underlying model for many of the methods described in later parts of the text.

The theory proposes that people are proactive in making sense of themselves and the world in which they live. They construct meaning from their experience and therefore an individual's particular way of making sense of the world will be personal to them.

The basic component of the individual's system of making sense of the world is the construct. This is a bi-polar dimension which provides a meaningful discrimination based on the individual's experience. The construct is based upon an entity and its opposite, which gives the basis for a discrimination of similarity and difference; one cannot exist without the other.

As a very simple example, if we were in a world where there was only a diffuse light then we could gain no useful information about our world through our visual channel. Consequently that sensory system would have no meaning or value for us. It is only when there is some contrast, or difference, within the experience that we can begin to make a discrimination (although this may or may not be meaningful). Until we perceive a contrast we cannot make a discrimination. The discrimination is meaningful if it is relevant to us personally. The construct then holds the basic unit of contrast, that is, it not only indicates what is implied but also what is denied.

At a more personally meaningful level I may describe a friend as 'compassionate'. In order to gain some sense of how I use this to discriminate between people it would be important to know what I am implying he is not. In other words, by describing him as compassionate what is the opposite that I am denying him to be?

The particular discrimination I am making is a personal way in which I discriminate between people. There is no assumption of generalisation between individuals.

The constructs are the dimensions which we use to construct meaning from our experience of the world. Our constructs enable us to create hypotheses about the world, and in that sense they are predictive; our predictions can be tested out against our experiences of the world.

Our system of constructs could be seen as forming our own personal theory of the world. The constructs are not only the basis from which we make discriminations about people and events in our experience, but also provide the basis for discriminations, and personal judgements about ourselves. Thus we are able to discriminate the sort of people we are from the people we are not, and the sort of people we would wish to be from the people we would wish not to be. This personal theory of the world is frequently referred to as the person's model of the world.

The first axiom presented earlier in the text is a key postulate of PCP in that an individual will behave in a way which is consistent with the way they make sense of themselves and the world in which they live, namely their model of the world.

An individual's constructs will not be independent of each other, but are organised (as a theory) so that there are hypothesised relationships between constructs, and particularly a hierarchical structure, from behaviourally specific discriminatory constructs, to more generally descriptive discrimina-tory constructs, with attributed values.

Given that a construct defines a contrast by which a discrimination is made, and an individual uses this discrimination as a basis for making sense of their world, then the discrimination reflects some sense of value to the individual, if it is to be useful and meaningful. Thus one end of the construct could be interpreted as the preferred pole, the contrast representing the less preferred pole. The construct provides a personally meaningful basis for making valuable discriminations in the world.

The basis for the preference of one end over the other gives one end of a 'meta' or higher order construct in the hierarchy. By way of example, if I take a construct I use to discriminate between people I meet in a social setting:

GENEROUS ———————— MEAN

I have a preferred end to this construct (generous). The basis, or underlying value, of this preference (what is of importance to me in my use of this construct to make discriminations) is that when people are generous I believe they are being 'open and honest'.

If I now consider how I would describe someone who is not 'open and honest' (the opposite or contrast), then this might be that I think they have 'something to hide'. I now have a construct operating at a higher level in the hierarchy (at a meta level to the generous/mean construct), that is:

OPEN AND HONEST ————————— SOMETHING TO HIDE

I could go on, expressing a preference for one end of this construct, establishing the basis of the preference, and then finding the opposite, to derive a meta construct to this one. This is one way of exploring the construct organisation, or system. A fuller description of exploratory techniques based on the work of Dr A.T. Ravenette is given later in the text. For the purposes here it is sufficient to have some appreciation that there is an organisation and structure to the personal construct system.

Although there is structure to the construct system, there may be a number of sub-systems, for instance I may make discriminations about people in different ways according to the circumstances in which I meet them. I may use different constructs to discriminate in my judgements about people I meet in a working environment from those I use when in a social setting. Constructs are said to have a range of applicability, or convenience, within the individual's experience. People may have a small or wide range of convenience for their constructs, or several or few sub-systems.

To the extent that we share similar constructs, and construct systems, with another person we are able to share in their model of the world. This is particularly pertinent to the earlier discussion on rapport building. Interactions are frequently about one person trying to understand how the other perceives the world, particularly as this understanding forms the basis for predicting their behaviour.

Core constructs

Core constructs are the constructs at a high level in the hierarchy, and have particular significance as they are the constructs upon which we make meaningful discriminations about ourselves, the people we are, and the people we strive to be. These are the constructs which serve to maintain the individual's identity and existence; they provide the basis for our sense of self, and the various roles we fulfil in our daily lives. Changes at this level will be very profound.

Lower order constructs, by virtue of the links as described in the earlier example, can have particular importance by the implications they have to the higher order constructs. For instance, if the construct sub-system, described in the above example, were applied to self, and I behaved in a 'mean' way, then the implication is that I *am not* being an 'open and honest' person. Note that the logical level has changed from a behaviour to an identity statement. If I strive to see myself as an 'open and honest' person then my 'mean' behaviour challenges this identity, and this I might find distressing.

Feeling states and core constructs

Confirmations or challenges to our core constructs from our experience of the world can be interpreted as underpinning a number of emotional reactions. Much of this links readily to cognitive dissonance described in Chapter 7.

Given that our identity is provided by the descriptions of the positive or preferred pole of our core constructs, then experiences which provide evidence that we are behaving, or viewed, in ways consistent with the non-preferred pole of the construct serve to challenge our identity and cause distress. Conversely experiences which tend to provide evidence that we are behaving, or viewed, in ways consistent with the preferred pole of the core construct will serve to confirm our identity, giving us reassurance.

It is not surprising that we would tend to prefer activities which are more likely to provide confirmatory messages of our identity.

On the other hand, if we are continually pressed to perform activities which present consistent challenges to our identity, then we may react negatively, due to the cognitive dissonance described in the previous chapter. In the light of the continual challenge we may begin to change our identity, as experience of the world renders the preferred end of those core constructs a less tenable aspect of our identity. The distress which then arises may be dealt with through a hostile determination to persist with the identity, or a change in identity based on other core constructs, thereby reducing the range of convenience of the core construct which has been challenged. A further possibility is a depression in which the individual attempts to reconcile not being the person they wish to be.

It is quite easy to see how this scenario may arise for a child who is failing to make adequate progress in a school situation. If consistently the child is unable to confirm the preferred pole of a core construct, then they may very easily be open to accepting the opposite pole of the construct as an alternative identity, particularly when very young and unable to take on alternative core constructs.

By way of example, take a child in primary school who is making poor progress in reading. If the system around the child (parents, school, etc.) is providing messages (at the level of values) that it is very important to learn to read, then the child is likely to have a core construct associated with reading well, as the child's model of the world is based on their experience of the world. This core construct could have some form such as:

GOOD READER ———————————— POOR READER

If the experience of the world for the child then presents evidence to the child that he is a poor reader, this will result in distress (as cognitive dissonance). This distress will need to be resolved.

The child may eventually accept the identity as a poor reader, but reduce the value and importance of this construct, so it is of less personal importance and no longer a core construct, although may still have a discriminatory significance in their understanding of the world. This seems to be a common occurrence, but requires that the system allows the child to no longer value reading.

However, this could be quite difficult if the system – teachers and parents particularly – seeks to maintain reading as a core construct, and could lead to considerable distress for the child. This could lead to the child taking on the identity of the non-preferred pole, with the construct remaining core. In this case the child is pressed into accepting evidence which challenges the higher construct in the hierarchy upon which the preference of 'good reader' vs. 'poor reader' was based. This, for young children, could be a highly significant construct such as 'good person' vs. 'bad person', which could then be very personally damaging.

Alternatively, and perhaps initially, the child may seek to defend his identity at the preferred end of the core construct, desperately demanding confirmatory evidence of being a good reader.

It is useful to consider how some specific emotional states can be interpreted in terms of core constructs of identity and particular experiences.

Guilt

Guilt can be considered as arising from experiences which provide evidence that the individual's behaviour has been consistent with the negative pole of a core construct. Thus they have behaved in a way which presents as a challenge to the way they would wish to see themselves.

Threat

Threat arises where there is the possibility that experience is likely to present a challenge to a core construct. The threat is that the experience will present evidence that the individual will be seen as being at the negative pole of the core construct.

A number of other emotional states can be considered in terms of the construct system as a whole.

Anxiety

Anxiety could be considered as occurring when events seem to be happening which are outside the range of the construct system. These are events for which there are no constructs through which to make satisfactory discriminations, and thereby adequate predictions about the world.

Hostility

Hostility could be seen as an attempt to preserve the use of constructs even in the face of evidence which suggests they are not providing satisfactory discriminations.

Aggression

Aggression is seen as either a positive or negative force where there is an attempt to extend the range of convenience of the existing construct system, to make discriminations in new areas of experience.

Hostility and aggression, in PCP terms, can both be seen as attempts to retain the existing construct system in the light of some evidence which may challenge the predictive validity of the constructs. In this sense they could be seen as attempts to change the experience in order to preserve the constructs!

The important issue to note in respect of feeling states is that they arise not in response to an event in the outside world, but as an implication of the event for the construct system.

Change work using construct systems

Although this is a brief consideration of PCP, it is useful to consider some of the potential initiatives, or directions, for change that the model offers.

Exploration and reframing

Exploration and reframing are looked at in more detail later on.

Exploration of the construct system refers to the investigation of the constructs themselves, that is, identifying opposite poles, and also the links between constructs. The implication of one construct discrimination in relation to a higher order construct forms the basis for the interpretation of experience both in relation to others and oneself. Offering alternative links between constructs, and within constructs, can present as powerful reframes in enabling alternative perspectives (or forms of discrimination) to be considered.

Exploration of the construct system also allows the client to investigate the implications of a particular change they may choose to make. This can be effective as change at an identity level (that is, constructs higher up the hierarchy) can be managed through investigating the implications for the more behaviourally oriented lower level constructs which are the concomitants of the higher level change. By exploring these behavioural implications of change, the client is then in a position of having the choice of change in the knowledge of what is involved.

In Chapter 10 consideration will be given to investigating the reference experiences which underlie the development of the elements of constructs. Reference experiences are those original experiences which have been fundamental to the development of the constructs, that is, the experiences which have validated the original discrimination upon which the construct was formed. In offering a framework for exploring reference experience the Meta Model from NLP provides an excellent complement to the PCP framework.

Alternative roles

There are many approaches to offering the client an opportunity to consider a change in identity, through exploring the alternative constructs that the change would imply, in terms of the identity, beliefs, values and behaviour. By considering the more behavioural implications of change the client has the opportunity for acting, or trying out, the new role this would imply. The key issue is that the client is not asked to give up an old construct, or construct system, in order to try out a new version, merely that they should put the old one to one side while they try out the new one. This presents less risk in experimenting with alternative constructions, and consequently can allow greater opportunities to explore change. The example of Tracey in Chapter 12 outlines this approach.

Changing the range of convenience of constructs

Another possibility for offering an alternative understanding of experience is to invite the client to consider applying constructs from one area of their life to make discriminations in a different area of their experience. For instance, in a work setting an individual may make much of a discrimination using the construct:

BUSINESSLIKE ———————— INEFFICIENT

which may be a useful construct. However, it may not enable them to fully appreciate the potential of their colleagues. Taking a construct which the client may use more readily in the social arena, for example:

ENTERTAINING ——————————— WITHDRAWN

and applying this to discriminations in the work experience, could give opportunities for perceiving colleagues more fully, and appreciating the qualities they have to offer. With the consequent change in behaviour that could arise from such a changed perception, there may be opportunities for difficult interpersonal relationships to be improved.

In this way, taking a construct used in one arena and expanding its range of convenience to another arena provides a more elaborated construct system, and thereby a more sophisticated basis for making discriminations about the world.

Conversely, reducing the range of specific constructs may also be a useful intervention in some circumstances.

Internal consistency

Exploration of the constructs can at times highlight internal inconsistencies in the client's ways of construing their experience, and themselves. This can lead to distress in the form of a dilemma arising through attempts to behave in accordance with the preferred poles of more than one core construct where there are different implications for behaviour arising from the different constructs.

Generally the PCP model offers a highly useable structure for exploring the client's model of the world. The particular value is the recognition that what is important is the way experience is construed rather than the experience itself. Indeed for every person we know who suffers from an experience or set of circumstances we can probably think of someone else who readily copes in the same situation. The problem is then not the circumstance or experience, but how we make sense of it. This offers a framework for working with difficulties that presupposes that problems are resolvable, because problems arise from the construction of the world, not the world itself.

CHAPTER 9

Methods for Gathering Information

In gathering information from the individual it is possible to use this to help generate hypotheses from both an individual perspective and a systemic perspective.

When using an individual perspective, it is useful to consider the logical levels in order to be aware of which hypotheses are developed and which require further information. Most of the models and techniques described earlier can be used to gain information at a number of levels.

Information about environment and behaviour may well be gathered through direct questions with members of the system, as well as with the child. Observation may also be helpful. Capability issues will be discussed at some length in Chapters 16 and 17. In this chapter the focus is on exploration of beliefs, values and identity, as a major part of the child's model of the world.

A child or young person's age and level of language will be important in determining the style of interviewing. Older and more verbally articulate children can easily be engaged in the language-based approaches supported with drawings. Adolescents are also generally quite happy to do drawing as part of the interview. Drawings provide important reference points during the discussion for both the psychologist and young person.

Exploring the model of the world

In interviews, and even general conversations, there are lots of opportunities for exploring an individual's model of the world. Indeed the whole process of communication is an attempt to share our model of the world with another person. The extent to which there is a shared meaning in language allows this communication between our models of the world; however, it also serves to cover up many of the inconsistencies between one person's model of the world and another's.

Basically an individual's model of the world is their version of reality, that is, their understanding of the world as they know it: the way it operates and how they themselves fit into it, including all the ways they generalise, delete and distort their experience of the world to establish and maintain their personal understanding of how the world works. The reality is an individual's personal experience and to this extent each individual's model of the world is different.

In communication language is shared and assumed to have a shared meaning; however, each person's underlying model upon which the communication is based will be different. The ability to use language constructively in communication probably reflects some similarity in our models of the world, but is helped by the lack of precision in language and our attempts to use it to represent our model of the world. This tends to give an illusion of similarity in our models of the world.

Much of the content of the model of the world will not be at the forefront of the individual's conscious mind. Many of the principal 'rules' within the model will have been established early in life, and the reference, or original, experience(s) upon which the rules are based will be long gone from the conscious mind. The 'rule' as a belief, value or identity may itself not operate at a conscious, linguistically articulated level, but may be at a more primitive level of feelings: what feels right or wrong, comfortable or uncomfortable.

In exploring an individual's model of the world, be that your own or someone else's, it is useful to have a structure to act as a guide for organising the exploration. The guiding structure is not the structure of subjective experience, but merely a model which helps us to investigate the model of the world. A distinction which is important to make (a quote from NLP) is that 'the map is not the territory'. This means that the model of the world is not reality; the guiding structure is not how people actually think, but is just a useful map to guide our exploration.

The 'rules' of the model incorporate the person's beliefs, values and identity about themselves and the world.

PCP, as previously described, gives a structure for exploring the individual's model of the world. To recap, the construct is defined by an entity and its opposite or, put another way, what is implied and what is denied. Given that for personal relevance there is a preference of one end of the construct over the other, a higher order construct can be established based on the preference. The behavioural basis of, or the behaviours implied by, the initial description can also be explored. The fact that a description is given by an individual validates it as relevant to their model of the world, and it can thereby serve as a starting point. To use the map analogy, the description having been elicited means a starting point on the map has been established.

Root questions

Ravenette (1992) presents three root questions which are very effective in eliciting descriptions related to identity. These are:

1. Who are you? – A question of personal identity.

2. What sort of person are you? – A question of personality.

3. What would other people say about you? – A question of self-perception.

Questions of this sort are very useful in the direct interview setting as they ensure that the exploration of the model of the world at least begins in the part which relates to the individual's beliefs about themselves. Less direct questions can be useful, but will sometimes require much further exploration. However, this may be more useful when the exploration has to be less overt, for instance in general discussions with teachers, parents or people in other arenas. Any questions which link to some form of personal value or belief can be a basis for further exploration. Even unrelated questions, such as those below, elicit some form of personal value judgement which represents the preferred end of a construct, and can be the starting point for further exploration and elaboration of the construct system. Any question asking for a judgement of some sort can yield a starting point for the further exploration. For example:

- How did you come to choose the car that you drive?

- How come you continue to work in the job you're in?

- What made you decide to become a psychologist?

- What made you decide to buy the shirt that you are wearing?

Exploratory questions

Once initial judgement or description has been given, PCP theory offers four directions for further explorations through asking questions:

1. Implies: finding out more of what is implied by the description.

2. Opposite: finding out what is denied by the description.

3. Importance: finding out what is important to the individual in this description (i.e. the basis of preference).

4. Behaviour: finding out what are the behaviours inferred from the description.

Each of these represents a direction for exploration. The direction which is taken is a judgement by the interviewer at the time; however, there is no wrong route to take. If a direction proves uninformative then choose another. Every new description elicited in response to a question becomes a point of choice in terms of the four directions. A diagrammatic description is given below of how the structure could be viewed.

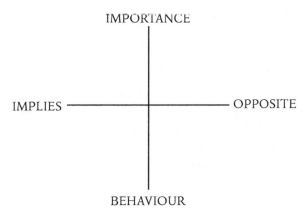

TYPICAL QUESTION STRUCTURES FOR EACH DIRECTION

Below are some of the types of question structure which will tend to elicit exploration in particular directions. The direction of the elicitation is not guaranteed, and often the question may elicit some unexpected direction. This in itself may be meaningful, or may merely suggest an alternative question may be more helpful at that time. The list is of course not exhaustive.

1. Implies

   ○ What else can you tell me about someone like that?

   ○ What does that mean to you?

   ○ What sort of person would say that about themselves?

2. Opposite

   ○ How would you describe someone not like that?

   ○ What sort of person would not describe themselves like that?

3. Importance

   ○ How is it important for you to be _____?

   ○ What is important for you about _____?

- How come it's important?

- What sort of person would describe themselves like that and then say it was/was not important?

4. Behaviour

- What would someone be doing if they were _____?

- How can you tell that someone is like that?

- How do you know you are that sort of person?

- What do you do that shows you are that sort of person?

Frequently an individual will respond with more than one description which is a useful starting point for further exploration. This becomes an enhancement of the choices and opportunities which are now available.

Keeping notes of the salient descriptions almost as if plotting out the exploration of the model of the world (in a way similar to the diagram above) is a useful way of organising your own thinking during the process. Noting how descriptions link together is particularly important as the basis of the links (the 'rules' by which the construct system is held together) may allow opportunities for productive interventions. This will be further elaborated through the chapters on interviewing techniques with the case examples and the sections on reframing.

CHAPTER 10

Further Exploration of the Model of the World

Language and the model of the world

Verbal communication, as a secondary, rather than primary, representation of experience, is a less than exact process. Even if we were all to use words in the same way, the meaning in the messages we send are based on the structure and content of our own model of the world, which have inherent differences.

An individual receiving any information makes sense of it by assimilating it into their model of the world. Similarly, in their own communication, they are making a verbal description of the content of their model of the world. In both these input and output processes the intended communication is subject to interpretation which deletes, generalises or distorts some of the content and meaning. The beliefs and rules implicit in the structure of the speaker's model of the world are also implicit in their spoken language. On hearing their communication we then interpret the content in terms of the implicit structures, or rules, of our own model of the world.

In the case of an interpersonal interaction the process is summarised in Figure 10.1.

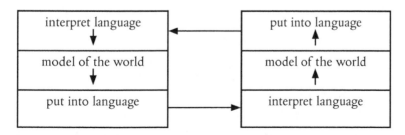

Figure 10.1 The interpersonal interaction process

It is a useful, and interesting, exercise to practise pure information gathering of another person's model of the world, attempting to avoid using your own model of the world in order to interpret and make links about what you think is going on in their model of the world.

People helpers tend to find this exercise very difficult, all too often attempting to present solutions (from their own model of the world) rather than really trying to find out what makes the problem a problem, in terms of capabilities, beliefs, values and identity issues, which form the structures within the other person's model of the world. Helping a person really explore what it is that makes their problem a problem can often be a major step in enabling them to begin to find solutions to sort out their problem for themselves.

As the sense of a communication is gained through assimilating it into our model of the world there is the illusion that we actually do understand what the other person means, and this gives the impression that our models of the world are the same. To the extent that there will be similarities in our models of the world, the consequences of our differing personal interpretations may not be of importance, and this does not normally present a problem.

If we want to be more precise and specific in our information gathering we need to ask questions.

Generally information gathering questions are those beginning with 'when', 'where', 'who', 'what' and 'how'. 'Why' is not included as this changes the level of response by seeking an aspect of belief structure, or seeks a justification. The 'importance' questions described in the previous chapter provide an alternative approach to seeking the higher order basis for a judgement.

A useful strategy for practising specific information gathering is to adopt the standpoint of an alien. Aliens, we can assume, have a good command of the language, but no actual knowledge about people or the world in which we live; in other words, if things are not put in sensory-specific terms they do not know what is meant. To behave as if your understanding of the world is from an alien's viewpoint is often a useful model to have available, to avoid the trap of assuming we know what other people mean, by interpretation from our own model of the world.

The universal modelling processes in the model of the world

To have an understanding of the world, from the mass of our experience of the world, we need ways of managing the wealth of information that bombards us through our senses. There are three ways of doing this which in NLP are called the universal modelling process. These are:

- deletion
- generalisation
- distortion.

Simply these can be thought of as the bits left out from the full representation, or what we choose to ignore (deletions); the non-specific descriptions, or that which we interpret as an example of a more general phenomenon (generalisations); and the explanations or 'rules' about how things fit together, how we understand the way the world works (distortions).

Here is an example story:

> I was driving along the road this morning, when this driver coming the other way suddenly pulled across the road in front of me. I could see he wasn't paying attention. Really people like that shouldn't be allowed on the road.

What are the deletions, generalisations and distortions in the story?

Deletions
This is basically information that has been omitted from that provided; that which prevents us from being able to gain a full representation of the experience in sensory-specific terms, for example 'What was I driving?' (deleted); 'Which road was I driving on?' (deleted). Clearly there is a mass of deleted information.

Generalisations
There are generalisations reflected in the language which represent beliefs about the content of our world. They are the stereotypes, value judgements and beliefs about what is or is not possible and desirable: our beliefs about how the world works. These are rules within our model of the world which may be operating at a conscious level, or may be reasonably accessible to consciousness. They tend to define the scope of our model of the world, for example 'people like that' (generalisation – this person is always like that; or this person is one of a particular stereotype).

Distortions
Distortions help attribute meaning to events based on existing beliefs within the individual's model of the world. These are the connections within the

model of the world, which form the structural rules of the model. They are the beliefs about what the world is and how it works. These rules probably operate at a much more unconscious level, and are less easily accessible to conscious awareness, for example 'I could see he wasn't paying attention' (distortion).

The distortion is that I am attempting to read the other driver's mind by the look on his face. This is a belief or rule within my model of the world which links a particular aspect of what I saw with an interpretation of what was going on in the other person's mind. This is a distortion in the model of the world. I have used my sensory experience to conclude something which I could have no direct knowledge of. My model of the world includes a rule that indicates that a particular look on the face *means* 'not paying attention'. The rule is an inference which is a distortion of the event: it is possible that the other driver was actually paying attention, despite the look on his face.

Surface structure and deep structure

The notion of surface structure and deep structure from NLP provides a distinction between the model of the world and the world of experience, which leads to a practical basis for working with individuals.

The surface structure of an individual's model of the world includes all their individual 'rules' of the world (derived through deletions, generalisations and distortions), involving their personal meanings about things, and with that the links between concepts that serve to provide the structure to their model of the world. The surface structure is in essence their everyday working model of the world with which they organise, understand and operate their life.

The deep structure on the other hand represents the original, or reference, experiences from which the rules in the surface structure have been derived. The deep structure is the validity upon which the surface structure of the model of the world is based. The deep structure is not directly in consciousness, and may or may not be easily accessible consciously.

Example

I may hold a belief that Fords are very good cars. I might use this rule when I think about buying a new car. This belief, or rule (that Fords are good cars), is a piece of the surface structure of my model of the world. The reference experiences in the deep structure which underlies this is derived, for example, from a trust in my father (who knows about cars). He has told me, at some time in the past, that Fords are good cars; in addition I have some positive personal experiences of having owned Fords before. The surface structure rule is maintained without challenge while there is no radically conflicting evidence, as I will tend to organise new information in terms of my model of the world.

The fact that my wife has had a Vauxhall for several years now, which has given sterling service, far better than my previous good experience with Fords, has not up to now challenged my belief that a Ford is a better car than a Vauxhall.

By considering the experiential basis for my belief in the deep structure, I now realise that it is a belief which has persisted over time, but has not been updated to check its current validity. Indeed I now realise, through exploring the deep structure of my model of the world, that my surface structure belief in the quality of Fords is based on experience of several years ago, and is not necessarily currently valid.

The example highlights the principle that beliefs or rules in the surface structure have some experiential basis, in the deep structure, which may not be consciously apparent until examined. Further this experiential basis may no longer be relevant, or valid, even though the belief persists in the surface structure.

Exploration of the deep structure of the model of the world can be a major help in coming to terms with problems. What makes a problem a problem frequently arises out of the beliefs, values and identity issues within our model of the world. Exploring the underlying basis of these 'rules' can often lead to a re-appraisal of the 'rule' which can be sufficient to begin to challenge the problem. The Meta Model from NLP is a linguistic model which highlights deep structure to surface structure relationships and thereby presents a particularly useful tool in the exploration of the model of the world.

The Meta Model

The Meta Model is a taxonomy of linguistic structures which identify elements of the surface structure of the model of the world from the language patterns used.

The Meta Model language patterns reflect the three universal modelling processes. The language patterns may focus on one of these modelling processes more than others, but frequently either explicitly, or by implication, will involve the three processes. Patterns which indicate omissions of detail tend to involve the modelling process of deletion. Patterns reflecting the (limitations of the) scope of the model tend to involve generalisations, and patterns reflecting connections in the model tend to involve distortions.

The Meta Model language patterns in detail

For each form of pattern an example structure is given with a typical response that may be used to recover the reference experience, and enable the individual to explore the deep structure, which forms the basis of the surface structure rules.

A. DELETIONS

These are language structures where some information has been omitted in the surface structure. The responses attempt to recover the sensory-specific detail from the deep structure.

1. Simple deletion

A structure where simply there is information omitted; for example:

> 'I am uncomfortable.'

- About what?

- In what way?

2. Lack of referential index

A structure where the referent is not specified clearly; for example:

> 'They don't listen to me.'

- Who doesn't listen to you?

> 'It doesn't matter.'

- What specifically doesn't matter?

3. Comparative deletion (good, better, worse, more, least, etc.)

A structure where a comparative is used but the standard by which the comparison is made has been omitted; for example:

> 'His behaviour is getting worse.'

- Worse than what?

- Worse than who?

- Worse than when?

4. Unspecified verb

A structure where verbs are used which do not provide a sensory-grounded description; for example:

> 'He disrupts my lesson.'

- What specifically does he do in your lesson?

B. GENERALISATIONS

These are language patterns where universality is implied. The response seeks to find counter examples or establish the deep structure basis for the generalisation.

1. Universal quantifier

A structure using a word of universality (e.g. always, never, all, every, nobody):

> 'He never listens to me.'

> - Never?

> - Has there ever been a time when he did?

> 'He shouts all the time.'

> - Is there ever a time he is quiet?

> - All the time?

2. Modal operator

A structure reflecting limiting beliefs in the individual's model of the world (e.g. cannot, must, should, impossible, have not, have to).

These limiting beliefs operate as either necessities (what ought, or ought not, to occur) or possibilities and impossibilities (what can, or cannot, occur); for example:

> 'I have to keep them quiet.'

> - What would happen if you didn't?

> 'I must be someone they respect.'

> - What would happen if you are not?

3. Lost performative

A structure which indicates some form of generalised belief or value judgement where the experiential basis of the judgement is missing; for example:

> 'Reading is more important than number work.'

> - How do you know that?

> - Who says so?

> - On what basis?

C. DISTORTIONS

These are the language patterns which reflect the beliefs which form the rules within the surface structure, namely the model of the world.

1. Cause / effect

A structure which indicates an implicit assumption that one thing is caused by another. The response may serve to explore the link or attempt to begin to separate the two elements. Frequently this structure will reflect an individual putting themselves in a position of effect, that is, perceiving themselves as being controlled by elements outside themselves.

The responses intend to recover the experiential basis for the cause/effect rule in the surface structure of their model of the world; for example:

'He makes me upset.'

• What specifically does he do that you feel upset about?

Words such as 'make', 'cause', etc. are particularly indicative of these sorts of structures.

2. Mind reading

A structure which indicates an implicit assumption that one individual knows what another is thinking or feeling. The responses invite the individual to explore the basis of the link between the sensory-based input and the interpretation of the other's thinking. In this respect a form of complex equivalence; for example:

'He doesn't like me.'

• How do you know that?

'His parents couldn't care less.'

• How do you know that?

• How would you expect them to be different if they did?

3. Nominalisation

A structure where a process has been turned into an object. In language a verb has been turned into a noun. The response serves to denominalise, by inviting the individual to consider the process again; for example:

'He has a communication problem.'

• How does he/should he communicate?

'He has dyslexia.'

• What do you mean by that?

• What specifically is he doing/not doing?

4. Complex equivalence

A structure where a behaviour, or phenomenon, is attributed a particular meaning. The response is intended to invite the individual to explore the deep structure of their model of the world to recover the experiential basis for this rule by which the attribution is made, and thereby establish the validity of the rule in the light of their experience to date; for example:

'When she uses that tone of voice I know she hates me.'

- How does her using that tone of voice mean she hates you?

There is also the option of attempting to find a counter example to the 'rule' from their experience; for example:

- Has there ever been a time when she has used that tone of voice and not hated you?

- Has there ever been a time when she has hated you but not used that tone of voice?

The complete counter example structure could be encoded as follows:

Complex equivalence:	X implies Y
Counter example:	Does X imply not Y?
	Does not X imply Y?
	Does not X imply not Y?

5. Presuppositions

These are structures where something is implicitly presupposed (in the surface structure) and not stated explicitly. If these structures are not picked up on, it is assumed that they are shared and accepted. They are frequently presented as a question, such that answering the question assumes acceptance of the presupposition; for example:

'Will you be here on time next week?'

- The presupposition is that you will be here next week.

'Is the head still having a secret affair with the caretaker?'

- The head has been having an affair with the caretaker.

'Can people's models of the world be the same?'

- People have models of the world.

The precision afforded by the Meta Model patterns is valuable in information gathering, identifying the aspects of language structures which reflect underlying beliefs and values, and uncovering the experiential basis on which those beliefs and rules are founded. The Meta Model provides information about how the other person is organising and structuring their subjective experience. A major benefit in having developed a working recognition of the Meta Model patterns is to be able to recognise them in another person's language in order to gain insights into how they organise their subjective experience within their model of the world. This avoids getting drawn into the illusion that we all have the same model of the world, which too readily leaves their problem thoroughly understood within your own model of the world, leaving a shared sense of being stuck and not finding a solution.

The Meta Model gives another dimension of rapport (through matching) and provides a beginning to helping others to explore and begin to solve their own problems. It is also helpful in expanding your own model of the world. Basically this latter aspect gives an extension to the psychologist's own flexibility and resourcefulness both for themselves and in their ability to work with others.

Becoming familiar with the Meta Model requires practice and time, but becomes a powerful tool in recognising the patterns in thinking and communication of the people we work with. A useful method for becoming familiar with the Meta Model is to choose one pattern to pay attention to in the language of the people you meet, and your own language. Practising each pattern for a few days will lead to relatively easy recognition of these patterns in language.

CHAPTER 11

Integrating the Two Approaches to Exploring the Model of the World

Two approaches to exploring an individual's model of the world have been presented, both of which can be seen as reasonably coherent wholes. However, they are compatible and each serves to enhance the value of the other.

In interviewing practice, the range of questions and directions to follow in exploring the individual's model of the world is increased substantially through having the two models. This provides a greater choice of options and opportunities to the interviewer and serves to enhance the quality of the interview.

In order to use the models, and questions they give rise to, most effectively it is useful to have a structure of how the models fit together. This gives the interviewer a broader framework for the exploration of their client's model of the world.

The basic structure given by the original root questions and exploratory directions was represented by the following grid.

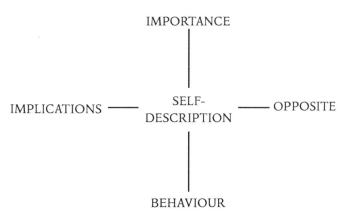

In terms of the universal modelling processes described earlier, the links between these descriptions are the distortions: the structural rules which form the model of the world. The exploratory questions serve to elicit the distortions which the individual uses to form the model of the world.

Any of the self-descriptions can form the starting point for this exploration in any of the four directions. The resultant description then forms the starting point for further exploration. The descriptions given by the client in this form of interviewing are surface structure descriptions. These contain the deletions and generalisations in their derivation from the deep structure.

In other words, the two-dimensional framework depicted above is effectively the surface structure which includes the distortions forming the links between the descriptions. This overlays the deep structure. Linking the two layers of surface structure and deep structure are the universal modelling processes of deletion and generalisation. A representation of this process is given in Figure 11.1.

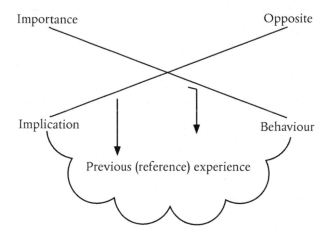

Figure 11.1 Surface and deep structure

It is important to acknowledge what this model represents. It is not a model of an individual's structure of subjective experience, that is, it is not the reality of how humans organise their beliefs, experience and memories of the world. The model serves as a guide to our questioning, as interviewers, to give directions to explore, and a sense of where we have come from. It enables us to keep track in our own mind where our interview is taking us. To use the previously mentioned expression 'the map is not the territory', in this sense the map is only as useful as it is helpful in guiding us in our exploration.

It is intended that the map should be as simple as possible and in this respect it is perhaps oversimplified at a theoretical level, but it is hoped that its relative simplicity will improve its usability in the practical situation of interviewing.

Distortions of the surface structure

The following language patterns were noted as reflecting the universal modelling process of distortion:

- cause/effect
- mind reading
- nominalisation
- complex equivalence
- presupposition.

It was noted that mind reading is a specific form of complex equivalence as both represent structures of the form 'X means Y'. In mind reading some, often unspoken, sensory experience is used to infer the other's thinking; this inference is a complex equivalence.

The cause/effect structure is also very similar to the complex equivalence, except that the link between the elements of the former is causal rather than equivalence. One creates the other, rather than infers it; nevertheless the structure of two elements with a link is similar.

These structures are the basis of the links between descriptions in the surface structure model presented earlier, the complex equivalence type of structures representing links on the vertical axis and the presupposition structures links on the horizontal axis. (Although this is probably an excessive over-generalisation, it is perhaps a useful simplification.)

The descriptions given in the surface structure will frequently be in nominalised form. Generally the descriptions will become less nominalised as the exploratory questions of 'behaviour' are used, and more nominalised as the exploratory questions of 'importance' are used, that is, more nominalised are higher up the vertical axis, and less nominalised are lower down the axis.

The combination of the two models provides a range of options and directions for exploration to the interviewer. These can serve as interventions and also present choices to the client, by prompting the client to explore their model of the world more fully. They also form the basis of the reframing methods which will be presented later in the chapter.

The implication is that, although we operate through our surface structure model of the world, the rules (distortions), which provide this structure, exist largely at an unconscious level. Thus our root questions and exploratory questions can frequently provide interesting insights for our clients.

Example

My earlier statement that 'Fords are good cars' is an example of a Lost Performative (generalisation), where an appropriate response may be 'on what basis?' My reply, by investigating in my deep structure, might be that I think they are 'reliable'. 'Reliable' is a useful description to work with in the surface structure; note that it is a nominalisation of a process, in the sense that 'reliable' is about the things that the car does (like starting when the key is turned, to explore the 'behaviour' direction), but it has been transposed into a quality that the car has.

I may then be asked the exploratory question 'What's important to you about things being reliable?', setting me up to provide a cause/effect or complex equivalent link up the vertical axis of the surface structure for my higher order belief/value. Alternatively I may be asked 'What else can you say about something, or someone, that is reliable?', gaining information about the 'implications'. Or I may be asked 'What can you say about something, or someone, that is not reliable?', gaining information about the 'opposites'. Seeking information in the 'behaviour' direction may use a question in the form 'How would you know if something was reliable?', which serves to de-nominalise the term reliable.

Information in the deep structure may be gained using the Meta Model questions, for instance 'Have you ever had a Ford which was not always reliable?', which would serve to challenge the implied universality of the initial statement that (all) Fords are reliable, all the time. Alternatively, 'How do you know that Fords are reliable?' serves to recover the reference experience which forms the basis of the judgement from the deep structure.

The combination of the two models gives the interviewer a wide range of options in the exploration of the client's model of the world. This provides a framework which helps to open up the exploration process and prevents the interviewer getting embroiled in the client's problems by interpreting the difficulty in terms of their own model of the world and potentially sharing in the client's inability to change. Exploring the client's model of the world in this way enables the client to discover the basis of their own difficulties, which can lead to new insights and previously unrealised options and alternatives. On occasions the new insights and understandings can lead to problems disappearing.

Case example: Graham

Graham, a 20-year-old, attended the Young People's Counselling Service with concerns about the organisation he had in his home. Both his parents had died, his mother within the last two years. He had previously attended a residential school for boys with emotional and behavioural difficulties. On returning from the school he had lived with his mother and an elderly male relative. Since his mother's death he and this elderly man had shared a flat. Both Graham's parents had suffered from mental illness, and spent time in psychiatric institutions.

Graham's concerns at home were that the elderly man, who exerted quite an influence on how things were done in the flat, showed little concern for ensuring that bills were paid on time.

The 'importance', for Graham, of ensuring bills were paid was that this would indicate he was 'coping'. The opposite, namely failure to pay bills, would result in services being cut off. This would then indicate that they were not coping. Coping was a description which frequently arose in the interviews with Graham, and seemed to be particularly significant. Its significance became apparent when the 'opposite' direction was explored. For Graham, someone who did not cope was 'mad'. Given his family history of mental problems this led to Graham's concern for a self-perception as 'coping'.

Exploration in the 'behaviour' direction about people who were 'mad', and some exploration of the deep structure, namely his reference experiences about 'mad' people, provided the basis for challenging his definition of madness – from a failure to pay bills to something quite different and less personally threatening.

This particular insight or intervention was a major point of change in the work with Graham.

Building complex equivalences

Complex equivalences are the key links in the surface structure. Some strategies for responding to complex equivalence structures have already been presented. In the next section the process of reframing will be considered as a further powerful means of responding to complex equivalent structures. The value of the reframing strategy, based on complex equivalence structures, is enhanced by being able to identify implicit complex equivalences in the surface structure. The exploratory questions can provide a vehicle for doing this quite effectively.

By way of example, I present a complaint about myself that 'I cannot manage to keep up with the amount of work that I get' as a problem I want to address. The importance of this problem can be explored with such questions as 'What is important to you in your job that you should be able to keep up with all the work that you receive?'; and 'What does it mean to you that you should keep up with all the work you are given?'; and 'What can you infer about a person who cannot keep up with all the work they get?'

A likely reply I may give is that it means I'm not very good at my job, or I'm not a good psychologist. This has then identified the implicit complex equivalence in my surface structure which forms the basis of my complaint, namely that:

> 'I cannot manage to keep up with the amount of work I get.'

means

> 'I am not a good psychologist.'

This complex equivalence can now be responded to as considered earlier, or with a meaning reframe as indicated in the next section.

Generally complex equivalences are of the form of a piece of behaviour or sensory-grounded information being inferred as equivalent to a statement at a higher logical level. In this respect any complaint which is expressed in terms of a behaviour or sensory-grounded experience needs to be explored using the exploratory questions in order to establish its significance at a higher logical level.

Reframing in the surface structure by offering alternative distortions

The elements of the surface structure have been presented as linked by distortions. These are predominantly reflected in language by complex equivalences or cause/effects. These patterns in the structure give rise to useful methods for presenting alternative perspectives to the client, through offering alternative complex equivalents and cause/effect links, in the form of reframes.

Reframing is a common psychological strategy which serves to present an alternative meaning to a behaviour or issue, or alternatively presents the behaviour or issue in a new light. This is sometimes called positive connotation, where a positive interpretation is made of a behavioural symptom. These two forms of reframe are presented here.

The meaning reframe

The meaning reframe works directly on the complex equivalence structure. The complex equivalence presents a structure in the form of 'X means Y'. The meaning reframe offers an alternative to this in the form 'X means Z' where Z is an alternative to Y, but importantly has already been found to be something valued by the individual through the exploration of their surface structure.

Here is an example to give the idea.

EXAMPLE

A friend tells me that he has a professional respect for a particular colleague because she is reliable. Reliability is important to him for various reasons which I have explored with him. I have also noted in further explorations of his model of the world that 'people who are effective agents of change (in casework)' is also an important description.

I could use this information to construct a meaning reframe based on this information.

The structure 'my friend respects his colleague *because* she is reliable' is a distortion in the form of a cause/effect: 'X implies Y'. The knowledge that my friend places a value on 'people being effective agents of change.' gives me a potential Z so that I can present the reframe 'X implies Z', as an alternative distortion, but one which matches existing elements of his model of the world.

I could then offer the reframe that 'although he says he respects his colleague because he thinks she is reliable, I wonder if really what he respects about his colleague is that she is an effective agent of change'.

Thus an alternative meaning is ascribed to his respect for his colleague.

Bandler and Grinder (1982) present a very extensive methodology of reframing including the meaning reframe. As an example of the meaning reframe in practice they present the following example of a piece of work done by Leslie Cameron-Bandler:

> Leslie Cameron-Bandler was working with a woman who had a compulsive behaviour… The rest of her family could function pretty well with everything the mother did except for her attempts to care for the carpet. She spent a lot of her time trying to get people not to walk on it, because they left footprints in the pile… When this woman looked down at the carpet and saw a footprint in it, her response was an intense negative kinaesthetic gut reaction. She would rush off to get the vacuum cleaner and vacuum the carpet immediately… She actually vacuumed the carpet three to seven times per day. She spent a tremendous amount of time trying to get people to come in through the back door, and nagging at them if they didn't, or getting them to take their shoes off and walk lightly.

The family seemed to get on fine if they were not at home, but at home everyone referred to their mother as being a nag... Her nagging centred mainly around the carpet.

What Leslie did with this woman is this: she said, 'I want you to close your eyes and see your carpet, and see that there is not a single footprint on it anywhere. It's clean and fluffy – not a mark anywhere.' The woman closed her eyes, and she was in seventh heaven, just smiling away. Then Leslie said, 'And realise fully that means you are totally alone, and that the people you care for and love are nowhere around.' The woman's expression shifted radically, and she felt terrible! Then Leslie said, 'Now, put a few footprints there and look at those footprints and know that the people you care most about in the world are nearby.' And then of course she felt good again. (Bandler and Grinder 1982, p.6)

This is an example of a meaning reframe where the 'X means Y' structure can be seen as:

X – the carpet clean and fluffy

Y – the mother's sense of being a mother and housewife

so that her sense of being a good mother is given by her experiential evidence of the clean and fluffy carpet. The alternative description Z is given in terms of the absence of the people she loves and cares for. The text indicates the woman's family is important to her, so this Z is going to be relevant.

The reframe 'X means Z' can then be offered giving a new meaning to the clean and fluffy carpet.

Meaning reframes offer an alternative link in the complex equivalence or cause/effect structure. To be successful, or accepted by the client, it is important that they fit well with the client's model of the world, and in this respect are another form of pacing and leading. The reframe can be conceived as leading onto new understandings, and therefore needs to have been adequately paced in order to be followed by the client.

The context reframe

This form of reframe positively connotes a behaviour by presenting it in a new light.

The context reframe works through the generalisation inherent in a statement. Many of the descriptions which are offered include, or at least imply, universal quantifiers; for example, the statement 'It is bad to be domineering'.

- It is implied that it is bad to be domineering at all times, in all circumstances, etc.

- The suggested response, in the previous chapter, to the universal quantifier was to check for contrary evidence in the client's deep structure, with questions of the form 'Always?' or 'Has there ever been a time when it is not?', i.e. attempting to find a counter example.

The counter example strategy was also considered as a form of response to the complex equivalence in the Meta Model.

The context reframe gives a new context where the particular link does not hold, rather like a counter example, but suggested by the interviewer, using important values from the client's model of the world.

The context reframe works by taking a description which is assumed to have a negative connotation and providing a context in which that behaviour would be viewed positively; for example, 'I wouldn't want to be thought of as a forceful and domineering person.'

The description indicates that being forceful and domineering is viewed as a negative self-attribute. However, by finding a context in which being forceful and dominant may be laudable attributes, in furthering some important value within my model of the world, it is possible to reframe the implied complex equivalence so that forceful and domineering do not mean something negative; thereby establishing a counter example, with which I am likely to agree. The key is that the counter example presented is related to something which is particularly important to me, as the client.

Very much like the concept of pacing and leading discussed in Chapter 3, it is crucial that, before the reframe (leading) can be offered, the model of the world has to be paced, and an appropriate match provided.

For example, I may be presented with a context reframe of this behaviour in terms of its being useful for me to develop the ability to be forceful, and even domineering, and recognise these as valuable skills in being able to handle situations where I would otherwise have to reluctantly compromise other important values. One situation which would have relevance to me would be where I discovered someone vandalising or taking my property. Being a forceful and domineering character in those circumstances would be quite an asset, as far as I am concerned.

Now I have such a counter example I can begin to examine the merits of forceful and domineering behaviour, and although my entire personality is unlikely to change, I have lost the complex equivalence of forceful and domineering behaviour being absolutely negative. I am able to bring to bear a sense of choice to my behaviour, according to circumstances, rather than have the restriction of the universal rule. This parallels the change in range of convenience in the PCP model discussed earlier.

There is a very simple example to illustrate the method. Again a therapeutic example is taken from Bandler and Grinder (1982, p.8). This is an example taken from the work of Virginia Satir. She was working with a banker and his family. Although the father expressed concerns about his daughter's stubborn attitude, the daughter perceived her father as the 'bad' person and sided with the mother although she acted like her father.

> The father's repeated complaint in the session was that the mother hadn't done a very good job of raising the daughter, because the daughter was so stubborn. At one time when he made this complaint Virginia interrupted what was going on. She turned around and looked at the father and said, 'You're a man who has gotten ahead in life. Is that true?'
>
> 'Yes.'
>
> 'Was all that you have, just given to you? Did your father own the bank and just say, "Here you're president of the bank"?'
>
> 'No, no I had to work my way up.'
>
> 'So you have some tenacity, don't you?'
>
> 'Yes.'
>
> 'Well there's a part of you that has allowed you to be able to get to where you are, and to be a good banker. And sometimes you have to refuse people things that you would like to be able to give them, because you know if you did that something bad would happen later on.'
>
> 'Yes.'
>
> 'Well there's a part of you that's been stubborn enough to really protect yourself in very important ways.'
>
> 'Well, yes. But, you know, you can't let this kind of thing get out of control.'
>
> 'Now I want you to turn and look at your daughter, and to realise beyond a doubt that you have taught her how to be stubborn and how to stand up for herself, and that that is something priceless. This gift that you've given her is something

that cannot be bought, and it's something that may save her life. Imagine how valuable that will be when your daughter goes out on a date with a man who has bad intentions.'

In this example the therapist has found a context where the complained-of behaviour could be viewed by the client in a different perspective. Thus the universal negativity of the behaviour is challenged. As Bandler and Grinder comment: 'Every experience in the world and every behaviour is appropriate, given some context, some frame.'

With imagination, and practice, context reframes can be used to begin to provide alternative perspectives within an individual's model of the world.

CHAPTER 12

Techniques for Eliciting the Model of the World with Children

When working with young children in particular, it is not always easy to use the highly linguistic-based methods which have been suggested in the last chapters. However, the conceptual structure which has been presented can still be used as a guide to the exploration of their model of the world, but methods less dependent on the intricacies of spoken language may well be more productive. In terms of representational systems, the techniques allow the visual and kinaesthetic modalities, in addition to the auditory digital, to be represented in the communication. This perhaps opens up new perspectives and gives access to new information. The methods are also very helpful in work with older and more articulate young people.

The methods presented in this chapter have been used by many psychologists over the years. Many of the methods have been devised by Dr A.T. Ravenette and are derived from PCP, which not only provides the theoretical underpinning, but also gives the basis for further exploration of the individual's model of the world.

The methods involve semi-structured drawing and talking exercises which serve as both root and exploratory questions. Root questions are those that elicit some initial form of self-description; exploratory questions provide a means to elaborate further the individual's model of the world from the initial root. Many of the forms of questions discussed in earlier sections can be used in the interview to elaborate further the child's model of the world.

None of the techniques in themselves yield information which should be considered in isolation, but all the information elicited should be used to generate hypotheses about how the child makes sense of the world in which they live.

Frequently similar descriptions will be elicited from a child in response to the exercises. This may infer a significance of the description for the child.

When conducting individual interviews with children or young people, it is important to work to develop a high degree of rapport. Establishing a shared understanding of why the interview is taking place, and at whose instigation, will be an important first step, in addition to conveying a respect for them as people.

1. Identifying the Concerns

Purpose

The initial stage of the interview involves establishing with the child what the purpose of the meeting is, how it has arisen and how it will be conducted.

Considerations

Psychologists will be aware that there are many issues to consider to create a satisfactory interview situation. When interviewing children in school it is important to recognise that they may very well not have any of the background information about why they are there, are unlikely to have seen the psychologist before, even around the school, and particularly be quite uncertain as to why they have been selected to be seen, and by whom.

It is useful to explain who you are; what your role is; how it was decided that they are being seen; and what you are likely to be doing in the interview.

Psychologists will have different approaches to this, and develop different styles for different situations. The beginning of the interview is also the crucial time for developing rapport with the child which will be essential if the interview is going to be maximally productive.

A useful approach is to let the child know that you see children frequently, and this is because schools, and parents, have expressed concerns about how the children are getting on in school. This can be followed by asking the child what they think the school or parents would be concerned about for them.

Some children will be very clear in their understanding of the concerns, whereas others will not have any understanding, or be reluctant to acknowledge difficulties at an early stage. In this situation providing options can be useful.

Options can be put in terms of general reasons why schools and parents would want a psychologist to meet a child, which could include:

1. where children find the work very difficult

2. where children get into trouble a lot

3. where children don't get on with the teachers

4. where children don't get on with the other children

5. where the children seem to be unhappy.

Inviting the child to say whether their teachers and parents would describe them in each of these terms can be useful in helping to identify the concern. Obviously the language has to be made appropriate to the age of the child.

The concerns can be further explored by asking who would be most concerned, and developing a hierarchy of level of concern. Additionally this may offer the opportunity for using exploratory questions to get a greater sense of the detail of concerns and the importance both they and others have about the concern.

It is important to stress what your role as the psychologist is in relation to the concerns. Often this can be most productively put as your involvement has been asked for in order to meet with the child and attempt to find the best way to help deal with the concerns.

Case example: James

James, a 12-year-old secondary school pupil, had been referred by his school because of concerns about his attitude to work, lack of homework, and particularly poor spelling.

At the beginning of the interview, after the initial explanations about the psychologist's role, etc., James was asked what he thought the school's concerns would be that had resulted in their asking for a psychologist to become involved.

James indicated that since he had been given a new homework diary, which both the school and home were monitoring effectively, his homework had improved. The relevant concerns now would be about generally getting work done and his spelling. He named the four teachers who he thought would be most concerned.

When asked who else would be concerned he named his mother, and noted that she would be more concerned than the teachers. He also commented that she would say that he could do his work and learn spelling if he put his mind to it.

When asked how concerned he was, James noted that he would be less concerned than both his mother and teachers.

When asked how concerned his father would be James noted that he was not very interested in school and wouldn't get involved, except if it was a question of behaviour, because his father would be very upset if he heard James had been badly behaved in school.

The question was put that, if James was more concerned than his teachers, how would things be different? He replied that he would put his mind to it, get higher grades and be able to read and spell.

The presupposition here is that James believes he could learn if he was to involve himself in the learning process, and this is something he could make a decision about. (In terms of the taxonomy of logical levels this is useful information about where to focus any intervention.)

He was then asked what 'putting his mind to it' would involve, and he replied: 'Have to do my work; learn; take more care over my work.' He was then asked what he would be doing differently if he decided to change. He replied: 'Not lounging around watching TV but doing homework; not saying, "Oh give it a few minutes then I'll do it"; not messing about.'

James was also asked who would be the first to notice if he decided to change. He replied: 'Teachers – because they would help me more because they would know that I was trying; Mother – because I wouldn't ask so much, but I would ask for help earlier; Nan – she would hear at parents' evening.'

These were only the first few minutes of the interview, but show the extent of useful information which can be elicited, and also highlights a number of avenues which may be worthy of further exploration in the interview and subsequent discussion with teachers and parents. They have direct relevance to the involvement the school and parents can have in promoting change, at least at levels of behaviour and values.

Two further useful questions to explore initial concerns are 'Tell me three things you like about this school', and subsequently, 'If there were three things which could be different about school, which would mean you would like it better, what would they be?' These root questions can often yield helpful avenues for further exploration.

2. Kinetic Family Drawing

Purpose

The Kinetic Family Drawing (KFD) was first suggested by Burns and Kaufman (1970). The technique was proposed as an extension of human figure drawings. Drawings can provide a wealth of basic information about the family in which the child lives, but a great deal of information is also available through interpretation of the content of the drawing, in addition to the drawing itself providing information about the child's approach to the activity. The drawing can become a particularly useful vehicle for the subsequent discussion about activities and relationships within the family, and the general functioning of the family, with both the child in the interview and the parents subsequently. The drawing and discussion opens the opportunity for generating and refining hypotheses, but it is important particularly with interpretative ideas that these be treated very much as hypotheses rather than assumed to be definitive. Thus with all interpretations it would be important to look for information from other sources to support hypotheses. Nevertheless, interpretations can be helpful as a basis for asking questions of the child, parents or teachers to ask them to consider tentative hypotheses or ideas.

Method

The technique is quite simple to carry out, involving asking the child to 'draw everyone in the family doing something'. This is the extent of the instruction. The child is provided with a plain piece of A4 paper and a pencil; rulers, rubbers, etc. are not necessary.

While the child is drawing they can be asked to talk about what they are drawing, or it may present as less of an interruption if they are asked to talk about the drawing on completion of each figure, or even at the end of the entire drawing. At times it is useful to consider who the child is likely to draw in the family, in terms of those living at home, or whether this should include members of the extended family. This is clearly a judgement to be made at the time.

Children on occasions have difficulty starting the drawing; this can often be helped by asking how many people are in the family, naming them, and then asking the child who they are going to draw first. Reluctance can also be expressed in terms of their lack of ability to draw, and particularly to draw people. This can often be overcome by indicating an acceptance that the drawing does not have to be perfect. If the child asks, it is important to indicate that the drawings should be more than matchstick people.

Basic information which can be asked of each of the figures drawn is name, age, relationship to the child, and what they are doing in the drawing. Information which is based on interpretation can be checked out with the child after the drawing has been completed.

Before working with this technique, particularly in any interpretative way, it is recommended that Burns and Kaufman's books are consulted (1970, 1972), as it is not intended to consider here the depth of the research they report. However, a few basic principles would seem appropriate to give some indication of the value of the information that can be derived, and the quality of interpretation that can be made.

At a relatively simple level interpretations can be made in terms of the verbal description of what is portrayed in the drawing. Some examples are given below.

1. PHYSICAL PROXIMITY

The physical proximity of individuals as they appear in the drawing could be interpreted as reflecting the closeness which is felt by individuals. The general layout of the individuals within the family may well reflect who is closest to whom in the family, and perhaps who gets in the way of others, in addition to noting who is central and who peripheral in the family.

2. BARRIERS

This is an extension of the above idea; barriers in the drawing, in the form of walls, furniture, etc., can represent impediments to a sense of closeness between individuals, very much a sense of 'something coming between them'.

3. COMPARTMENTALISATION

This is almost a special case of the above, in which children or others in the family seem to isolate themselves (and their feelings) from other members of their family. The compartment is a barrier around the individual, perhaps also showing the family functioning more as a number of distinct individuals existing within their own world, with less emphasis on the family as a unit. Compartmentalisation may be seen in ways other than individuals drawn in boxes, but could include people drawn in cars, or on the bus; these examples have the added indication of leaving, going somewhere, or possible abandonment.

4. SIMILARITIES

Similarities in the drawings of one individual with another suggest a sense of identification.

5. SHADING

Heavy shading is frequently associated with anxiety. The shading may denote a preoccupation with the particular area shaded.

6. POSITION

The position of individuals on the page can be interpreted as having importance, not only in terms of relative position as already noted, but in relation to the page. Generally those who are higher up the page tend to be seen as more dominant, those in the centre more central, and those to the outside more peripheral.

7. ACTIONS

The actions which particular individuals are involved in can be a particularly useful source of interpretative information, for instance how one individual's activity relates to another person, particularly involving objects or projectiles. The direction an individual is facing, particularly towards or away from the family, is important. Are individuals involved in activities which include them in the family or show them removing themselves from the family?

General points of interpretation

A useful strategy in interpreting information from the KFD is to take the picture quite literally. Frequently literal descriptions of aspects of the picture in words and phrases can provide useful interpretations to check out. In the case example of Steven (Chapter 13), the picture of Steven in the top right-hand corner shows him bouncing on his bed leaving him 'up in the air', a phrase which tended to make some sense to the adults around him. Children have drawn pictures where members of the family have 'turned their back on them', which again have turned into apt descriptions of family life.

It is important that interpretations are not taken as definitive statements about the world of the child. The KFD represents a source of information which can be extended in its scope with interpretation. The interpretations have to be recognised as suggestions arising from the picture and as such have no higher status without confirmatory information. The value is often not necessarily in the immediate information, but as the vehicle the KFD provides in enabling a discussion at a considerably more sophisticated level with the adults in the system. This can happen even without offering interpretations, but where interpretations are offered their status does need to be acknowledged.

The books by Burns and Kaufman give much more detailed consideration to interpretations and are recommended reading.

Case examples

KFD 1 (Oliver) shows figures in compartments (Figure 12.1). Oliver (on the left in the drawing) described himself as having a strong bond with his father, which is characterised by the great similarity in the drawing of him and his father. However, Oliver rarely saw his father who was separated from the family, and who now had another family which he lives with, and is perhaps a reflection of the additional person in his father's compartment. Oliver did not get on particularly with his mother and sister, which is reflected by the compartmen-talisation and also his positioning most towards the outside of the family. Oliver throwing darts in the direction of his mother could also be interpreted as anger directed to his mother. Possibly Oliver sees his mother and sister coming between him and his father. The fact that all members of the family are compartmentalised perhaps also reflects that the family generally functions in a way which does not encourage members to share their feelings with each other, but to operate in relative isolation.

The value of the drawing in this case was not the interpretations, which were developed through the drawing and discussion, but more that the drawing provided the opening to discuss these issues sensitively with both Oliver and his mother, allowing them to acknowledge the situation and then open up opportunities to consider possible intervention strategies.

Figure 12.1 KFD 1

KFD 2 (Paul) shows Paul with his mother and two younger sisters (Figure 12.2). Paul generally was very isolated within his family. There is a resemblance between the two sisters and the mother, with Paul drawn differently. The mother and sisters are drawn higher in the page suggesting their relative importance to Paul. Paul's very poor relationship with the eldest of his sisters could be reflected in her foot being superimposed on his face. The overlap perhaps also indicates a sense of there not being room for both of them in the same family. The scored-out drawing was Paul's first attempt at himself which, part way through, he stopped as he realised there was not enough room, as it would overlap with his mother. Perhaps his mother was too much of a figure to have such a conflict with, in terms of room in the family, and his position changed to where he was in conflict with his sister for the space.

Figure 12.2 KFD 2

The drawing again served as a useful vehicle for checking some of the suggested hypotheses with both Paul and his mother. The interpretations were very relevant and allowed an in-depth discussion of family functioning. The interpretation and discussion session was shared with the special needs co-ordinator in the school, which enabled a greater understanding of Paul's personal world, enabling a more positive and sympathetic attitude to be cultivated with school staff.

The drawing also shows an example of what Burns and Kaufman describe as the 'ironing board or X syndrome'. They describe the ironing board below the mother with an 'X' as a constant theme with children attempting to control sexual impulse.

KFD 3 (John) shows his father with the dog walking to the shops past the pub (Figure 12.3). John is drawn on his bicycle, with his mother, drawn much less carefully, between them, and in front of the pub. Discussion with John about the family drawing and using other interview techniques described in this chapter suggested that John was particularly close to his father, whereas his mother seemed 'to get in between them'. John described his mother as not doing very much because she was always drinking.

Figure 12.3 KFD 3

In subsequent discussion, using the family drawing as the vehicle for the discussion, it allowed the mother to indicate the considerable marital difficulties the parents were experiencing. The initial impressions generated from the drawing did not seem to be confirmed in the details by the mother, but nevertheless the KFD did provide a very effective opening to discussion of some of the very serious underlying difficulties which seemed to be a major source of distress in the family.

3. A Drawing and its Opposite

Purpose

This is a technique which can be used to explore with the child their model of the world beyond the superficial level and to provide a basis for interpretative hypotheses. In PCP theory terms, it is a vehicle for exploring similarities and differences through themes which are represented in both pictures, or noticeably absent from the pictures; that is, what the pictures imply and what they deny.

Method

By example – a Year 3 boy at a secondary school had previously been referred when he was at junior school, and again at the secondary level, because of his very worrying temper tantrums. When seen for the first time at the secondary school, it soon became very apparent that his anger was a concern for him, but that he could talk around this endlessly without addressing the real issues. He was asked to draw what his anger had looked like to him, when he lost his temper when he was in the junior school (this being safer than using the present). He produced picture A (Figure 12.4), which seems quite explosive and uncontained. He was then asked to draw a second picture which was the opposite of the first and he drew picture B (Figure 12.5). His comment as he drew picture B was 'putting out the flames and using the energy positively'.

Figure 12.4 A Drawing and its Opposite (A)

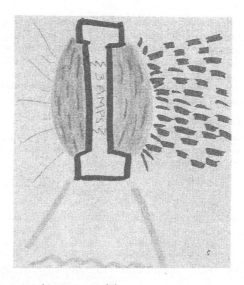

Figure 12.5 A Drawing and its Opposite (B)

Observations

1. Picture A seems very much more out of control and angry. B appears to be much more contained within and by the structure of the fuse (but of course, a fuse has the potential for blowing if the external demands are too great).

2. Picture A has no external forces to control the uncontained anger, whereas B has the external rain which has a 'dampening down' effect.

3. Picture A represents a potentially destructive force, whereas B acknowledges the positive and creative potential of an appropriately contained energy.

These pictures offer a non-verbal vehicle for tapping into a richness of verbal metaphor, which can be used with the child to establish a shared understanding of their view of the concern. In this case the child was enabled to go on to say that all his life he had thought that his parents had been on the verge of splitting up and this, in his view, was because of him. When this information was shared with the parents, they were horrified. They acknowledged having had difficulties, but had no idea that their son viewed their marriage and home life in this way.

It was agreed that they would talk to their son about their arguments and reassure him that they were to do with their relationship and not attributable to him, and that they had no intention of separating.

The school subsequently reported that the boy's temper significantly reduced and was no longer a concern. No further tantrums were experienced.

A second method

This second method is started by drawing a line, such as that given in Figure 12.6, and inviting the child to use the line to produce a drawing which includes four people who are important.

Figure 12.6 Line for elaboration

The child is then asked to do a drawing which would be the opposite of the drawing they first drew. Through discussion, the content of the drawings can be established and the two drawings used as a basis for developing themes with the child, making note of the similarities present and possibly any significant omissions (e.g. an absence of people from both pictures) in addition to the differences.

Given that these similarities and differences can represent constructive understandings, perhaps in metaphor, the drawings present a non-threatening basis for enabling the child to explore their view of the world which they might otherwise find difficult to articulate. This may also allow the psychologist to share in this understanding and offer possible alternative perspectives for the child to consider.

A third method
PURPOSE
This latter method is very clearly structured from PCP with explicit instructions and questions intended to identify similarities and differences in the drawings elicited, and using the opposite to further clarify.

METHOD
The child is asked to draw a picture; this may be as a free choice or, as in the example presented above, a picture which includes four important people. When the drawing is finished the child is asked to describe what is happening in the drawing. If they have difficulty doing this, questions which elicit what people in the drawing are thinking, feeling and doing are useful exploratory questions.

Once the child has given a description of the drawing, which has allowed them to explore the content reasonably thoroughly for themselves, they are asked to do another drawing which represents the opposite of the first drawing. Frequently they will need to spend quite some time in determining for themselves quite how to interpret this.

When the two drawings have both been completed, the child can be asked to describe three ways in which the drawings are different, which represent them being opposites. After this they can be asked to describe three similarities of the two drawings.

The major part of the psychologist's role at this stage is to help the child put into words in a meaningful sense what are the pertinent issues upon which they are making the distinctions of similarities and differences. This can be done by feeding back the distinctions they are making, but not by leading them into the understandings that you as the psychologist would make of what they are saying.

Once the similarities and differences have been isolated reasonably clearly their opposites can be identified. On some occasions it may be useful to derive opposites earlier in order to more clearly identify the original definitions of the similarities and differences.

At this stage a number of constructs have been identified which can be checked back with the child as to their pertinence as important dimensions or value judgements which they use to make sense of themselves and their world. One particular way in which this can be explored is by gaining some understanding of how important it is for the child to aspire to one end of the construct rather than the other.

When the constructs have been elicited in this form further exploration of the model of the world can be considered using the exploratory questions described earlier.

4. Salmon Line

The following technique originally comes from the work of Phillida Salmon (1988), and links to later work on scaling from other solution-focused models.

Purpose

This technique elicits bi-polar constructs from the child around the perceived problem in order to explore with them where they see themselves in relation to the two poles and the possibilities for change.

Method

Having established with the child what they think the concern is (from other techniques described earlier), draw a line:

If the child has said, for instance, 'reading is hard', use this as one end of the construct and ask the child what the opposite of 'reading is hard' might be. This might be 'reading is easy'. Any other form of description may be used either from a direct question or a description elicited from any other technique.

Let the child choose which end of the line to put each of the descriptions; for example:

reading is _____ / ____ / ____ / ____ *reading is*
    easy   *hard*

Having divided the line into sections to give the idea of a scale, ask the child if they can think of anyone at home or at school who finds that 'reading is easy'. Once they have thought of someone invite the child to mark where this person would be on the line (A).

Do the same for someone who finds that 'reading is hard' (B). Then ask them if they know anyone who is in between (C). Ask the child where they think significant others might be; for example, where would Mum be on the line, where would Dad be, where would brothers and sisters be? Finally ask the child where they think that they would be on the line.

Then ask the child if they think that it is possible for things to change for them, and whether they think they can move up the line towards the 'reading is easy' end. If the child says things can change, ask them how far up the line they think they could move and ask them to mark this on the line. Join the position the child sees themselves at present with the position they see themselves being in the future with a dotted line. (This allows the possibility of change to be seen.) Then ask the child what will have to happen for the change to occur.

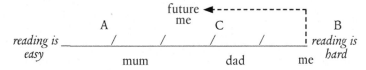

Alternatively, if the child says that they do not think that things can change, this gives the opportunity for exploring, with them, what they believe prevents change happening (challenging the Modal Operator of Possibility in Meta Model terms). This exploration might take place at a number of the logical levels, namely environmental, behavioural, capability, belief and identity. For example, a child might say that things cannot change because they have nowhere to study, nobody has shown them how to study, they have a damaged brain, or they cannot be a better reader than Dad.

Of course, 'reading is hard' and 'reading is easy' are just examples of poles for a construct, and any other opposites elicited from the child can be used in exactly the same way.

5. Portrait Gallery

Purpose

To explore the child's sense of themselves in relation to their experiences in their world.

Method

Initially, draw the outline of a face with hair. Although the picture is not of the child themselves, ensure that at least the hairstyle resembles that of the child, as in Figure 12.7.

Figure 12.7 Outline drawings for Portrait Gallery

Ask the child to fill in the face so that it looks like a happy face. When this is done, write 'happy' under the face and say, 'Tell me three things about someone who would have a happy face like that.' Write down the child's answers.

Draw another outline face and ask the child what the opposite of a happy face is. For most children 'happy' and 'sad' are opposite ends of a construct and they will respond by saying 'sad'. Ask the child to fill in the face so that it looks like a sad face. When this is done write 'sad' under the face, and ask the child to tell you three things about someone who would have a sad face. Write down the child's responses.

Say to the child, 'Happy and sad are feelings that people can have. Can you think of any other feelings a person might have?'

Accept their answers and draw as many outline faces as feelings they name. Ask for three comments for each face using the form 'Tell me three things about someone who would have a face like that'. If the child cannot think of any feeling states, or you have a sense of the child's affective state, you could suggest that some children might feel _____, and ask the child to draw a face that would represent that feeling. Continue the process as above.

A further step with this technique is to explore how the child perceives themselves as being viewed by others. Using the set of portraits of feelings, ask them which their mother would say was most like them (if the child says they do not know, ask them to guess). Repeat this for the father, siblings, teacher, head teacher and any significant others in the child's life. Also ask for the child's own view of which is most like them, and which they would most like to be.

Another approach to this, if the feeling state can have identified opposites, is to set them out as constructs on the Self-Description Grid, which is described at the end of these example techniques.

This can also be done for the referred problem and its opposite, noting which affective state is associated with each pole.

The method can be used to provide a discussion about change and the implications of change in one area. Again the exploratory questions and the use of the Meta Model become the tools for the exploration, with the 'Portrait Gallery' of faces a visual reference for the discussion.

Exploring possibilities for change

The technique can be extended to explore the possibilities for change using the principles of the scaling described above in the Salmon Line.

Ask the child to fill in the face of a boy/girl who has the child's identified problem (see the earlier section on Identifying the Concerns). Typical examples may be:

- a boy who fights in school
- a boy who finds reading difficult
- a girl who is naughty in class.

Again three descriptions are elicited.

The contrast can then either be provided by you or by the child by asking, 'What would somebody be like who did not fight in school/find reading difficult/be naughty in class?' The face is then drawn, filled in by the child and three descriptions elicited.

The descriptions, of course, may offer the opportunity for exploring any issues as they arise and seem pertinent. The value of further exploration is always a matter of judgement at the time. Discussion linked to the faces helps de-personalise the problem which facilitates the child to look at the situation a little more constructively without being defensive about their own position.

A scaling line is then drawn between the two faces, similar to the Salmon Line previously described.

Once this has been done, the child is reminded of the extreme ends, problem and opposite, emphasising the extremity of the very end point (e.g. always gets in trouble vs. always perfectly behaved). Then ask the child to mark on the line where they would see themselves currently. Also mark where they would like to be able to put themselves. (If the child would like to be nearer the negative end this gives the opportunity for exploring how this would be better for them – and what is good for them about being at the problem end.)

Referring to the two opposite faces, you can ask if it is possible for the first child to become like the second (e.g. 'Can the boy who finds reading difficult become like the boy who can read easily?'). If not, it is important to find what stops this from happening, and further work on belief change may be important; stories and metaphor may be particularly useful.

This helps identify at which logical level to concentrate on promoting change in order to help make a difference for the child.

If change is possible, the next stage is to explore the possibility of making a small incremental step from where the child is on the line now in the direction of where they would like to be.

Referring to the small step change on the scaling line, we can explore in detail how the change might occur, how it may be supported, and note particularly the degree to which the child sees it within their power to bring about the change.

The following questions are useful for this exploration:

- How will the change begin to happen?

- What will you be doing differently?

- Who can help?

- What will they need to do?

- Who will be the first to notice?

- What will they notice?

- Who is most important to notice?

- How will you know they have noticed?

The answers to the above questions can form the basis for an action plan drawn largely from the child. This plan outlines how the system around the child needs to respond, in order to initiate and maintain their own efforts to bring about change. The key people the child identifies are likely to be parents as well as teachers; the information can provide a useful basis for discussion with them to arrive at an action plan at a later stage.

The pro-forma in Figure 12.8 can be used as a prompt for the technique.

Change
1. Is it possible?
2. How will it begin to happen?
3. What will you be doing differently?
4. Who can help?
5. What will they need to do?
6. Who will be the first to notice?
7. What will they notice?
8. Who is most important to notice?
9. How will you know they have noticed?

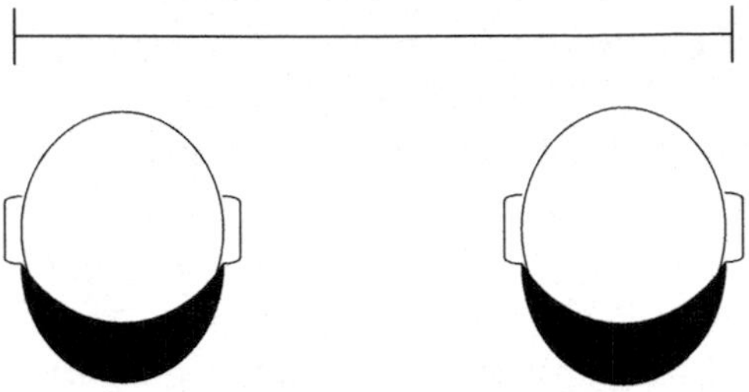

Desired state

1.

2.

3.

Current state

1.

2.

3.

Figure 12.8 Pro-forma for action plan to bring about change

6. Three Comments

Purpose
To explore the child's perception of themselves through their perception of how they are seen by others.

Method
Having previously noted in the interview with the child that their parents have agreed to this interview, note that you will be meeting with their parents later.

The following provides an adequate introduction to the task.

> *'If when I meet your mum (and gesture towards an empty chair) I ask her, "Mrs X, what are the three most important things you could tell me about [child's name] that would let me know what sort of a person [child's name] is", what do you think she would say?'*

If the child replies that they do not know, ask them to guess. Write down the child's responses. It is helpful to give an explanation for writing down what they say, in terms of its importance and that you do not want to forget it.

The question can be repeated for all members of the child's family (note KFD), class teacher, head teacher and significant others, and for the child's view of what they would say about themselves. Animals (and maybe, even, inanimate objects) can also be considered if they are important to the child, and would give a view of the child if they could speak.

An extension of this is to ask how the child would like to be, or what things they would like to change about themselves if they could. It is important that this is worded so that it seems to be quite normal to wish to be different, and there is no implication that there is something wrong with the child. The following question conveys this:

> *'All of us have things that we would like to be different about ourselves. I can think of ways in which I would like to be different. If you could have three ways in which you could change, in what ways would you like to be different?'*

Significant themes are often apparent arising from the descriptions through assumed commentaries of different people. The commonality across commentaries may suggest particular descriptions are important or relevant for further exploration, although any description can be further explored using the exploratory questions described in the earlier chapters

Case example: Ruby

Ruby, an eight-year-old, was referred because of concerns regarding her reading and writing. She presented as an articulate and able child. Ruby's parents had expressed concern initially about medical problems and as those were resolved they focused on her literacy skills.

To the questions outlined above, Ruby gave the following responses:

MUM

1. She works.
2. She reads.
3. She writes.

DAD

1. Good at work.
2. She plays a little bit.

OLDER SISTER

1. Sister helps Ruby work sometimes.
2. She works a lot at maths.
3. She's good at writing.

TEACHER

1. Behind in my work.
2. Good at writing.
3. She's trying to read.

RUBY

1. I like reading.
2. I like writing.
3. I like maths.

Ruby was then asked to describe someone who is not like her, and she said:

1. Nicer than me.
2. They know more than me.
3. They are kind to me.

When Ruby was asked what things she would like to be different, she said:

1. Like to learn.
2. Like to know more things.
3. Be a bit taller.

For these to happen she said the following would have to occur:

1. Have to concentrate more.
2. Listen a bit more.
3. Have to grow.

The views that Ruby perceived were held by Mum, Dad, sister, teacher and herself clearly indicate the importance of academic issues. The description of the contrasting person suggests that, in order for Ruby to see herself as being a 'nice person', it would be necessary to separate 'niceness' and academic achievement.

The frequent description of herself in terms of her ability with respect to reading and writing were presented to her parents as representing crucial aspects of Ruby's self-perception, and reflected some of the anxiety and concern she has around these areas.

Through discussions using this information, it was possible for her parents to acknowledge Ruby's concerns and to appreciate that it would be crucial that any interventions would have to incorporate ways of reducing her anxiety. The parents were then able to relieve some of the pressures she felt from home. With the help of a structured programme implemented by both the school and home, the parents were able to provide constructive help for Ruby's reading, in a relaxed and comfortable setting.

7. School Situation Pictures

Purpose

The School Situation Pictures can be used to explore the child's world, particularly as they relate to school activities, situations and difficulties. They can also be used as a vehicle for exploring alternative ways of dealing with these difficulties.

Method

At the end of this section there is a copy of examples of the School Situation Pictures (Figures 12.9 and 12.10), which can be photocopied (enlarged) and mounted on card. Present the pictures to the child and ask them to choose any three, so that they can make up a story about each of them. Then put the others away.

Present the pictures in turn, in the order that the child selected them. Ask them what is going on in the picture and allow the child to describe the situation. Tell the child that in the picture there is someone who is upset, and ask them who they think it would be. Use the following questions to expand upon the story.

'What are they doing?'

'What has made them upset?'

'How would this person feel?'

'What might they be thinking?'

'What could they do to try to make things better?'

'Who could they ask to help them?'

'What might that person do to make a difference?'

'Would it work?'

'Who else could they ask?'

'If the person in the drawing came to you and asked what you thought they should do, what would you suggest?'

'Would that work?'

'Do you know anyone who would know what to do?' If the child says 'No' to this question, you might like to suggest that they think of a television or cartoon character who might know what to do.

'What would they suggest?'

The same process can be repeated for each of the pictures selected. The technique can elicit issues which present as difficulties the child encounters, or situations which cause them upset. It can also open up how the child has become stuck in ways of operating which are not helpful for them and present an opportunity to begin to explore possible alternative ways of dealing with things. The information may effectively be fed back to the school and carers to enable them to form an understanding of the child's perspective of their situation and to prepare the way for an effective intervention.

Case example: Jack

Jack, a ten-year-old, had been physically abused by his father; the school had informed Social Services of this and the case was taken to court. The outcome was that Jack was placed with his maternal grandparents with supervised parental access. The educational psychologist became involved because of Jack's very challenging behaviour in school, which had resulted in his being permanently excluded. However, the school's governing body overturned this and agreed to Jack being allowed to return to school, provided that the father agreed to the involvement of an Educational Psychologist (without consultation with the EPS). Despite the psychologist's misgivings about the process, Jack was interviewed in school.

One of the methods used to interview Jack was the School Situation Pictures (Figures 12.9 and 12.10). The following is a description of just one particular picture. This was picture number 7 in Figure 12.10, which is set in the classroom.

Jack described a situation where people were working, and one person had to sit by themselves because they had been 'bad'. They had thrown something in the classroom, and they had done this 'because they were bad'. There was no reason why they were 'bad', they were just 'bad'.

Jack initially said that the person who would be upset would be the teacher, but he quickly changed this to 'Mum and Dad, actually'. He also said that Mum and Dad spoil him; for instance, 'they let him go downtown' and 'they give him anything he wants'.

Since Jack felt that it was the teacher who was upset in the story in the picture, he was asked what the teacher could do to try to make things better. He suggested that the teacher could see the 'bad' boy's mum and dad, and that Mum and Dad would have to be strict to help the boy to decide not to be 'bad'. If the parents started to be strict, it would be much better for the boy as well as for the teacher.

During the feedback session with the father and head teacher, which took place in school, the extent of the animosity between the school and the father became clear. This was particularly fuelled by the father's anger towards the school for having made the referral to Social Services. Although it was necessary to be careful about the use of the word 'strict', the feedback from this part of the interview with Jack highlighted the importance of the school and father working in partnership to enable Jack to decide to change his behaviour.

Initially the father agreed to have a further meeting in school, to discuss setting up a home/school book to monitor Jack's behaviour. This became reasonably effective in bringing about sufficient change for Jack to be positively engaged in school, but was only achieved by setting up a series of regular in-school meetings with the father, to keep him fully engaged, and to ensure that Jack knew that the home and school were no longer fighting, so that he could maintain the changes he had achieved. It should be noted that these review meetings continued to be held over an 18-month period. By the end of this period there was a considerable shift in the father's attitude to the school, even to the extent that he volunteered to come into school to help with the music classes with the children.

It seems that Jack was placed in the very uncomfortable position of being in the middle of a dispute between his father and his school, where he could only engage his father by setting the school up to fail, just as, in a sense, the father had failed in the eyes of the school.

Figure 12.9 School Situation Pictures 1–4

Figure 12.10 School Situation Pictures 5–8

8. Self-Description Grid

Purpose

The Self-Description Grid has some similarities to the Salmon Line, and other scaling approaches. The grid is intended to give a visual representation of previously elicited constructs. This gives a useful basis for the child to appraise their own self-perception in relation to their constructs. It can provide a vehicle for considering the possibilities for change.

Method

Bipolar constructs which have been previously elicited, either through exploratory questions or any of the other techniques, are written into the spaces on the sides of the grid.

The child is then asked to indicate where various significant others would place them on the 11-point scale for each of the constructs, by putting in that person's initial. The significant others may be members of the family, peers, teachers, etc. Who the significant others are will be determined from information gathered earlier in the interview. Particularly important placements are where the child would place themselves (S), and where they would like to be able to put themselves (Ltb).

Once the grid has been completed in this way, it can be used as a vehicle for exploring what changes the child may wish to make for themselves, or what changes they would wish to make in others' perception of them (this latter recognising that they can only make changes to their own behaviour, but acknowledging how their behaviour can be effective in changing other people's perceptions). The mismatch between 'Self' and 'Like to be' can highlight particular areas which may represent a useful focus for change.

Change initiatives can include many of the principles already considered in other chapters, for instance the use of personal resources from other situations, and consideration of what the client would be doing, thinking and feeling differently if they considered themselves in a different position on particular constructs.

It is quite useful to determine the most effective change to consider, in terms of how a change on one construct may have corollary changes in other constructs. This may suggest concentrating on one particular change as a powerful focus, and also make the potential change much more appealing to the client, as the potential change can be seen to have extensive beneficial implications for the client.

Case example: Tracey

Tracey, a 13-year-old girl, attended secondary school. Her head of year expressed concerns about her relationships with her peers, in that she was not particularly friendly, and had a rather surly nature which was evident with teachers as well as peers.

Root and exploratory questions were used to elicit self-descriptions from Tracey, and it was particularly noticeable that with questions in the 'importance' direction the questions and responses seemed to go round in circles returning to a 'Fat' vs. 'Not fat' construct. It was decided to use the Self-Description Grid to work with the elicited constructs, even though the constructs themselves did not seem to be particularly core (to the psychologist!). (See Figures 12.11, 12.12 and 12.13.)

The constructs which had been elicited which the exploratory questions seemed to return to frequently were:

Fat ———————————————— Not fat

Walks properly ——————————— Walks like Mum

Polite ———————————————— Ignorant

Care about themselves ——————— Don't care about themselves

Gets on with others ——————— Bullies

Talks properly ——————————— Shouts

Can admit when wrong ——————— Always has to be right

A further dimension which was added to the grid was:

Likes Tracey ——————————— Doesn't like Tracey

Tracey was asked to make judgements of how a number of significant others would see her on each construct and mark these on the grid. These included her parents and brothers, and some classmates and teachers with whom she got on well and some with whom she did not get on well. She was also asked to put in where she would rate herself (Me), and where she would like to be able to put herself (Ltb).

It was apparent from doing the exercise that the construct of 'Fat' vs. 'Not fat' was particularly important to Tracey (Figure 12.11) and this was closely linked to her description of how much she liked herself. Change along this construct would very much drive change on other constructs.

The 'Likes Tracey' vs. 'Doesn't like Tracey' construct was given because it seemed that this largely determined whether people would rate Tracey at the positive or negative end of any of the other constructs. A further point worthy of note is the way that Tracey produced quite polarised discriminations on the grid. Almost all the ratings are at the extreme ends of the dimensions in the grid. This form of discrimination tends to suggest a degree of immaturity, the discriminations showing little sense of uncertainty. This immaturity is also reflected in the descriptions of the constructs which are very behavioural.

The Self-Description Grid shows clearly Tracey's high rating of herself as 'Fat' and 'Not liking herself' (Figure 12.11).

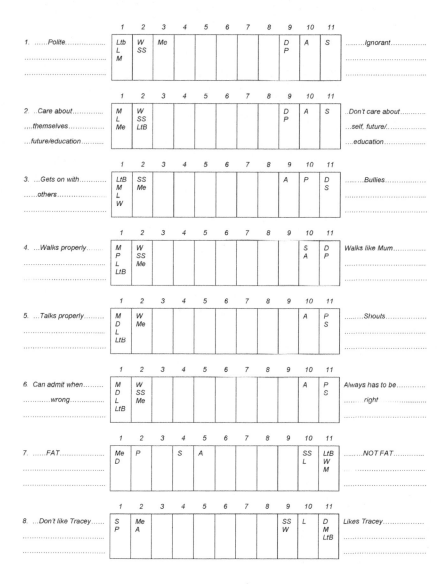

1. Polite — Ignorant

1	2	3	4	5	6	7	8	9	10	11
Ltb L M	W SS	Me						D P	A	S

2. Care about themselves future/education — Don't care about self, future/education

1	2	3	4	5	6	7	8	9	10	11
M L Me	W SS LtB							D P	A	S

3. Gets on with others — Bullies

1	2	3	4	5	6	7	8	9	10	11
LtB M L W	SS Me							A	P	D S

4. Walks properly — Walks like Mum

1	2	3	4	5	6	7	8	9	10	11
M P L LtB	W SS Me								S A	D P

5. Talks properly — Shouts

1	2	3	4	5	6	7	8	9	10	11
M D L LtB	W Me								A	P S

6. Can admit when wrong — Always has to be right

1	2	3	4	5	6	7	8	9	10	11
M D L LtB	W SS Me								A	P S

7. FAT — NOT FAT

1	2	3	4	5	6	7	8	9	10	11
Me D	P		S	A					SS L	LtB W M

8. Don't like Tracey — Likes Tracey

1	2	3	4	5	6	7	8	9	10	11
S P	Me A							SS W	L	D M LtB

Figure 12.11 Tracey's initial Self-Description Grid

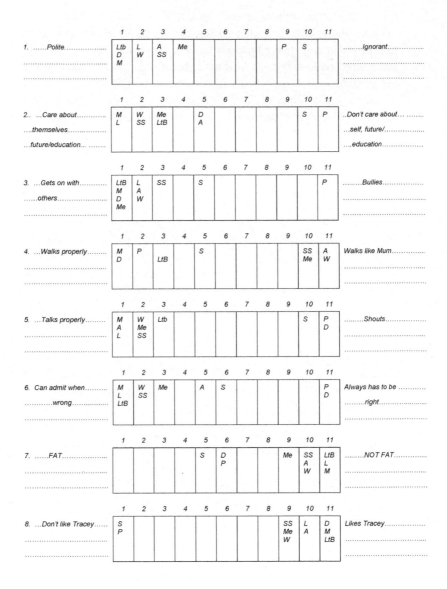

Figure 12.12 Tracey's Self-Description Grid at review

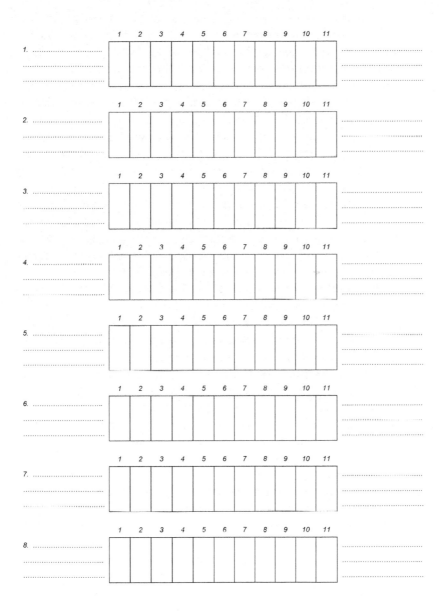

Figure 12.13 Blank Self-Description Grid

The implications of change were discussed with Tracey in terms of what would be different if she were suddenly not fat. This, in essence, amounted to her being able to have a new start because people would not recognise her so she would be able to establish better relationships with them. Not being fat had implications of talking differently, walking differently and having a different hair style; the change then would be quite substantial.

Given Tracey was now talking about how she would establish better relationships with others, questions were asked to get her to be specific in behavioural terms about how she would be doing things differently, particularly in terms of how she would behave differently to others. Once the new role had been clearly established by Tracey the issue was addressed as to whether she actually needed to become less fat in order to start changing. Tracey agreed that she could try out the new behaviours over a two-week period before a review meeting to see how she had got on.

Tracey's head of year was given feedback about the interview and asked especially to be aware of any attempts Tracey seemed to be making in terms of changes in her interpersonal behaviour with either peers or teachers, and to make comment to Tracey to let her know that these changes were being noticed.

Two weeks later Tracey's head of year had noted changes in Tracey's behaviour. Tracey herself was aware that her attempts were being recognised, and she was happy to continue to develop this new role further for a longer period of time. It was agreed that there would be another review meeting after a further month.

At this second review meeting it was noted that the changes had still persisted and during the interview a second Self-Description Grid was done using the same constructs as in the original interview (Figure 12.12). In the second Self-Description Grid it can be seen that generally there is a slightly greater weight of descriptions towards the more positive ends of the constructs. Most noticeably, and possibly significantly, there is a change in the shift of Tracey's self-perception in terms of how much she likes herself, from 2 to 9, and also in her self-perception of Fat, from 1 to 9. The second grid also shows slightly less polarisation in the discriminations.

While Tracey was not thin, she did not present as noticeably overweight, nor was there any indication that she had lost any weight over the period of involvement.

At a meeting some months later with Tracey's mother, it was noted that Tracey's behaviour and attitude had persisted in a more positive vein. Her mother also noted that Tracey had become more willing to stick to her diet. She had previously had diets for several years but had shown little tenacity in keeping to them.

Although much of the work done used many of the approaches outlined previously, Tracey's example perhaps shows more than anything that there is no set method which should be applied, but rather emphasises the necessity for the psychologist to have guiding principles within a framework with some techniques which help to structure the interviews.

The Self-Description Grid itself was not the key feature of the work with Tracey, except that it provided a structure within the interviews. It did serve as a valuable vehicle, providing a visual representation on paper of some basic structure within the interviews which served as reference points for both psychologist and client.

CHAPTER 13

Case Example: Steven

This case is taken as an example, not because it represents a case with a particularly outstanding outcome, but it demonstrates the use of a number of the interview methods used together. The approaches were used at quite a simple level, and there was little questioning during the interview to elaborate Steven's model of the world (he did not have a very sophisticated level of language), but the information obtained formed the basis for generating hypotheses.

This provided a useful perspective of Steven, and also presented this perspective very powerfully to Steven's mother, which was important in gaining her commitment to an intervention which required changes in her behaviour.

Initial information

Steven was an eight-year-old boy attending junior school; his mother and father were separated. Steven had an older sister, about 14 years old, who lived with her grandmother. It was thought that this was because she did not get on with her mother.

From initial discussions of concerns in the school it seemed clear that Steven's mother was having difficulties in managing his behaviour at home. She had taken Steven to the GP because she suspected that he may be hyperactive; the GP had suggested that he may be schizophrenic. The mother had seemed quite pleased with the diagnosis and had consequently accepted a referral to the local Department of Child and Family Psychiatry, although work did not seem to be progressing.

In school Steven presented as disruptive with a worried, insecure grin. He was responsive to praise, and could work well in a one-to-one situation. The school's view was summed up in the comment 'he seems a nice boy underneath, but screwed up'.

Steven had previously had a transfer of school, but this did not create any significant changes, and he returned to his original school with continuing difficulties. Steven's mother seemed to assume that the difficulties were because of the school, and seemed to accept little responsibility for the difficulties, or involvement in working on them.

The school's final comment had been that Steven was 'excessively lovable', and also that he seemed to be rather 'too well informed about sex'.

In terms of anticipated outcomes for the work, the school were keen to identify ways to improve Steven's behaviour and understand his anxieties. The school also wanted to develop a more constructive working relationship with Steven's mother as they also saw this as a key way to impact on Steven's behaviours in school and at home and address the emotional concerns they had for Steven.

Interview information

A number of interview methods were used to attempt to gain some understanding of how Steven was making sense of himself and his world. These included:

- Identifying the Concerns
- Kinetic Family Drawing
- Family Interaction Matrix
- Three Comments
- Portrait Gallery
- School Situation Pictures
- Draw a Person.

The following information is taken from the interview notes, and where appropriate needs to be looked at in conjunction with the drawings, etc.

Identifying the Concerns

Of the list of concerns that were offered to Steven as potential reasons for the interview he suggested the school and his mother would be concerned because he:

- finds the work too hard
- gets into trouble in school
- school and his mother would think he was unhappy
- doesn't get on with other children (but he does get on alright with his teacher).

Kinetic Family Drawing

Figure 13.1 Steven's Kinetic Family Drawing

The following information is Steven's description of his family as he drew them in the KFD (Figure 13.1). The basic information is who each of the people are, their age, and what they are doing in the picture. Other comments Steven made during the exercise are also noted.

1. Sister (15 years old), Wendy
   - dancing

2. Little brother (1 year old), Terry
   - running about in my bedroom
   - he pulls my stereo about
   - he sleeps in my bedroom
   - I've got four bunk beds in my room

3. Little brother (2 years old), Kevin
   - he usually does the table up for my mum

4. Self (8 years old), Steven
   - playing about on my bunk bed
   - jumping on the bunk bed
   - my sister sleeps on her own bed

5. Big brother (16 years old), Steven

   ○ same name as me – Steven's a Scottish name

   ○ he's doing my mum's car

6. Big brother (19 years old), Mark (after some thought)

   ○ sitting down on the chair

   ○ he watches videos – horror films

7. Mum

   ○ doing the cooker

8. Dad

   ○ playing football with friend.

Family Interaction Matrix

Although not covered in the earlier text, this technique was included in the interview. The matrix is derived by asking Steven about each member in turn to find out who they get on best with in the family. A second part can be included for who each member gets on least well with. (It is often useful to introduce a general comment that in all families some people get on better with each other than with others.)

Within his family Steven described the following relationships:

Steven (self)	– gets on best with –	Mum
Kevin	– gets on best with –	Steven (self)
Terry	– gets on best with –	Steven (self)
Wendy	– gets on best with –	Mark
Mark	– gets on best with –	Steven (self)
Steven (brother)	– gets on best with –	Steven (self)
Dad	– gets on best with –	Steven (self), Mark, Terry
Mum	– gets on best with –	Steven (self) – 'cos I don't swear or do naughty things that much

This was followed with an unsolicited comment: 'I love all my family'.

Three Comments

Steven was asked what he thought other people would say if they were asked to describe what sort of a boy he was.

MOTHER'S COMMENTS

'She works from 7 in the morning to 1 o/clock at night' (Steven's comment).

Steven is:

1. usually good

2. usually naughty

3. cuddly.

FATHER'S COMMENTS

'He [father] doesn't know where the school is' (Steven's comment).

Steven is:

1. really good

2. he sits on my shoulders to see the cars

3. he [father] lets me on the ramps at the garage (Steven described father working in a garage).

CLASS TEACHER'S COMMENTS

The class teacher would say of Steven:

1. I've been good

2. I've been naughty

3. I usually sit my bum down.

STEVEN'S COMMENTS

Steven would say of himself:

1. Usually I watch tapes

2. All the time I go home and eat my bar of chocolate

3. I eat all my dinners up at home.

Portrait Gallery (see Figures 13.2 and 13.3)

Mad	Angry	Sad	Happy
1. Mad cos he chucked a stone at the window when he went to the shop.	1. His mum was angry at him, he was angry at his mum. Hungry – never eat his dinner up. M angry – wanted his dinner.	1. Mum chucked dinner in the bin.	1. Just got home in time for dinner.
2. Mad that he broke his bunk bed.	2. His mum threw his sweets.	2. Sad he moved cos it was a nice house and mum wanted to move.	2. Got a friend they met another friend.
3. Cos somebody took his stereo M.	3. He got happy at last. That's the end of that one.	3. Lost – at home can't find their way home.	3. Hungry – and it's just as well they've got food at last. Happy – Birthday Christmas New school Moved They're warm.

Figure 13.2 Steven's Portrait Gallery 1

	Naughty	Good
Change – No	1. Punched his mum	1. His mum bought
Can't change – what	in the mouth.	him a P.E. bag.
stops?	2. Gave his mum a	2. Mum bought him
his face	punch on her car.	Kinder egg.
His bones make him	3. Good after all.	3. Mum bought him
stay angry.		new coat cos he
Have to go to doctor		was good eating
to change him into		his dinner.
happy.		

Cheer his self up to be
good.

Figure 13.3 Steven's Portrait Gallery 2

School Situation Pictures, Numbers 5, 4, 3 (see Figures 12.9 and 12.10 in Chapter 12)

The questions asked and Steven's answers are summarised below. Steven's answers are not verbatim, as they were supported by gesture and pointing; they have been expanded slightly to give the reader a better idea of the content.

PICTURE 5: THE CLASSROOM
Where are they?

- in the teachers' room

What's happening?

- the teacher is writing, doing adding and taking away

- everyone is sitting down

If somebody was unhappy why would that be?

- they don't like doing the work

What could they do for things to be better?

- cheer them up

How?

- give them money

How would that help?

- because then they could buy things

'That's the end of that story' (Steven's comment).

What could the teacher do to help?

- cheer them up
- give them a new pencil

How could Steven help them?

- that would help them (i.e. what the teacher had done).

PICTURE 4: THE PLAYGROUND

If someone was unhappy why would that be?

- because they haven't got a friend to play with
- they can't get up the slide

What could they do for things to be better?

- they couldn't get up (the slide)

How could they be helped?

- getting a friend
- somebody to help them get down and play together

If you were there what would you do to help?

- cheer them up by playing with them

'That's the end of this one' (Steven's comment).

PICTURE 3: THE PLAYGROUND AGAIN

What's happening?

- they're all playing together

Which one's upset?

- the one on his own

How come they are upset?

- upset because they can't get down from a chair
- someone should come over and help him

Who?

- Steven.

Draw a Person (Man)

draw him sad (Q why)
– can't get in the house

Figure 13.4 Steven's Draw a Man picture

The 'Draw a Person' exercise (Figure 13.4) is a very useful source of information. As the Goodenough–Harris Draw a Person test, it offers norms in terms of cognitive functioning. These can be useful as the exercise can offer a child with limited language an opportunity to show their skills.

The 'Draw a Person' technique has also been studied extensively relating aspects of the drawing, and drawing style, to personality characteristics. Burns (1982) is a very useful reference.

As he was doing the drawing Steven made the following comments:

- do him sad

Why?

- he can't get in the house any more
- put on monkey bars.

The last comment did not make sense in the interview, and despite asking Steven for further elaboration no further sense was gained.

Case notes

The following are the case notes, written soon after the interview. These are written to provide an aide memoire for the psychologist, on file, available for future recall, and also an opportunity for clarifying thoughts, developing hypotheses, and planning the direction of possible interventions.

General impressions

Steven seemed keen to talk, and have the interview, although he seemed unclear about why he was being interviewed.

Poor vocabulary and difficulties understanding grammatical constructions of sentences may have formed a basis of some misunderstandings.

Kinetic Family Drawing

Steven drew a large family including his sister, two younger brothers, two older brothers (including one with the same name as himself) and his mother and father.

The school reports that Steven lives alone with his mother and perhaps her boyfriend. His sister lives with her grandmother, but this seems a largely fictitious family.

Family Interaction Matrix

Steven gets on best with his mother; everyone gets on best with him except his sister.

POSSIBLE INTERPRETATION

Is Steven expressing a desire for a family life around him where he is loved and appreciated? Note his comment here that 'I love all my family'.

The figures in the drawings are very similar; however, Steven is distanced from his mother by objects and a number of fictitious others.

It is also notable that Steven draws a 'brother', Steven (aged 16), who is specifically helping the mother by washing her car. This Steven is closest to the mother. Is this perhaps an idealised position he would like to achieve?

The mother is lowest on the page – perhaps reflecting a powerlessness?

Steven himself is highest on the page – jumping up in the air from his bunk bed – is he quite powerful in an uncontained sort of way? (Perhaps he is rather 'up in the air'.)

Steven also said he had four bunk beds in his room – is this a sign of him wanting to have a family close to him? He noted his sister had a separate room (perhaps why he is not the one she gets on best with).

Steven also talked about his little brother taking carrots off his fork when they were eating and this made him angry.

Food is a common theme, but is a fictitious brother pinching it?

Three Comments

Here Steven shows good and naughty sides, but also closeness to his mother with cuddles – and a closeness to his father who takes him to the garage where he works.

The mother and father are unable to come to school. The father does not know where the school is, and the mother works from 7 a.m. in the morning to 1 a.m. at night. Does this serve to prevent the fictitious family being discovered and thereby challenged, and also express a sense of distance between the mother and Steven (as she is not there)?

Note Steven bringing out food as a common theme in his own comments about himself.

Portrait Gallery

Many of the examples given reflect basic needs:

1. food

2. home

3. importance of mother.

The mother certainly comes across as the provider of the basic necessities, Steven showing a concern for her as the provider of his needs and nourishment. In terms of Maslow's hierarchy of needs, Steven's concerns are at a basic level.

GOOD/NAUGHTY

Again reflects an omnipotent mother, and her key role as determinant of what Steven does and provider of the consequences. Her involvement is the only key element for Steven.

School Situation Pictures

Troubled children need to be cheered up. This can be done by:

1. giving them something – money, a pencil

2. having a friend to play with.

Draw a Person

The man is sad because he can't get in the house – again reflecting basic needs, and concerns about being a part of home/family?

Issues around bed

Particular comments about bunk beds were noted in relation to the KFD: how many there were; jumping on them, etc.; room for his brothers. Again sleep and bed could be another issue of basic needs being met, or there could be other reasons for further exploration.

Summary

Key themes

1. Basic physical needs such as food, home, sleep and love are particularly prevalent in Steven's responses.

2. Role of the mother as key provider of all of these, Steven's need for his mother, his sense of dependency on her, and a sense of her not being there for him emotionally.

3. Need for a family to care for him and contain him. Is this a reflection of others between him and his mother?

4. A desire for there to be others around him who will look after/like him – be his friends (as School Situation Pictures).

5. Need for 'unconditional positive regard' – given his need levels are so basic, is this a major first step in helping him develop as a person? Is this what cheering up would address?

6. He sees basic needs as met through good/naughty in some instances, but also very much outside his control. Perhaps he sees himself as having little influence ('up in the air' rather than powerful).

7. Does he crave cuddles and love? (Does he get any?)

The basic hypothesis at this stage was that Steven seemed to focus very much on his mother and seemed to need his mother's affection, positive regard, etc., but something seems to be getting in the way, or he feels that his access to this was not within his control.

Other supplementary hypotheses are, perhaps, also in mind, and further information gathering when meeting the mother would also be concerned with the development (or not) of these. The most important at this stage was a very unspecific consideration about Steven's sexual knowledge (as reported by school), and a number of references to bedtime, etc.

The focus of an intervention would therefore be to attempt to encourage the mother into promoting a closer relationship between Steven and herself.

The intervention

Given the information provided from the interview and the hypotheses suggested, the following is intended to give an indication of how the information was used to try to create change. This was done in a meeting which included the mother, head teacher and psychologist.

After basic introductions and sharing of information of concerns between the school, parent and psychologist (which did not change the basic hypothesis substantially, and in fact seemed confirmatory), an introduction was given to the content of the interview. This particularly reflected the fact that the information available would have to be interpreted and this would then be in the form of hypothesis, and should not be seen as definitive, the purpose being that we could use this information to add to what we knew about Steven already. This new information, and hypothesis, may give rise to ideas about how we could work to best help the situation.

This sets up a situation where the hypotheses can be put forward or generated so parents in particular do not feel they have to defend themselves against any view being given. However, as previously noted in the earlier chapter on the Meta Model, if the hypothesis, as a presupposition, is not challenged, then by implication it is accepted.

The content of the interview was fed back to Steven's mother, particularly emphasising the themes of:

- her importance
- his desire for food
- his desire (and need) for love and cuddles.

The former was readily accepted by the mother; the second confirmed by her in terms of Steven enjoying food. Although this was not taken as a serious issue by Steven's mother, it was useful in terms of providing a match to the mother's view of Steven.

The third theme was introduced gradually, and the mother acknowledged that Steven was quite a caring and loving boy, although not one who liked close physical contact very often. The position of the 'elder' Steven in the KFD was presented as perhaps reflecting the position where Steven would like to be if he knew how to be like that, namely close to his mother.

This introduced the suggestion of the need to enhance the mother/child relationship, but at this early stage removing responsibility from the mother by putting the reluctance for the relationship onto Steven, because of his lack of ability in knowing how to behave in a close manner. This helped to avoid the mother's possible rejection of the hypothesis, by presenting the difficulty as Steven's, although the mother by implication has the responsibility for changing her behaviour in her role as the adult who has to intervene to help him overcome his difficulty.

This allowed the discussion to focus on the difficulties some children have in maintaining close, affectionate, physical relationships with their parents, although noting that frequently these children would like a much closer relationship, but have difficulty knowing how to go about getting it. The children themselves feel uncomfortable with close physical contact, even though ideally that is what they want. This then gave the opportunity to relate the story of Abdul (which is presented in Chapter 19). The story is about the importance of the mother/child relationship, and how a mother can bring about change in this through developing a closer physical relationship with her son.

Some further work and discussion about monitoring Steven's school behaviour followed with the mother agreeing to work with Steven to draw up a small behaviour monitoring chart to act as a reward system for his school behaviour, and this forming the basis for the mother and school to develop a closer working relationship.

The hypothesis and intervention were relatively simple in concept, but putting it over to the system, and in this case particularly the mother, seemed to be the key issue in working to bring about change. The drawings and comments from the interview were key to presenting a hypothesis to the mother about Steven's world which had implications for how she could be effective in working towards change.

CHAPTER 14

Case Example: Gordon

Background

Gordon, a boy in Year 5, was raised as a concern at the consultation meeting by his junior school. The major concerns expressed by the school were that he was frequently in trouble in school through threatening behaviour, swearing and shouting. He had previously had two fixed term exclusions. The school's view was that he was an able boy, although underperforming in academic areas. They also sensed that he tended to keep away from his younger siblings.

At home he is the oldest of three children in his family. His father is no longer at home and both the mother and father had previously had substance abuse issues. Gordon's mother had told the school that things had been very stressful at home prior to their overcoming their problems, and that might have rubbed off on Gordon. She was very pleased to have the psychologist involved as she was concerned to address Gordon's needs.

In terms of outcomes, both the school and mother were keen to improve behaviour in school and find ways of reducing Gordon's anger and stress both at home and school, which they saw as underpinning the behaviour difficulties.

It was agreed that the psychologist should meet with Gordon and then have a subsequent meeting with Gordon's mother and school staff.

Interview

In interview Gordon presented as engaging, and open to talking about how he was getting on at school.

Identifying the Concerns

Gordon indicated concerns in school would be that:

- he gets in trouble a lot

- he is naughty – swearing, hitting, threatening

- he has had three warnings and penalty points.

He also indicated that he has trouble getting on with mates, for example Sean – he doesn't stop talking.

He has friends (Bill, Ian and Carl) in his class, and other friends in another class (Alan, Tony and Callum). He had also made a new friend in his neighbourhood when his family moved house.

WHAT HE LIKES ABOUT SCHOOL

- science

- DT

- art – 'do colours of your feelings and do things how you like'.

Gordon likes these because:

- 'you get to work with each other'.

Following further exploration he confirmed that he likes things where he can think things through and work it out, and has some level of choice about how he gets his work done.

CHANGES GORDON WOULD LIKE AT SCHOOL

- More classes – so he could have Year 7 at this school – he doesn't want to move schools (to secondary school).

- Doesn't like the idea of being with new people (despite having met a new friend when they moved house).

- Bigger pond – more room for the animals that live in it – this would mean that treat time would be better if there were more animals.

- Nicer Year 6 teachers – they are strict, shout and scream – Gordon doesn't fancy Year 6. First thing he heard when he came to this school was shouting – he was worried the teachers might not be nice.

Kinetic Family Drawing

Gordon's Kinetic Family Drawing is shown in Figure 14.1.

Figure 14.1 Gordon's Kinetic Family Drawing

KFD DESCRIPTION

1. Mum – feeding pet snails (four African Land Snails). He has had them 3 days. They came from a friend.

2. Jenny (5) – little sister painting Gordon a picture. He has drawn her crying – she is always crying for nothing.

3. James (3) causes trouble – hits people (with Jenny – they are always crying together).

4. Nanny – driving the car (lives on the other side of town).

5. Granddad – had a heart attack couple of weeks ago – needs more exercise – building a cage for my guinea pigs.

6. Snails.

7. Uncle Paul – lives at Nan's – bald – cleaning his car.

   ○ Question – where are *you*?

8. Gordon drawing the picture.

9. Guinea pig – Harry.

   ○ Who knows Gordon best? (Mum, Jenny and James – all live in the same house.)

WHO GETS ON BEST WITH WHO?

Mum	– gets on best with –	Gordon
Jenny	gets on best with	friends in school + teachers
James	– gets on best with –	Mum and Gordon
Nan	– gets on best with –	Granddad
Granddad	– gets on best with –	Nan and Paul
Snails	– gets on best with –	each other
Paul	– gets on best with –	Gordon and Granddad
Gordon	– gets on best with –	everyone
Harry	gets on best with	no-one

Three Comments

MUM

- I like playing on my game cube.

- I never come out of my room.

- I always tell my brother and sister to go away – I like time on my own – peace and quiet and can choose what I do (hypothesis check from preferred approach to work in school).

GORDON

- I like time on my own.

- Like quiet.

- Like cars (q) – speed – favourite Ferrari. [(q) means that the interviewer asked a question to prompt further information.]

LIKE TO BE

- Get out of my room – spend time with brother and sister – they don't behave if I do – like to spend more time – but have fun.

- Stop Mum smoking so she doesn't get cancer and die – and don't have to walk through smoke.

Portrait Gallery (see Figures 14.2 and 14.3)

Worried

Angry

Sad

Happy

Worried	Angry	Sad	Happy
1. Jenny and James – when Mum is furious – they get in trouble – I get into trouble for smacking sister's bottom.	1. Me – when get bullied – sometimes hit back – or tell teacher – both work.	1. Granddad – when he can't make something properly.	1. Me – cos I'm always happy – at least when not getting bullied. Three people get bullied by Year 6 boys.
2. When they see my football heading to them – kicked it hard.	2. Me – when Jenny and James don't behave – I smack their bottoms – not hard – get angry.	2. Me – when sister won't shut up.	2. Nan – always happy – likes driving her car on a sunny day.
3. I am jumping on the trampoline and I mustn't land on Mum.	3. When Mum hears crying – she gets angry then she smokes.	3. When M says eggs in snails tank – have to stamp on them.	3. Snails always happy.

Figure 14.2 Gordon's Portrait Gallery 1

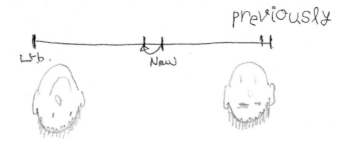

Change	Gets on well in school	Gets in trouble in school

• Possible? – yes
  ° start doing work properly
  ° start reading better
  ° start writing better
• get more treats
Notice?
• Gordon – thinking about behaviour
Next?
• Teacher – work getting better – behaviour better – sit better
Next?
• Miss S (TA) – writing improving – working harder at it
Next?
• Mum – behaving with brother and sister
Know they had noticed?
• better marks
• Mum would ask me to do jobs around the house, e.g. dishes/hoovering
	1. happy – not been naughty – not told off
	2. get treats – money – ice cream – from Nan/Mum – book in class
	3. not behaved well – get penalty points (sense of defeat and overwhelmed by it)
		1. bored – cos always told off
		2. it serves him right for being naughty – (how come decides to do it?) – silly – bit of a doop
		3. bit of a doop myself – cos get into trouble

Figure 14.3 Gordon's Portrait Gallery 2

Gordon was keen on the idea of the scaling line in Figure 14.3, and the sense of progress being recognised for small step changes. This perhaps will help address his sense of despondency if success isn't full and consistent over time.

Summary discussion with SEN Co-ordinator following meeting with Gordon

Gordon acknowledges issues raised by the school:

- behaviour – swearing, hitting, threatening
- not getting on with peers – he talked of bullying by older boys but also has some friendship groups.

Things Gordon likes:

- things where he has a level of choice/discretion
- where he can work things out himself
- time on his own – peace and quiet – shuts himself away from problems of siblings.

Things Gordon dislikes:

- worries about new situations
- doesn't like shouting and screaming.

Siblings issue:

- having to manage them – finds them difficult to manage – they cry – he is responsible – so he shuts himself away as he can't manage to control them.

He can be positive, but can readily have a sense of despondency if he gets overwhelmed or if his efforts to make things good do not promptly result in successful outcomes.

Summary of Gordon's view of what would bring about change

- Gordon sees improving reading and writing as important. Help with writing will help with behaviour.
- Gordon needs to be recognised for trying. There is a need to reward his effort and small steps to success.

- Gordon would like to have responsibility around the house which he can manage and succeed at – for example, hoovering/doing dishes – but not responsibility for his siblings.

- Rewarding his choice of time out when he needs to calm down.

- The value of a scaling line or similar to contextualise his progress to his target.

Notes from meeting with Gordon's mother

Current situation

Gordon's mother attended the subsequent meeting, including the school special needs teacher, the learning support assistant (LSA) who mainly worked with Gordon, the psychologist and for the latter part of the meeting Gordon. (Gordon had said he would like to attend the meeting with his mother when asked in the meeting with the psychologist.)

In the initial part of the meeting both Gordon's mother and the school were invited to say what their concerns were for Gordon. In addition to sharing these concerns and background information, Gordon's mother was willing to acknowledge family issues which she felt would also have had an impact on the situation for Gordon.

The meeting was able to use this information, in addition to the feedback from the psychologist's interview with Gordon, to develop shared ideas for what we saw as likely issues for Gordon and how they might impact on his behaviour in school and at home.

These were summarised as:

- Gordon acknowledges that his behaviour can cause him trouble in school.

- The school recognises issues of poor self-esteem.

- Both the school and Gordon's mother noted that he can get upset and angry at times.

- Gordon likes things where he can have some element of choice.

- Gordon likes having time on his own and appreciates peace and quiet.

- While Gordon can frequently work positively, he also can feel despondent when things don't work out. Recognising his efforts to work and behave well would be important even if he is not always successful.

- Gordon finds having responsibility for looking after his brother and sister stressful, and while he would like to help in the house he would prefer to do this with things he feels more confident in coping with.

- Gordon worries about his mother and the impact of additional stresses on her.

The following actions were agreed as an intervention plan.

Intervention plan
1. HOME TIMETABLE
Gordon's mother agreed to develop a home timetable with him. This would include the following features:

- It would be designed with Gordon.

- It would give 1:1 time for Gordon with his mother.

- It would ensure Gordon does not feel responsible for Jenny and James.

- It gives Gordon responsibilities he can cope with to show he can help.

2. USE OF A FEELING CHART
Both the school and Gordon's mother were keen to use a feeling chart to help Gordon communicate how he felt and to monitor how he was coping with any stresses. This was to be used at home and in school in the following ways:

- to build self-awareness

- when Gordon indicates he is stressed in the morning at home then Gordon's mother would let the school know through a home/school book

- to use at the end of the day at home to review the day and how he has felt about it.

3. SCALING LINE
Gordon had indicated that the idea of the scaling line (from the final part of the Portrait Gallery interview technique) was something he would like to use to see his progress, and break progress down into manageable chunks. The school agreed to draw this up with Gordon, with the focus on trying:

- to recognise progress

- to help Gordon see that progress can be in small steps.

4. REVIEW
It was agreed to hold a review after four school weeks.

Review of progress

The review meeting was held after the four weeks as agreed and included school representatives as previously, Gordon's mother, Gordon and the psychologist.

Generally in school Gordon was reported to be more positive in approach and attitude. He seemed less stressed and things were much better at home as a consequence. However, he had been excluded (fixed term) following an incident with a dinner lady, although the school felt confident about how this had been managed and that there were learning experiences to be gained. It was felt that the situation had been addressed and unlikely to re-occur.

At home Gordon's mother had concentrated on:

- confidence building

- recognition of efforts at home

- giving Gordon time.

In school there had been very positive days, but also a number of single incidents which were largely around unstructured times such as breaks and lunchtimes. Gordon had been given a ten-minute session in the playground at lunchtime to minimise the risk of problems arising.

Agreed actions

1. Gordon's mother will continue with the approach she has adopted at home.

2. Gordon's LSA will continue with Gordon into the Year 6 class which will support his transition.

3. Gordon's LSA leaves the classroom at 3.00 pm. Before she leaves she will use the last few minutes to give Gordon a structure and plan for the expectations for the final 30 minutes of the day.

4. Gordon's LSA will also work with him and friends just before lunch to help them plan what games they might play for their ten-minute

lunch break. The special needs teacher will support initially with playing games to give them ideas for constructive play together.

5. At lunch time Gordon will go out for ten minutes to play. He will pass a card to the dinner lady. After the ten minutes he can come into the school for an activity club. The card will remind the dinner lady to prompt Gordon when it is time to come in and also to give a smiley face if the session has been positive.

6. The school will contact Gordon's mother to ensure there are positive messages going home.

Review

As it was felt that progress had been substantial, it was agreed that there did not need to be any further review meetings including the psychologist. Reviews were to be arranged between Gordon's mother, Gordon and the school. The psychologist would be updated at the autumn term school consultation meeting.

CHAPTER 15

Ability and Strategies

The following presents some issues in relation to children's educational difficulties, and expands the range of hypothesis-generating frameworks, with a focus particularly on the capabilities element of the logical levels.

Educational difficulties: Child or system

In the introductory chapter we considered whether children's difficulties can be considered a consequence of intra-child problems rather than the child's response to the system in which they live (which also includes the education system). This is particularly pertinent to the realm of learning problems.

Many psychologists' and teachers' experience challenges the conventional educational view that children show poor educational achievement because of their intrinsic learning difficulties. Their successful interventions are based on a range of different approaches including, for instance, Feuerstein's Instrumental Enrichment, NLP, Accelerated Learning, etc. Other teaching and instructional approaches which also show excellent results, for instance Solity's Early Reading Research, with a focus on effective instruction (Solity *et al.* 2000), also challenge the view that intrinsic learning difficulties have an overwhelming impact. The common presupposition of all these approaches seems to be that the child has the resources to learn and change, given that the system provides appropriate experiences for them to change. This has been presented earlier as the second axiom.

It is generally recognised that there is a correlation between intelligence as measured by IQ tests and school achievement (correlation in the region of 0.7). This means that nearly 50 per cent of the variance in learning outcomes for students can be linked to the variance in the psychometric measure IQ, though it does not necessarily imply a causal link, and there will be many factors which have a common effect on both attainment and measured IQ. This poses two issues:

- What factors are associated with the other 50 per cent of variance in achievement and how can these have an impact on improving achievement?

- What can be done to improve achievement even where there is low measured IQ?

These fundamental points, amongst others, have been key to challenging the value of the use of psychometric tests in particular and intrinsic learning difficulty in general. Nevertheless many educationalists readily adopt a perspective based on intra-child limitations when they have failed to enable the child to learn effectively. Such a perspective or belief held by the system (whether it be correct or not) can then create the limiting belief for the child, which can lead to a self-fulfilling prophesy.

Impact on educational progress of logical levels

Identity, values, beliefs and behaviour

Some of the other factors which have an impact on educational achievement, and indeed will also impact on measured IQ, are described by the logical levels outlined previously in Chapter 7, namely identity, values, beliefs, capability, behaviour and environment.

A powerful example of the impact of beliefs and identity on educational achievement is provided by the West Dumbartonshire Project (e.g. MacKay 2007). The early work for the study demonstrated the powerful impact on reading accuracy and comprehension of attitude change and self-esteem. In addition to changing attitudes and adopting clear teaching approaches and early intervention, the main study also highlighted the powerful impact of children's self-declaration of their intention to learn to read as an identity statement.

The study has been replicated on a smaller scale by Allen (2009) who demonstrated enhanced literacy levels in young children who made bold 'declarations' regarding their future reading achievement. In his further study he demonstrated that declarations which attributed future reading achievement to effort (behaviour level), rather than ability (identity level), seem to have greater impact in improving literacy skills and self-concept. In addition he suggested the attribution at the behavioural level in the declaration guards against possible learned helplessness (identity level), by ensuring the more favourable attribution of effort, rather than ability, for any possible future failure.

The study suggests that, although positively focused identity, values and beliefs are important in achievement, there is a need to also be engaged at the behavioural level (effort) for the maximum impact of the intervention.

The focus on behaviour provides a fail safe to identity, beliefs and values if success is not forthcoming. Interestingly, Allen also found that where attribution of effort was the basis of the declaration this led to positive gains in self-concept. This suggests the experience of achievement through effort offers a more robust positive identity than where success is attributed to ability. This possibly also reflects the greater sense of locus of control, as effort is under the personal control of the individual where ability is not.

The studies (by MacKay and Allen) offer a clear indication of the importance of a focus on all the logical levels in addressing learning issues.

The danger in the assumption that cognitive assessments are measures of cognitive ability is that this creates, or possibly colludes with, a limiting belief in the system about the child, with the possible consequences of a self-fulfilling prophesy of failure, as the child takes on this identity-level view of themselves.

Professionals can exacerbate the situation for children with the use of diagnostic terms, such as disturbed, conduct disordered and dyslexic, which are statements of identity. These identity statements are generally based on an inference drawn from presenting behaviours and often show a failure to explore the logical levels which may provide more hypotheses, from which to derive interventions. Allen's study highlights the value and importance of the attribution of both success and failure to the behavioural level, recognising the possible detrimental effects of attribution to ability at an identity level.

It could be suggested that diagnostic terms, as identity statements about children, are functional in serving the status quo of the system. They provide an intra-child explanation for the system's failure to make a difference, rather than press for further investigation and alternative, more constructive, hypotheses to promote change in the system to help the child.

Capability level: Strategy or ability

The descriptions of the above studies have been focused on identity, values, beliefs and behaviour.

When considering learning, it is important to also reflect on the level of capability. This is distinct from inherent ability as assumed to be measured by psychometric approaches. In Chapter 7, where logical levels were introduced, 'capability' was described as knowing how to do something, an issue of thinking style or strategy. It is about the skills to achieve something or behave in a particular way.

Although many psychologists use psychometric tools to produce assessments of children's ability, there is wide recognition of the limitations of both the tests and the concept of inherent ability. Many psychologists will have examples from their own experience which demonstrate these limitations and indicate the importance of thinking style and strategy in cognitive performance.

Case example: Gary

Gary, a nine-year-old, was carrying out the Recall of Designs scale of the British Abilities Scale. On the first sub-scale he struggled, clearly using a primarily verbal strategy, talking himself through the designs.

Earlier in the interview he had been taught the NLP spelling strategy (see Chapter 17), a largely visual-based strategy involving the use of an internal visual representation of the word to be learned. He had done this quite successfully.

It was suggested that he use the spelling strategy in doing the second sub-scale of the Recall of Designs, which seems to be a more efficient strategy for this visual recall task. He did this, clearly showing appropriate eye movements (Chapter 16), indicating his use of an internal visual representation. His score on the first sub-scale yielded a centile of 26 whereas the centile score on the second sub-scale was 93. Clearly Gary's ability had not changed, although his strategy had.

A colleague (Max de Luynes – personal communication) described a second example, using the British Abilities Scale Block Design sub-scale. He has found on a number of occasions that merely saying 'Take it one step at a time' can make a significant difference to performance. Again this does not alter the child's ability, but even such a simple instruction can effectively change their strategy.

These descriptions involve instructions which are divergent from the test instructions. However, if simple instructions can yield such improvements in performance, this must question the assumption that ability is a stable concept which can be measured.

These examples indicate that performance on a task is dependent on the strategy used, rather than the limits of the child's ability. To some extent what the test measures may be the child's choice of an efficient strategy for the particular task. Ability is not necessarily the key issue, as is clear from the examples; when a child is directed towards a more useful strategy they may well be able to use it successfully.

Using cognitive assessments to find deficits in a child's functioning ignores the consideration that the results of an assessment may be more about the child's ability to select successful strategies. The child's selection of a particular strategy is possibly a result of their habitual use of a strategy for a particular task, rather than a selection of what could be their optimum strategy.

This further case example demonstrates this.

Case example: Chloe

Chloe (16), generally academically successful and articulate, was seen in order to provide an educational psychologist's report to the examination boards, to support the school's request for examination concessions in the light of her spelling difficulties. In considering her spellings it was clear that Chloe's strategy for spelling words was more or less exclusively auditory, except for some words with which she was particularly familiar. This was exemplified when she was asked if she thought some of the words she had attempted were correct from how they looked. She seemed confused by the question to the extent that she found the notion of a visual check of her spellings as quite unheard of.

The opportunity was taken to teach her the NLP spelling strategy (Chapter 17), which is primarily visual. She was quite able to take on this approach and learned the words in the demonstration effectively.

The interesting issue which Chloe demonstrates is her habitual use of a strategy for spelling which was clearly not working well. She was quite capable of using another strategy, but had not done this prior to it being suggested quite explicitly. How Chloe had developed her strategy is unknown, but frequently in education the emphasis in teaching has not been placed explicitly on *how* to think and learn, but *what* to think and learn, leaving children to devise their own strategies.

In terms of logical levels it seems to have been very easy for somebody, even as academically successful as Chloe, to understand her spelling difficulties in terms of a belief about spelling, or as an identity issue in terms of her belief about herself as a poor speller. She did not perceive the difficulty in terms of an issue of capability and therefore had shown little attempt to try alternative strategies. In terms of an intervention it was important to ensure that Chloe would also make the necessary changes in terms of belief and identity and make appropriate attributions for her experience of success and failure.

Exploring strategies and other factors in learning

In Chapter 16 we will look at representation systems as the basis for our internal representations of our world. This provides the basis for looking in detail at thinking and task-focused strategies in Chapter 17.

Perhaps an indication of a child's ability could be related to their range of strategies, incorporation of new strategies offered or openness to develop new approaches. However, this form of argument needs to be approached with scepticism, particularly when the information is taken in isolation. We have already considered how the other logical levels can impact on task performance and learning achievement.

Although the argument put forward here is for consideration of strategies rather than a focus on abilities, this is not to deny that there are children who do have limitations to their ability. However, by considering an approach based on strategies, there are greater possibilities to develop individually focused interventions.

Dynamic Assessment

In addition to the elicitation of strategies in assessments, constructive information to support hypothesis development and intervention planning can focus on a number of other important parameters of the learning situation and the child's approach to it. This approach is particularly emphasised in Feuerstein's Instrumental Enrichment Model. The model also provides a constructive approach to intervention and rejects the static concept of ability assumed in traditional psychometric assessment.

The model is based on three broad preconditions for learning:

- *Input.* This is the process of gathering and assimilation of information which requires: close focusing; precision; and impulsivity restraint.

- *Elaboration.* This involves interpreting and understanding information which requires: problem definition; selection of relevant information; identification of relationships; choosing; planning; hypothesising; and seeking evidence.

- *Output.* This involves reaching and communicating conclusions.

Assessments based on this model look at the child's approach to the learning situation in terms of these three parameters. It is referred to as Dynamic Assessment because it is a consideration of the dynamics of the learning paradigm and the teaching approaches, or mediation, through which the individual child can be most effectively supported in their learning situation.

It is not intended to look at this model in detail in this text as psychologists will already have more than a passing acquaintance with the approach. It is included in this chapter, albeit briefly, to highlight the importance of Dynamic Assessment and the features of learning assessment it offers.

CHAPTER 16

Representation Systems

The main approach to considering strategies introduced in the previous chapter comes directly from NLP. The work on strategies will be taken further in the next chapter, based on representation systems which are outlined here including an introduction to sub-modalities and a basis for individual intervention.

Information quality

Our sensory apparatus enables us to access five qualities of information about our environment: visual, auditory, kinaesthetic, olfactory and gustatory. In NLP, the assumption is made that, given we have information about our environment in terms of these five modalities, then the internal modelling of our world will also use these five qualities of information. Our subjective internal experience is made up of the pictures, sounds, feelings, smells and tastes that we can both recall and construct out of our prior experiences.

This is quite a simplified view and a number of further points could be included to make the model more sophisticated, for which reference to the NLP texts is recommended. However, two further issues are worthy of note. First, the kinaesthetic modality reflects tactile, proprioceptive, visceral and emotive forms of feelings, and needs to be acknowledged as a multi-faceted representation system. The tactile, proprioceptive and visceral aspects of the kinaesthetic system are direct experience, whereas the emotional kinaesthetic is a response to the experience, and consequently not a part of the direct experience. For this reason it is sometimes referred to as a 'meta' kinaesthetic, that is, it is how we feel about the experience.

A second consideration is the function of spoken language. People will readily acknowledge their internal dialogue (or monologue) as part of their thinking processes. However, in terms of the external world, and the internal world, the language element is a mediator of, or commentary on, the experience, that is, it serves to communicate about the experience rather than actually being the experience itself. Thus in terms of our individual models of the world, the spoken word represents a communication about, and thereby an approximation to, our direct subjective experience of either the internal or external world to which we are referring. Language is then seen as a secondary representation of experience, whereas the other representation systems are considered to provide a primary representation of experience.

In NLP, spoken language, either as internal or external experience, is referred to as 'auditory digital' in order to indicate a distinction between the language (digital), content and the tone, tempo and volume (analogue) characteristics of the auditory modality.

Identification of representation systems
Predicates
The representation systems or modalities to which we attend in our internal experience correlate with our external behaviour in several ways. For instance, if we are focusing on internal visualisations in our thinking, we are quite likely to be using words which suggest visualisations in our linguistic descriptions of our thinking. These sorts of words we call visual *predicates*; similarly we will find auditory predicates describing our internal auditory experiences, and so on.

The modality predicates we use in our language will then tend to give some indication to the type of internal experience we are paying attention to at a particular time.

In Table 16.1, there are a number of words which are typical examples of predicates of each of the three major representation systems.

Table 16.1 Predicates of the representation systems

Visual	Auditory	Kinaesthetic
clear	quiet	soft
bright	scream	rough
colourful	crackling	hurts
focused	sounds	hold

Whole phrases are often interesting in giving representation system distinctions; for instance:

I think I can *see* the sense of what you're saying but I'm not *clear* about the detail yet.

I'm *quietly* confident that if we *sound* out the proposals there will be a *resounding* approval.

I feel we are on *firm* ground with the *point* we are *pushing*.

Not all words are predicates; there are non-specific words, such as think and wonder, and other words which are ambiguous, such as light (visual or kinaesthetic?).

Eye access cues

Another cue to representation systems, and probably the most well known from NLP, is the eye access cue.

Although there are common generalisations here, the important rule to remember is not the generalisation but the fact that there is a rule. In other words everybody does not have the same eye movements correlating with the representation systems, but there will be a consistency within an individual between their eye movements and the modality of their internal representation.

Another feature of internal experience which needs to be introduced is the distinction between recalled experience and constructed experiences. That is, those internal pictures, sounds, feelings, etc. which are recalled from memories, in contrast to constructed pictures, sounds, feelings, etc., which are fabricated to produce new internal experience (although presumably fabricated out of previous experiences, but not a memory from the past).

As an example of the distinction, the visual recall experience of remembering what the view from your bedroom window looked like in the place where you lived as a child could be contrasted with the visual constructed experience of imagining what the area you live in would look like if you were a bird flying over it (assuming you have not flown over before in an aeroplane and have a memory of it).

Despite the reservations about generalisation, Figure 16.1 sets out the most frequently occurring pattern of eye movements to representation systems which has been estimated to be consistent for a majority of the population, though not a specific pattern for all.

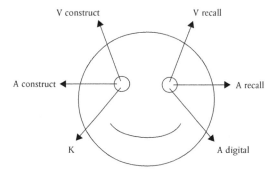

Figure 16.1 Eye movement patterns

Eye movements can occur quickly, and need to be noticed when the individual is attending to their internal experience, not when their attention is directed to their external experience and their eyes are directed to something they want to look at.

In attempting to identify an individual's pattern of eye movements in relation to the modality of their internal experience, asking directive questions and watching for the eye movements can be useful.

Example forms of directive questions are given in Table 16.2.

Table 16.2 Directive questions

Questions	Construct
What colour is your father's car?	visual construct
Can you imagine how the world would look if all the grass was red?	auditory recall
How does your favourite song go?	auditory construct
How would the Prime Minister's voice sound with an American accent?	auditory construct
How do you feel when you wake up and realise it is Saturday?	kinaesthetic
What was said the last time you spoke with your mother?	auditory digital

Other cues

Many other facets of an individual's external behaviour can be indicative of the representation system of internal experience. These include postures, gestures, breathing location, depth and rate, colouration, etc.

A summary table of indicators is given in Table 16.3.

Table 16.3 Summary of indicators

	Visual	Auditory	Kinaesthetic
Postural variations	Head up Shoulders back	Shoulders hunched Head rests on hand Hand on chin	Hand over heart/ chest

	Visual	Auditory	Kinaesthetic
Gestures	Point to eyes	Point to ears	
Intonation	Higher pitch	More rhythmic	Low pitch
	Fast tempo	Slow tempo	
	Loud volume	Quiet	
	Fewer pauses	More pauses	
Breathing	High in chest	Deep breaths	In abdomen
	Fast		Slow rhythm
	Momentary		
	Holding of breath		

Generally it is important to use a whole range of cues to identify the modalities that an individual is using.

Frequently, children will show overtly in their behaviour the representation systems they are using, for instance children carrying out tasks will often talk themselves through it, showing small lip movements as they silently talk. Kinaesthetic modality use can often be identified by hand and finger movements as these trace the direction of the child's attention, through an activity.

Sub-modalities

Within each representation system, or modality, there are structural elements which can be used to change the form of the representation of an experience. For instance, changes in the structure of an internal visual representation may be made by altering:

- brightness

- colour intensity

- size

- focus

- distance

- depth

- dimensions (two or three)

- shape

- perspective (associated or dissociated)

- contrast

- texture
- border (bordered or panoramic)
- location
- movement (movie or still).

Similar structural sub-modality distinctions could be made within the auditory and kinaesthetic modalities. Some auditory sub-modality distinctions are:

- pitch
- tonality
- melody
- inflection
- volume
- tempo
- rhythm
- duration
- mono/stereo.

Examples of kinaesthetic sub-modalities are:

- quality (warm/cold, sharp/blunt, relaxed/tense, etc.)
- intensity
- location (where in the body)
- movement
- direction
- speed
- duration (continuous/intermittent).

Making changes to the sub-modalities of a represented internal experience can produce quite profound changes in how the individual subjectively experiences it, particularly in terms of the 'meta' kinaesthetic or emotional association. The sub-modality changes can directly change the intensity of the primary representation of the experience either attenuating or intensifying it, this then attenuating or intensifying the emotional association.

Sub-modality changes can be very powerful in reducing the emotional reaction to the relived memories of previously traumatic, or upsetting, events, or alternatively enhancing the positive states engendered by pleasant memories. Representations of beliefs, doubts, confusions, understanding, etc. all also have sub-modality structures which can be changed to good effect.

For instance, a simple exercise is to investigate the sub-modality distinctions of confusion and understanding. Make a visual representation in your mind's eye of some process you understand well, and note the sub-modalities of the visualisation from the list above.

Next make a visual representation of some process you find confusing. An important point here is to make sure it is the process you find confusing (i.e. a lack of understanding rather than a lack of information). Again note the sub-modalities of the visualisation of the confusing process. Identify the sub-modalities which are different between the visualisation of the understood process and the confusing process, for instance is one brighter, more colourful, larger, closer, in a different position, etc.? One by one change the sub-modalities of the confused visualisation to the sub-modalities of the understood visualisation, and with this the confusing process will become clearer! (Or, alternatively, identify what further information you need.)

An important aspect with sub-modality work is to identify the sub-modality which makes the difference. This is frequently referred to as the critical sub-modality. Taking a visualisation of a pleasant experience, go through the visual sub-modalities changing each in turn. Find which sub-modalities make the most significant difference to the pleasurable feeling, when they are changed. Frequently the critical sub-modality will be the one which tends to create other sub-modality shifts at the same time. That is, it tends to be the one which drives the others. The critical sub-modalities will need to be investigated for each individual and experience.

Swish Pattern

The Swish Pattern is a very effective change pattern which can be used to change the feelings associated with an experience and enable the client to respond differently in the future. It can form a very effective intervention for both children and adults.

The procedure involves first the client identifying a situation where they would like to respond differently, both in terms of their personal feelings and how they react.

The client is asked to find a visual memory of this situation. It is important that the representation is associated, that is, the perspective of the picture is from their own eyes as they are in the situation. The picture also needs to have a border (for instance, like a picture frame). Check that this picture does have the negative feeling associated with it that the client wants to change.

Having established the picture, it is necessary to go through the sub-modality distinctions in order to identify a critical sub-modality. This is a sub-modality which when changed creates a significant reduction in the intensity of the feeling associated with the experience. Once this has been done this picture can be put to one side.

The client is then invited to create an alternative picture of this situation in which they are dealing with things in a way they would wish. They can be as inventive and creative as they wish in constructing this image. They can have all the personal powers and resources they would wish; it is not necessary to be bound by the limits of reality with this picture (whoever's reality that might be). This picture needs to be dissociated, that is, the perspective needs to be that of an observer to the situation, so that the client can see themselves in the picture, with all their resources and powers. Again this picture needs to be bordered; also check that this picture does have an associated positive feeling. And again, go through the sub-modality distinctions to identify a critical sub-modality. However, in this case it is only necessary to go through the sub-modality distinctions which were significant in changing the feeling in the first picture.

The goal is to identify a sub-modality which can be changed in one direction to reduce the intensity of the negative feeling associated with the first picture, and changed in the opposite direction to enhance the positive feeling associated with the second picture. (Although this sounds a laborious procedure, in practice it is generally very easy to identify such a sub-modality.)

The next step is to set up the following procedure with the client.

Taking the first picture, make the sub-modality change (which reduces the feeling) all the way so that the picture disappears. For instance, if the sub-modality is distance, then have the picture shoot off into the distance so far that it disappears; or if it is brightness, have the picture darken, or brighten, as appropriate to reduce the associated feeling, so that the picture disappears. Once the picture has disappeared have the sub-modality change back from the point of disappearance, so that the second picture returns into view, reappearing with the increasing positive feeling associated with the increasing sub-modality.

The client then stops, and clears their visual field.

To establish the Swish the client is asked to repeat this last step ten times, each time more quickly, so that after ten trials it happens almost instantaneously. Between each of the ten trials the client has to stop so as not to reverse the process.

The effectiveness of the work can be checked by having the client think of the first picture again. If the work has been done well then the client will not be able to keep this picture and the associated feeling; the transition will happen automatically.

The work should be future paced, that is, the client is asked to think of another similar situation where this would happen and check that the changed feeling occurs.

For ease the steps are summarised:

1. Have the client find a visual memory of the situation where they want to change the way they feel. Check it is an associated picture, it has a border, and the negative feeling is produced by it.

2. Go through the sub-modality distinctions to find which sub-modality changes have a significant effect on the feeling.

3. Have the client create a second picture of how they would like to be in this situation. Check the picture is dissociated, it has a border, and a positive feeling is produced by it.

4. Go through the previously identified sub-modalities (from 2) to find which have a significant effect on the feeling.

5. Choose one of the identified sub-modalities to be the vehicle for the transition from the first picture to the second. Explain the process to the client, then ask them to do it. The process involves changing the sub-modality for the first picture to the extent that the picture disappears, and then changing the sub-modality back again, but so that it is the second picture which reappears.

6. Check the client understands the instructions, then tell them to do it.

7. Tell them to repeat the process ten times, but after each time stopping when the second picture has appeared.

8. Test the effect, then future pace using a similar future event.

Case example: Alfie

Alfie, aged ten, was referred by his school because of his disturbing behaviour. He had previously been excluded from school, and had attended appointments with a child psychiatrist. His teachers described him as rude, disobedient and aggressive and, in relation to others, self-centred, selfish and violent.

In the interview, Alfie acknowledged his difficulties in school, attributing them to his uncontrollable temper. He was keen to do something to control his temper, but assumed this was something he would have to live with. The issue of his temper was explored more fully at a further stage. It seemed very appropriate to use the Swish Pattern as Alfie was clearly identifying his desire to change, and also identifying that there were situations where he would like to behave and feel differently.

Alfie accessed his experience of 'anger' by visualising a typical situation where he would feel angry. To ensure a good quality of experience he was directed to recall the fully represented experience by directing him to attend to the auditory and kinaesthetic components of the experience.

In the second, more constructive response, visualisation was then developed.

Brightness served as a significant sub-modality to create the transition from one picture to the other, by darkening the first picture to the point where it became completely black, and then brightening again to reveal the second picture. This was repeated ten times.

Although there was more to the interview than the Swish Pattern, this had been the only part of the interview which was a direct intervention.

Subsequent reports by Alfie's teachers after three, five, and eight weeks indicated Alfie was showing distinct and successful changes in his reactions to situations where he would previously become angry.

Although this presented as a successful outcome in the short term, it unfortunately was not sustained in the long term. Attempts to establish good working links between home and school were not successful, and there was clearly a significant degree of disagreement between these parts of the system.

While Alfie remained at the primary school, his behaviour deteriorated gradually, but slightly; however, this escalated considerably when he went on to secondary school some 18 months later.

Although the Swish Pattern served as a very effective intra-child intervention, this was not supported by changes within the system. Alfie's changed behaviour was in isolation and thereby was not sustained.

CHAPTER 17

Strategies

Representation system information is particularly useful in eliciting the strategies individuals use to carry out tasks. In progressing through a task an individual will not only have aspects of their external environment that they pay attention to, but also significant parts of their own internal experience.

A major area of work in NLP has been to elicit the detailed strategies of competent performers in particular tasks, in terms of the sequence of relevant aspects of both their internal and external experience which they attend to. This allows the identification of efficient and effective strategies for specific tasks. Some of these identified strategies will be considered in some detail later in this chapter.

Once a strategy has been elicited in detail it is possible to model the strategy; in other words, to teach either yourself or others how to do the same task in exactly the same way the competent performer carried it out, by paying attention to the different modalities of the internal and external experience in precisely the same order as required for the competent performance.

Modelling in this form is a key principle in NLP, but follows the same basis as proposed by social learning theorists (e.g. Bandura and Walters 1963). The significance of modelling in NLP is the focus on eliciting the strategy from the competent performer which includes their internal experiences, in addition to the externally observable behaviour.

The behavioural correlates of the internal representation systems described earlier help in eliciting this detailed information, although verbally checking the subjective experiences of the performer is important. Well-developed strategies are frequently effectively streamlined with practice, so the behavioural cues to representation systems can be useful in indicating aspects of strategy of which the performer may not be consciously aware.

Strategy elicitation can be a very useful tool and a number of useful principles of effective and efficient strategies are highlighted later in the chapter. However, for a more detailed text on strategy elicitation, the book *Neuro-Linguistic Programming 1* (Dilts *et al.* 1980) is recommended reading.

An awareness of strategies based on representation systems, and the cues to detecting them, provide an added dimension to the psychologist's perspective and information gathering in the individual interview.

This provides a basis for the use of assessment tasks in identifying the strategies a child selects in attempting to carry out different types of task. Individuals will frequently show the use of particular types of strategy which they will habitually use, even though the strategy may be quite inefficient for the task. Some examples of this have been noted in previous chapters. The Feuerstein Learning Potential Assessment Device (Feuerstein, Rand and Hoffman 1979), briefly described previously, adopts a similar principle of approach to assessment.

Teaching new strategies can be a particularly successful approach to begin to make significant changes to a child's learning, not only in terms of improving their capability at the task, but also changing their beliefs about learning and themselves as learners. Providing evidence of competence can be a significant challenge to their previously held negative beliefs and identities. MacKay's work on personal declarations (MacKay 2007), described in Chapter 15 has shown the importance, value and impact of identity and belief statements in relation to literacy attainment.

The principles of strategy elicitation have been used by researchers in NLP and a number of strategies have been identified with a particular relevance to educational achievement.

Strategies in themselves often seem to be exceptionally simple, and frequently teachers and parents claim they have been teaching their children in this way. However, there is an important distinction between the way material is presented and the process by which a child is taught to learn the material. With the spelling strategy (see below), teachers and parents may comment that they have already used 'flashcards' to no avail, assuming that the presentation of the material is the key element of the spelling strategy. In considering strategies it is how the individual manages the information in the external world and the links to their own internal experience that is the crucial aspect of an effective strategy, and this is not necessarily governed by the actual presentation of the material.

Merely presenting a child with words to learn using flashcards does not presuppose that the child will use a visual internal representation to learn the words. The child will use whatever strategy they have evolved in order to learn the words.

Teaching strategies is about how children are taught to learn, as an effective learning process, rather than focusing on the content of the material.

Spelling strategy

The spelling strategy is perhaps the most well-known piece of strategy work in NLP with education. A number of NLP users in education have different versions of the strategy which best suit their own use, and reflect the range of creative opportunities that can be brought to bear in teaching strategies.

The basic spelling strategy derives from a contrastive analysis of the spelling strategies of 'good spellers' and 'poor spellers'. Generally it is found that people who are able to spell well remember words as internal visualisations which are associated with the auditory presentation of the word and a kinaesthetic indicator giving a sense that the spelling is correct. In contrast, poor spellers tend to attempt to learn words in a number of ways but do not to use this sort of strategy.

From experience, poor spellers often have a visual strategy for spelling words which they have learned particularly well through frequent exposure to the words. Even highly phonic-based spellers can often spell phonically irregular words such as 'the'. However, on investigation they generally say they 'just know the word' which on elaboration often amounts to remembering what it looks like. When they are asked to learn new words they tend to revert to non-visual strategies and perform poorly.

The spelling strategy for learning words is a sequence of external and internal experiences the individual is given to carry out as follows:

1. Hear the name of the word.

2. See the word (written on a piece of paper).

3. Make an internal visualisation of the word as it is written down.

4. Check the internal and external visuals are the same.

5. Have a positive kinaesthetic experience to indicate the internal picture matches that presented on the paper, i.e. is correct, or

6. Do not have the positive kinaesthetic experience indicating the internal visual is not correct, in which case return to 2.

The key part of the strategy is that people who learn words effectively tend to store the information in a visual format. Thus if they subsequently try to remember a particular word for spelling, they will do this by internal visualisation. The correctness, or incorrectness, of their visualisation is indicated by an internal kinaesthetic, a sense of 'Does it feel right?' This is the 'meta' kinaesthetic associated with the experience.

The strategy is quite simple to teach to children, or adults. Initially it is important to get across the notion of making internal pictures. As this generally is not the level of discussion we have with each other, phrases such as 'See it in your mind's eye', or (with younger children) using the analogy of a camera inside your head to take pictures, can be very effective in establishing the principle of internal visualisations.

Some children will readily be able to do this, whereas others will not, probably partly determined by the habitual strategies they have developed for a wide range of tasks. There are occasional times where a child will have developed very verbally oriented strategies and may find it quite unusual to work in a visual modality. Even children who have developed very capably in their use of visual strategies can get fixed into the idea that learning words is a verbal activity and they will concentrate on verbal letter lists and phonic attempts to learn words.

The spelling strategy is not an attempt to intervene in a dispute between phonic and look and say methods, but an acknowledgement that both visual learning and phonic decoding are two different strategies both of which are valuable and serve different purposes. The visualisation serves the function of remembering and retaining words; the phonic strategy is an important decoding method to attempt unfamiliar words, but does not present as a viable method for retention of words.

Teaching the strategy, once the principle of visualisations has been established, is relatively straightforward, and demands explicit instruction to the child to learn the word as presented as an internal picture in their 'mind's eye'.

Once the child has got the picture of the word in their 'mind's eye' then they need to let you know so that you can remove the presented word from their sight and they can read off the letters of the spelling of the word from the picture in their 'mind's eye'. Assuming their response is correct, then they need to have this acknowledged so that they are able to get a feeling of having the right response, that is, the positive kinaesthetic component of it 'feeling right'. Should the response be incorrect, they should be invited to look at the stimulus word again and note how it is different from the picture in their 'mind's eye' and make the necessary changes.

A subsequent activity is to ask the child to read off the letters in the reverse direction. This serves two purposes. First, this is your check that the child has used visualisation, although you will probably notice this from the eye movements. If the word has been remembered as a verbal letter list, this exercise is very difficult. Probably more importantly, however, this part of the exercise seems to be that which particularly impresses the child about their ability to learn words. If they have successfully learned a relatively long word both forwards and backwards, this can be the point at which the strategy as an intervention begins to challenge negative self-beliefs about their ability to learn, and becomes an intervention which, as most do, crosses a number of logical levels.

A handout, written for parents to use the spelling strategy with their children, in conjunction with the school, is given in Appendix 2. This is a programme based on precision teaching principles with the purpose of enabling the child to develop and practise the strategy so that they can become able to use it readily for remembering new words they come across. It has been used quite successfully as a programme carried out with the parent and child, with links to the school, as a four-week intervention with the intention of developing the child's use of visualisation in their repertoire of reading and spelling strategies. This could then be followed up with the reading for pleasure strategy.

Reading comprehension strategy

A successful reading comprehension strategy has been elicited which has proved helpful in giving a strategy to children who are able to read text reasonably accurately, but fail to remember or take in what they have read.

Basically the strategy involves a transfer of experience from the external visual input of the written words to form internal auditory digital language. This is used to create an internal visual constructed image. A subsequent kinaesthetic component should also be included as a check to indicate if the visual image is consistent in the context of previously established visual images from the text.

As the reader becomes more skilled and proficient, the strategy may be streamlined and avoid some of the auditory digital language element, but this is at the level of speed reading and is quite an advanced skill.

The steps may be summarised as follows:

1. See the text on the page.

2. Read the text to derive the internal auditory digital language.

3. Construct an internal visual representation from the internal language.

4. Kinaesthetically check that this visual image is consistent with the previously established context of the story.

This strategy has been used successfully with children. A useful exercise to give practice in developing and using the strategy is to invite them to read some text, but after each sentence for them to draw on paper what is happening in the story. In this way the child effectively converts the story from the written text into a cartoon form. Again, as with the spelling strategy, explicit instructions to follow in terms of how the child is to 'think' about the strategy are crucial.

Following verbal instructions strategy

This strategy is useful for helping children who have difficulties following verbally presented instructions because they have difficulty remembering the instructions. It is not a strategy to get children to follow instructions they do not want to follow! The strategy is very similar to the reading comprehension strategy, in transferring auditory digital language information into a visual format.

The strategy is as follows:

1. Hear the verbally presented instruction.

2. Construct a visual image from the verbal instruction.

3. Combine the visual image with preceding images to form either a series of stills (as a cartoon), or a movie, in internal experience.

4. Kinaesthetically check that the visualisation is consistent with the context of the preceding information.

The cartoon or movie is a visualisation which can hold a considerable amount of information. In contrast, children trying to remember instructions in the auditory digital language modality will tend to have to rehearse the instruction internally, which will then lead to subsequent instructions being ignored, or they will pay attention to the subsequent instructions, failing to retain earlier instructions as they fail to rehearse.

Reading for pleasure strategy

Although not particularly a strategy from NLP, this is a useful and popular strategy for developing expressive and receptive vocabulary, developing sight recognition skills and aiding comprehension. It is not a set strategy in the sense of those above, but basically uses paired reading as a vehicle. It is particularly useful where reading at home is becoming stressful to both parent and child.

The strategy may be summarised as follows:

1. The parent and child sit comfortably together with the reading book.

2. At its easiest, the parent reads the passage or part of the passage to the child.

3. The parent and child talk about who was in the story, what they did, what happened, etc.

4. The parent uses the discussion to identify any words the child does not understand and explains their meaning within the context of the story.

5. The parent identifies key words in the story which have occurred reasonably frequently and points out the particular word in the text to the child.

6. The child is asked to try to spot where that word occurs at other places on the page.

7. The child then might be asked to draw the story in cartoon form as in the reading comprehension strategy.

The emphasis placed on different elements in the strategy will depend on what aspect of the child's learning is most relevant to focus on. The discussion (3 and 4) may be the key element if language development is a focus. The word spotting (5 and 6) may be more important if developing sight vocabulary and visual word learning skills are the focus. The discussion (3) and drawing (7) may be emphasised if reading comprehension is more of a focus.

The key element of the strategy may be in enabling the child and parent to carry out reading activities together which can be pleasurable, meaningful and not as fraught as some reading attempts where parents feel under pressure, or are unclear what to do.

This strategy may be more appropriate than the spelling and reading comprehension strategies described above if a greater emphasis is to be placed on reading as a pleasurable activity. The selection and focus of any of the strategies will depend on the case issues and the degree to which the adults will be engaged with a strategy, depending upon which makes most sense to them.

Some general points

In working with strategies it is quite easy to create useful new strategies for children who have developed relatively inefficient ways of going about tasks. One way of doing this is to identify how you do a particular task yourself, provided it is not an area that you have difficulty with. Often working with a colleague can lead to a satisfactory strategy which a child may find helpful. There are some useful general points to bear in mind when developing, or for that matter eliciting, strategies.

Each of the strategies presented above utilise a kinaesthetic component to provide a form of check within the strategy. This is a very common element of the kinaesthetic component to strategies.

It is important for strategies to have some form of decision point in them, as strategies which operate without checks or decisions would present as uncontrolled habits without any sense of choice or control by the individual. It is also worth noting that strategies are best designed to include at least all of the three major representational systems, that is, visual, auditory and kinaesthetic.

Generally strategies which utilise visualisations for holding information will be more efficient than using the auditory digital language modality. The visual system can hold information simultaneously, whereas language is of essence sequential. Further, visualisation is direct experience, be it internal, external, remembered or constructed. In contrast the auditory digital language represents a commentary on experience rather than the direct experience itself, and as secondary experience loses some of the richness.

Case example: Developing a bespoke strategy

Andrew, aged 14, was raised as a concern by his secondary school because of his spelling difficulties, and his depression and anxiety in relation to his poor spelling skills. Both the school and Andrew's mother had been working together on a number of approaches to attempt to help Andrew learn to spell. However, this had not been successful and Andrew seemed to have decided that he was not likely to be able to learn to spell. This was causing him distress, and he showed little commitment or enthusiasm to work with support staff to develop spelling.

The psychologist's involvement was focused at helping to develop some new strategy in relation to spelling which may give success, and to help give Andrew a sense that learning to spell was a possibility through exploring any belief, value or functional issues which may have a negative impact on his capability to develop spelling skills.

In interview Andrew was initially quite upset and tearful, indicating that he had been worried about meeting the psychologist. He expected he was going to be tested and he was worried whether he would pass or fail. He acknowledged a sense of importance to this, but could not put into words what was important.

He was quickly able to identify his spelling as an area of concern and that this had several ramifications for later life.

He noted his reading had improved considerably and that this had been accomplished because he had been taught by his teachers and mother. (It was significant that he perceived this as him having been taught rather than him having learned. This issue of him as a passive recipient in the process rather than the active element was a recurrent theme through the interview.)

In relation to spelling, he managed to spell the following words from the British Ability Scales spelling test: the, up, sit, box, was, play, come, new, pie, walk, soil, catch. His mistakes were the following: brige, cicule, treasuer, Quaroled, begining, convenent, phesersas. He was able to identify all the words which were correct and those misspelt, although this did not help him identify the correct spelling.

In looking at the word 'brige' he recognised that it was misspelt. When given the correct spelling he recognised this. He was asked to learn the word by visualisation (based on the NLP spelling strategy), and was able to do this easily. The missing 'd' was made more memorable by using colour and brightness sub-modality changes. Despite this he indicated that he expected he would have forgotten the spelling after only a short time. When asked the basis for this pessimistic view, he indicated that he had been taught by this method before, and he had not retained the words (this method being a common approach, amongst others, in the school's SEN department).

Given that he could develop visualisation approaches quite readily, and was also verbally able, it was decided to experiment with meaningful visual pictures to support the spellings.

The picture support shown in Figure 17.1 was used for the word 'bridge'.

Figure 17.1 'Bridge'

The representation is of a suspension bridge. The two towers derive from the upper parts of the 'b' and 'd'. The visualisation therefore requires that the 'd' must be present.

This is slightly different from making a picture out of the word to aid memory, as it is designed to have the picture support the element of the spelling which is not correct.

A further example was then used (Figure 17.2).

Figure 17.2 'Quarrelled'

This was supported with the phrase 'It takes two to quarrel'. The problem had been to remember if there were two 'r's and/or two 'l's. The visualisation and sentence focused on this aspect of the spelling to make it memorable.

Andrew was reasonably convinced that if asked the next day he thought he would remember the correct spelling for 'bridge' and 'quarrelled'.

A number of pieces of further work were done to explore Andrew's beliefs about himself. This generally suggested that he was usually quite a happy person except in relation to school. He also described himself as kind, but 'always carrying the world's guilt on his shoulders', an example of this being that he would feel sorry for homeless people.

Exploration of emotional states (using Portrait Gallery) did seem to suggest Andrew operated at effect rather than cause in relation to the world (generally indicating that he seemed to have little sense of his personal locus of control and ability to bring about change himself). In some ways this seemed to parallel his concern for homeless people, who had been dealt a poor lot, and presumably by circumstances beyond their control.

The homeless were used as a metaphor to describe situations where some people chose their circumstances; others get to a stage where things aren't going well for them but this can be the turning point to work towards a better life for themselves. It was suggested they are homeless while they work out a strategy of getting out of the situation they are in. While this happens they may feel like they have given up, but it is just because it is taking them longer to find a way out. At times they may think there is no way out, but eventually they will come across something.

In the final discussion of the possibilities for change, Andrew was still quite passive in his attitude to the possibilities that he could be effective in learning to spell. He indicated that change would only be promoted through teachers, parents and friends lending a helping hand. Although he did not know what he would have to do to promote change, he did acknowledge that a new way of learning would be important. He also indicated that an incentive would be necessary (external and concrete); this again seemed to reflect his lack of conviction that anything would work, so this extra was needed for motivation.

In terms of noticing any change, he considered that teachers and parents would be the first to notice, not him. He agreed with the suggestion then offered that, when there is so much sadness, depression and worry, it is perhaps difficult to notice any changes.

Andrew agreed that in the meeting the following day with his parents he would be happy for a programme to be organised based on the word learning strategy we had devised and he would carry it out with his parents. He was clear that he did not want to be part of the meeting (again a reflection of his sadness and his sense of not being personally effective in the process).

At the meeting with his mother and father on the next day the programme was agreed. Each day Andrew, with his parents, would learn one new word. This would be done by analysing where he had difficulty with the word and then developing some creative visualisation and/or mnemonic to retain the correct aspect of the spelling.

Words previously learned would be tested each day and the number of words recorded graphically to show progress.

There was general agreement, although some sense that the father had some reservations about Andrew's ability to learn spellings at all. This did leave some despondency with both the school staff and psychologist about the likely effectiveness of the intervention. A review date was agreed for about six weeks' time and an invitation given to Andrew (through his parents) to attend if he could.

At the subsequent review Andrew attended and took a willing part; he displayed the pack of word cards he had developed with the word pictures indicating the mnemonic phrase where applicable. The graph of words learned clearly showed a rise as more words were learned and retained.

Andrew was clearly much more positive and confident in this meeting and showed a more positive proactive approach to the programme than in the initial meeting with the psychologist. His father also was much more positive about Andrew's ability in general and to learn spellings.

Andrew's mother, who had done most of the supporting at home, indicated that the word learning took time because of finding what precise aspect of the word was the difficulty and required the support, and because thinking of the creative visual/language mnemonic as the support also took time.

Andrew was keen to continue the programme for another six weeks up to the end of the term and was also happy to review the progress then with his parents and the school. He did not feel the need for the psychologist to be present as he was confident that progress would continue.

Subsequent to the involvement at an informal meeting between the school and psychologist it was indicated by the school that Andrew continued to make progress, and continued to demonstrate a more positive attitude and happier emotional state.

A hypothesising strategy

As a final part of this chapter a possible strategy is included for the psychologist which has been found useful in developing hypotheses about a child's functioning.

The strategy is for the psychologist to use the available information to attempt to create internal visual constructed images of the child in their environment, including the way the child and others are behaving, particularly in terms of the concerns expressed. These visualisations are dissociated, that is, they are as if observing the child, rather than from the child's perspective. The visualisations need to include a number of aspects of the child's life including school, home and other situations the child is likely to be in, for example with friends.

The strategy is as follows:

1. Having constructed a number of these visualisations, make the picture associated, that is, step into the picture momentarily seeing life from the child's perspective. Become aware of what the child sees, hears and feels in these situations.

2. Given our basic axiom that the child's behaviour makes sense in terms of the world they live in and the understanding they have of it, check if, while in the child's perspective in the visualisation, the way the child is behaving, in terms of the concerns expressed, makes sense as an appropriate way to behave given an understanding of the world from that position. If the behaviour does make sense to you

in that situation, then it is likely that your visualisations do represent a hypothesis worth considering further, and also perhaps allows some further appreciation of the child's predicament. This may also give indications about what changes in the system, and the child's understanding of the world, may have beneficial effects.

3. If the behaviours do not make sense, then try constructing some new visualisations, or perhaps you need to acquire some new information about the child and the world in which they live. The sources of this information may be the parents, school or the child themselves. If the visualisations are unclear, difficult to construct or require a great deal of personal content, then this is likely an indicator that more information is required in order to create the hypothesis.

The value of any strategy is in its usefulness. It has been presented here as an invitation to try out and find out.

CHAPTER 18

Developing Interventions

In Chapter 1, the outline of the PDR process and the problem solving model provided a basic introduction to interventions.

Many of the subsequent chapters have provided methods and models for gaining information from both an individual and systemic perspective. This information provides a basis for generating hypotheses to gain an understanding of the concerns about a child and offering opportunities for interventions.

Hypotheses may be generated from a range of perspectives, with those arising from more systemic thinking based on concepts introduced in Chapter 6; or from an individual perspective based on the logical levels and using concepts introduced in Chapters 7 to 11.

The focus of the intervention could be seen as linked to the degree of the young person's *locus of control.*

Locus of control

Locus of control refers to the level of personal control the individual has in a particular situation. This is relevant in thinking about the degree to which the child/young person can take responsibility for change, and the extent to which the system needs to take that responsibility.

For younger children, the child's world is predominantly defined by the system. The adults define what is right and wrong (values); the way the world is (beliefs); and the child's sense of identity.

The child has less personal locus of control and, in terms of responsibility for change, the adults need to see themselves as the key players. While the child may be an active participant in voicing and understanding the concerns, defining the sought-for outcome and developing the interventions, the adults need to take responsibility for initiation and maintenance of the process. The implication is for greater systemic working, that is, changing the way the world works around the child.

Older young people have a greater personal locus of control, and while this may enable a greater level of personal responsibility to be given to the young person, it needs to be paralleled with a greater engagement with them in defining the problem, and the problem solving process. However, there also needs to be recognition that aspects of the system could be a force to promote change, a barrier to change, or represent inertia to change.

For older young people, their world is likely to be defined by a broader group of influences, media, peers and a range of adults beyond parents and teachers. The system is much harder to engage in the change process, and this provides a practical reason for a greater focus on individual work. Nevertheless it will be important to ensure that the key players in the system are engaged as a force to promote change and support the intervention.

Interventions for change

The hypotheses linked to the intended outcome for the involvement will inform the focus of the intervention. The psychologist may have some hypotheses they would not wish to share directly with the system, but may inform how the intervention is focused. This will be important as considering the relationships and dynamics within the system could be crucial to the effective implementation of the intervention. In addition, it may be that any intervention plan can also have a beneficial effect on systemic aspects as well as being directly targeted to the child.

Interventions can be targeted to address change at a range of levels. For instance, a psychologist may be working to enable the parents and school to put together a form of supplementary work package for the parents to work with the child at home, under the guidance of the school teacher. The psychologist may see a significant focus of the intervention as facilitating improved communications between home and school, whereas the school and parents may see the sole purpose as applying the teaching method to address the child's difficulty; both foci are valid to target the agreed intended outcome of the involvement. However, it could jeopardise the intervention for the psychologist to disclose their underlying systemic hypothesis overtly.

Most interventions will operate at many levels. For instance, the spelling strategy programme described earlier in Chapter 17 is an intervention which could potentially create change in any number of the following ways:

1. Direct teaching of word spellings to the child.

2. Development and practice of the word learning strategy for the child.

3. Relieving the child's anxiety about learning words.

4. Changing the child's beliefs about their ability to learn words.

5. Changing the child's beliefs about the ease of learning words.

6. Changing the child's self-perception, or identity, in relation to learning, their competence and their value as a person.

7. Changing the parent's beliefs about the ease of learning words.

8. Changing the parent's belief about their ability to help their child learn.

9. Relieving the parent's anxiety about the child's learning of words.

10. Enabling the parent to do, and believe they can do, something in a constructive way to help their child.

11. Enabling the parent to provide an appropriate positive learning environment for the child.

12. A number of similar changes in the beliefs and behaviours of the teachers in relation to the child.

These potential areas of change relate to the logical levels framework. In addition this same intervention could be seen from a systemic perspective as potentially creating the following changes:

1. The relationship of child and parent through giving the opportunity to work on something constructively, where the high degree of structure in the task allows a relatively unstressed environment, and where both can experience success through their combined efforts.

2. The relationship between parent and school where the school is involved in supporting the programme to some extent and facilitating the parent and school working together, thereby changing attitudes and perceptions.

3. With a little constructive reframing, to engage a perhaps distanced parent by emphasising the need for the child to have the additional reinforcement of both parents working with them.

The list is not exhaustive, and is included merely by way of example. It is not that the spelling strategy programme particularly addresses all these issues, but it can be used to do this. It is important for the psychologist to consider how to focus an intervention to ensure it targets the range of hypotheses which are pertinent in the particular case.

The reading for pleasure strategy described in the same chapter has a much greater emphasis on the systemic elements and beliefs and values level, where the development of strategy is still apparent, but may be seen as more incidental. Indeed all interventions, be they focused on educational achievement, behavioural or emotional concerns or any other issue, should be made to be effective at a number of different levels, and create a systemic change. What seems important is that as psychologists we are aware of our underlying hypotheses, and can ensure that whatever interventions we use we seek to be influential across the range of issues highlighted by our hypotheses.

In a number of the case examples described in the text, it has been noted that changes in the individual child's behaviour have been apparent but these have not been sustained on a reasonably permanent basis. It has been significant in these cases that despite the changes in the individual child's behaviour there has been little change in the functioning of the system around the child, so the system has not reinforced the change, and effectively may be seen as continuing to provide the context for the previous behaviours to be maintained. It is important that interventions do focus on the changes in systems and relationships around the child.

Setting the intervention

There are a number of features to successfully setting up an intervention which are worth considering. Many of these points have been raised in previous chapters, but it is useful to bring them together.

The concern to the hypothesis

Has the concern of all participants been explored, shared and acknowledged?

If the concerns of participants have not been recognised and taken seriously, they are unlikely to feel committed to the process and unlikely to take an effective participatory role. If the psychologist has not been directly involved in seeing the child, as is the case where work is with school staff and parents, are the child's likely concerns known and acknowledged?

Does the hypothesis present as a credible understanding of the concerns for the participants, particularly the adults? The acceptance of a hypothesis, which can often be overtly offered as a *working* hypothesis, will depend to some degree on the level of rapport which can be developed by the psychologist with the participants.

The credibility of a hypothesis to the adults will also be improved by engaging their own thoughts and the information they provide. Where an interview with the child has taken place the information provided, and the formation of this information into a coherent hypothesis (or hypotheses), can be highly compelling to the adult participants.

Hypothesis to outcome

Are agreed outcomes for the involvement agreed by all participants? Participants not committed to the outcome of the involvement will not be committed to any role they may be asked to take in a proposed intervention.

Does the hypothesis link to the agreed outcome credibly for the participants?

Hypothesis to intervention plan

Does the hypothesis and agreed outcome(s) link to the proposed intervention credibly for the participants? The participants' acceptance of the intervention will be enhanced by the level of rapport achieved, as well as the degree to which the link is established in a convincing way.

Interview information available from a child interview can be important in engaging the participants in the hypothesis and intervention. The Portrait Gallery extension technique (Chapter 12) which outlines the conditions for change from the problem state to the desired state can provide very convincing feedback from the child to the adult system about the conditions for an effective intervention.

Intervention plan to intervention action

In addition to being committed to the intervention plan, participants need to be clear about who needs to do what and, in particular, how information is communicated between the adults in the system and between the adults and the child.

Adults need to take responsibility for the intervention and not leave elements of the management of the intervention to the child. A frequent breakdown of intervention occurs where the child is used as the conduit for communication between the adults, particularly the parents and school. An example would be where a child carries a home/school communication book. If the book does not arrive at home, the parents need to take responsibility to contact the school, and vice versa; if the book does not arrive at school the school needs to take responsibility to contact the home. Anticipating such details in planning can be important in preventing interventions from breaking down.

Where tasks are to be carried out, it is important to spend time to ensure that all participants are clear about their own task and what others will be doing. Not only is this of practical significance, it will also provide the child with a sense of the system around them working coherently and in the same way, frequently an important element of change for the child.

Noticing change

Interventions can be hard work and both the child and the adults need to be able to experience success for the effort to be sustained. Often the intervention can be seen as joining up the efforts of the child to change, with the adults in the system ready to acknowledge those efforts and encourage and reward them.

It is important to build into the intervention ways in which change and effort to change is noticed by the system and communicated between the adults and to the child. In the Portrait Gallery extension technique the following questions are used:

- How will the change begin to happen?

- What will you be doing differently?

- Who can help?

- What will they need to do?

- Who will be the first to notice?

- What will they notice?

- Who is most important to notice?

- How will you know they have noticed?

These questions are key ones to address in the detailed planning of the intervention, if the technique has been used the responses from the child will provide the model for the intervention plan.

Review

The review was discussed in Chapter 1, in the outline of the PDR and problem solving approach. The review serves many purposes; it is crucial in bringing closure to the intervention. The intervention can be demanding on the adults in the system. If they are to persist with the intervention it is only respectful that this is carried out for an agreed period of time prior to a formal review. Participants will commit to carry out an intervention if they know it is only for a few weeks, whereas this would be unlikely with open-ended recommendations.

At times, the length of the intervention period prior to review can be an important judgement in promoting the commitment to intervention. An intervention period of less than a week is rare, but at times may be necessary to ensure it is carried out, particularly if the participants are less than completely committed to the intervention. The psychologist's diary management has to be less of a consequence than a 'failed' intervention where the failure arises from its not being carried out.

The review also acknowledges that the intervention is based on a hypothesis from information gathered, and psychological models, theories and frameworks; it is not a truth. The review is a review of the information, hypotheses and intervention. Our honesty that psychology leads us to hypotheses, not truths, is acceptable because the review allows validation of our involvement against the achievement towards the agreed outcome for the work.

CHAPTER 19

Elements of Interventions

Introduction

In this chapter we look at various issues and techniques to gain commitment to create and implement interventions.

Time for change

Although for a psychologist a new piece of casework is part of daily life, for most of our client group, be they children, parents and sometimes teachers, the involvement is quite unusual and has the potential to be a significant life event and point of change.

The individual interview techniques described in earlier chapters give the child or student the opportunity to review their perception of the world and themselves which can be a significant event in itself. In terms of their understanding and beliefs this offers the potential for individual change. Similarly discussing issues with parents and teachers, especially when supported with information of the child's world and perception, can lead to insights which will promote change within the system.

Appendix 3 describes research to identify points of change in the behaviour of students in secondary school and the possible prompts for the change. The study arose following a number of colleagues' anecdotal experience that, in the lead-up to the psychologist becoming involved in direct casework with an individual child, changes had already started to occur, particularly in relation to emotional, attitudinal and behavioural issues.

The study looked at detailed daily records of secondary school students' behaviour in class over a year, and identified those students for whom significant behaviour changes had occurred. This was based on intensive data collection in one secondary school. The change points for individual students were identified using a statistical procedure which also indicated if the changes were statistically significant. The interesting conclusion from the study was that where change occurred, for better or worse, the nearest event to the point of change (as identified from the student's school file) was contact between the school and parent. Where outside agencies were involved, this generally occurred after the point of change.

Subsequent work suggested that the key elements of the school/parent contact at the (positive) change point is when the school and parent begin to share a common understanding of the difficulties, developing a sense of working together, and this may well be promoted or supported through the agreement to involve an outside agency. The conclusions stress the importance of the level of rapport established between the school and parents, and their commitment to a common aim.

Certainly for many cases, the coming together of parents, school, psychologist and possibly the child can be a unique opportunity with a sense of the potential to create change. Exploring possibilities for change with a child in an individual interview, and following this up with the system to promote, enhance and support the child in change, can make our limited involvement a significant point of change for the case. Our ability to develop a powerful rapport with the child and the adults in the system will be crucial in impacting this point of change in the child's educational career.

Although our involvement, or potential involvement, could be the spur to change, our key goal must be that the change is then sustained and maintained over time, and is likely to require change at a systemic level. The ongoing PDR cycle should support the impetus of the change to become embedded in the functioning of the system.

Themes

Themes drawn from information in the individual interview with the child, and/or meeting the adults in the system, form the basis for hypotheses, setting directions for change, and framing up an intervention. Reviewing the information from an individual interview with a child prior to feeding back to the system allows clear themes to be outlined as a basis for hypotheses. The themes, demonstrating credible hypotheses about the child and their world, allow the psychologist to engage the adults in constructive thinking about interventions.

The information feedback needs to be carefully considered to highlight the appropriate themes which will promote the direction for change towards the outcome, and enable or persuade members of the system to view potential interventions as appropriate, possible and worthwhile.

Describing to the adult members of the system how the individual child seems to make sense of the world can be a very powerful tool in promoting change, particularly where direct quotes can be given. The way this information is presented is the psychologist's responsibility, and therefore needs to be done in a way that facilitates the direction of change. The case examples described in Chapters 13 and 14 show how the information collected from an individual interview with a child can be developed into themes for presentation in feedback, with a view to promoting different behaviours from the adults in relation to the child.

Tasks

An intervention plan will involve adult members of the system in various tasks or activities. Tasks may be based on systemic or individual-based hypotheses (or ideally both). The interrelationship of the individual and the system means that the task necessarily will have an influence on both the system and the individual. It is also important to consider how an intervention task can have an impact at different logical levels in order to attempt to maximise its effectiveness.

The detail of tasks is best negotiated with the participants rather than prescribed in detail, although this will depend on the particular case. Occasionally some adults do value and respond to a prescriptive approach. However done, it is important that the details of the task are established, all issues or difficulties which can be anticipated are addressed, and communication routes are established to ensure that any other issues can be dealt with as they arise.

The form of tasks which may be used will be dependent upon the participants, the hypotheses and the psychological framework the psychologist adopts.

Behavioural principles can be important in setting up details of tasks with the system. These can provide a powerful rationale to engage the system to carry them out. Although they overtly focus on changing the behaviour of the individual, the fact that the adults around the child are responding differently means there will be systemic change at some level.

Keeping a systemic perspective in setting up behavioural interventions is important so that all significant members of the system are included in the intervention. The clarity of purpose, actions and contingencies which behavioural interventions generally include can be particularly helpful in providing a controlled and contained reorientation of the functioning within the system.

The range of types of tasks that can be set up by the psychologist and the system will be as wide as their creativity allows. Some examples are given below:

- paired reading or other work with parents
- precision teaching

- playing organised games within the family/school/class

- creating behavioural rituals within the family

- behaviour monitoring shared between the school and family

- home/school liaison, through visits, books, telephone

- setting up or agreeing positive contingencies for the child's behaviour by the parents and school

- programmes for giving the child messages about their personal value

- programmes for giving the child messages about the value of school (or other specific) activities

- programmes for giving the child messages about their competence

- family reinforcement of the child's behaviour or learning progress in school.

In considering the logical levels, interventions can be devised to make changes to any and all aspects of the child's view of themselves and the world they live in. The system in which they operate is the basis of their model of the world, so setting the system the task of presenting a different view of itself to the child, or presenting the child with different messages about themselves, can be the basis of significant intervention.

Tasks to present coherence in the child's world

Conflict and discrepancies between the child's school and family systems can be significant in exacerbating the difficulties in school. Bringing a sense of coherence to the child's world can be a major feature in relieving stresses, frustrations, tensions and unhappiness for the child. These can impact on all aspects of behaviour, emotion, attitude and learning. Engagement of the family and school together in the shared enterprise of an intervention can give the child that sense of coherence in their world, enabling them to engage more effectively to make positive changes themselves. The experience of working together and sharing success can also be a powerful vehicle for establishing a longer term positive relationship between the school and home. The case example of Jack (see School Situation Pictures, Chapter 12) is an example.

Stories

For the psychologist, creating the optimism that change can take place, that the effort of the intervention is worthwhile and that the adults working in partnership is a viable and positive option to achieve a positive outcome can be a challenge in some situations. The reasons for these challenges may be variously linked to the perceptions, beliefs, values and self-identity of each of the adults involved as well as other systemic issues.

As noted previously, in developing successful interventions, frequently the difficult issue is not what needs to be done, but gaining the co-operation and enthusiasm from those in the system to do it.

However, changing the behaviour of the adults in the system may not require a change in their perspective from an intra-child basis for the difficulty to an acceptance of a systemic perspective. Change may be readily achieved by doing something differently, and the adults may need reassurance or convincing that this is feasible. At times the adults may see themselves as powerless to make a difference in respect of the child's difficulties.

Stories can be powerful tools to challenge beliefs, provide a rational for intervention, and gain commitment to carry out an intervention. They are an exceptionally useful and creative tool for psychologists in their work with people in all situations, be they adults or children. Themes presented by stories may reflect both individual and systemic hypotheses.

Stories are a powerful vehicle for a message to create a significant change in perspective and behaviour. It is not the intention here to go into the theory about how stories work, but generally they retain a similar structure to that in the perceived 'real' situation. That is, they offer an analogy allowing a message to be given which relates to the situation but through a different content. Even though the content presented is different from the recipient's experience of the 'real' situation, the recipient can only make sense of the content, through reference to their own experience and model of the world. Although the principles of the intervention message are delivered through the structure of the story, with a different content from that of the 'real' situation, if the analogy is good, it will be interpreted within the context, and have significance to the 'real' situation.

The term 'real' situation is used in this context to distinguish between the situation where the work is being done and the situations depicted in the story. The quotes have been put in to indicate that the actual situation is only as interpreted or understood by the individuals in it and there is no absolute reality.

The story is more powerful than directly presenting 'advice'; the latter can easily be disagreed with, challenged or sabotaged. The story cannot be challenged as untrue, if told as of personal experience; or alternatively the truthfulness may be irrelevant if it is presented and acknowledged as a fiction, or metaphor. At worst it may be considered as irrelevant, but even so the story has been told and received. Stories and metaphors tend to be appealing and memorable, so even if initially dismissed by the recipient they may still provide material for subsequent thought.

The story has an ending, either positive or negative. This allows consequences to be outlined in a way that cannot be contradicted because it is inherently only a story. In contrast giving direct advice in relation to the 'real' situation can only relate to the hypothetical consequences which may result. These are easily challenged; our clients know we cannot predict the future!

Successful delivery and use of stories requires rapport. The story needs to pace the recipient's experience in order to lead them to new perspectives which will be developed through their interpretations of the content of the story.

There are a number of important features which should be considered in using or creating stories to enhance their impact.

1. Structural matching

The structural matching (or extent of analogy) of a story to the 'real' situation is particularly important. This is essentially the issue of pacing the recipient's experience of the world, so that the story contains the same sort of patterns, perhaps through symbolism, as are apparent to the recipient in their model of the world.

The story has a representation, possibly symbolic, of the people, places, understandings, life situations, etc. as in the recipient's 'real' situation which serves to pace their model of the world. This pacing should be at a level of the deepest patterns or structures within the situation, rather than superficial details.

This representation and symbolism can be seen in Milton Erickson's use of metaphor (see Haley 1973). An excellent and frequently quoted example is from his work with his client Joe, an elderly man and ex-gardener who was terminally ill and in pain. Joe's family had asked Erickson to use hypnosis with Joe in order to help alleviate the pain, although Joe himself was adamant that he did not want to be hypnotised.

Erickson talked to Joe about a tomato plant. He used the tomato plant as an analogy for Joe so that in talking about the plant he was able to offer Joe some considerations about his situation and predicaments, even considering how possible it is for a tomato plant to feel comfortable.

Erickson's structural matching in the use of this analogy of the tomato plant for Joe is worth considering. Both are individual entities taken out of a group context. An individual tomato plant is unusual on its own; they are usually grown in numbers to provide a crop. They are vulnerable if not cared for. Their carers are remote and do not appreciate their internal experience. They are relatively unable to exercise control within their own environment.

In all these respects the tomato plant provides a good match as an analogy for Joe, as one of a species known for their social grouping; and as a family man, he is on his own, going in the individual and fatal direction of his own death. He is becoming dependent on the care of others who are remote (the doctors such as Erickson); and is losing the ability to exercise control within his own environment, to the extent that he is brought for hypnotherapy against his wishes. Once these structural similarities are established then it is possible to provide a range of messages about the tomato plant which relate to Joe and his situation.

EXAMPLE STORIES

A number of stories are presented in Appendix 4 which can be used constructively in structurally similar situations to enable the recipient to gain new insights into their own situation. These were presented at the AEP Conference in 1991 by Nigel Mellor, an educational psychologist in North Tyneside, based on the work of his colleague Eric Harvey, who had used them very effectively with parents to engage them in developing behavioural interventions with children. Stories of this sort can provide a useful range of possible tools for the psychologist in their attempts to create change in the system around a child.

A further source of useful stories comes from personal or casework experience. Personal experience stories are useful in that they are easy to deliver congruently, namely as true stories, and believably so. Even 'true' stories attributed to others are effective as they are easy to present congruently. Completely fictitious stories paraded as real life examples can be difficult to present congruently unless well practised. Completely fictitious stories are best presented as such; they can still be powerful, and delivered congruently.

An alternative often used by Ravenette (1988) in individual work with children is to invite the child to make up a story, and in return offer to make up a story to tell them. The appropriate structural similarities of the story can be included with the desired outcome. Fairy stories can often be seen as operating in a similar way with children, and could be an additional resource.

The following is a story from a piece of personal casework which has often been used in subsequent cases, with some appropriate modifications, to promote change in adults' responses to their child. It is particularly helpful when a mother has concerns about her son's behaviour, and where the difficulties and worries seem to override the bond between them.

Case example: Abdul's story

Abdul was about seven years old when he came to this country with his family from Germany. His father had started his own business in England. His mother was at home as Abdul's younger brother, aged four years, had not started school. She was a college graduate.

Abdul was referred to the psychologist by the school because of concerns about his behaviour in the classroom, and his poor educational progress. He was now aged nine years, and in the two years since arriving in this country he had become quite fluent in English.

Following an individual meeting in school with Abdul, there was a meeting in school with his mother. Feedback from the individual interview to his mother had elicited further information from her.

While the family had lived in Germany, Abdul had been closer to his father, and the mother had been closer to a younger brother. This younger brother had been killed in a road traffic accident. This had been especially traumatic for the mother, who had lost the son she had been particularly close to, Abdul being closer to her husband. In her grief, the mother became remote from Abdul. Subsequently a new younger brother was born, and he was seen by the mother as the replacement for the child she had lost.

Not only had Abdul previously been less close to his mother, but in the time since the accident his mother had found herself less and less able to feel affection for him. In England the father's business kept him away from home for long hours and Abdul's main contact with his father during the week was by telephone in the early evening before he went to bed, his father returning home too late at night to see him.

At home the mother had some behaviour management problems with Abdul, although these were not too serious.

The mother was upset and felt guilty about the situation and the difficulty she had in feeling affection towards her elder son. She also recognised that, even though this was not in any sense Abdul's fault, it was going to be detrimental to him in the long term.

In the meeting it was suggested that the mother could perhaps begin to develop some relationship with Abdul by learning to cuddle him. It was anticipated that while both of them would undoubtedly find this very difficult to begin with, and feel very uncomfortable, it would be important to develop some means of giving Abdul the sense that there was some positive feeling about him from his mother. The mother agreed with the idea, but did not feel she would ever really be able to love her son properly. Nevertheless for his sake she decided that she would attempt to do this, even though it would be hard for her, and Abdul may also find it uncomfortable. It was agreed that she would find two times each day when she would cuddle Abdul, when he arrived home from school, and when she tucked him into bed at night.

It was reiterated that initially the cuddling would seem very strange and probably quite uncomfortable for both the mother and particularly for Abdul. It was predicted that he would probably become quite rigid and unresponsive, initially wondering what was happening. We agreed to meet again in two weeks' time to see how things were going.

Two weeks later on arrival at school, the school staff noted that Abdul's behaviour in school had changed quite significantly for the better. On meeting the mother it was apparent that she had carried out the cuddling intervention as agreed. Although she had actually found this quite difficult to do, as had Abdul, she had persisted and gradually she had found it easier. Abdul, also initially confused and unresponsive, had gradually come to enjoy the cuddles. His mother still did not believe she would feel real affection for him, but she had noticed sufficient changes at home to continue and begin to extend the behaviours she was developing to at least 'show' affection for him.

That is the basic 'story' from the case; the actual details of the case and particularly the success of the outcome can be modified as necessary to improve the structural match of the analogy.

Perhaps an important aspect of the story is the terrible negative consequences it portrays of what is probably every mother's fear: the death of their child, whom they love. This is intermingled with the failure of the mother's love for the child.

The story has also been used successfully on a number of occasions with single parents with their son. Although there are other characters in the story, they merely set the scene for a story about a mother and her son in isolation (the basic structure). In this story the structure is of a mother and child; the family is part of the content but not inherent to the structure.

Cases and personal experience can provide useful content for stories. An important consideration is determining the direction for the story, in terms of behaviours to be encouraged or avoided. This issue of direction is either 'away from' or 'towards'.

2. Towards or away from

Stories, in promoting change in behaviour, can also focus on the motivation for the change. Abdul's story above generally sets a direction 'toward' establishing a better mother/child relationship, with the promise of working towards all the advantages that will provide for the mother, son and school.

On the other hand, stories can be created which work in an 'away from' direction, indicating the terrible consequences of behaving, or failing to behave, in particular ways.

An example of this is a story Richard Bandler uses of a wood cutter who accidently cuts his finger off on the power saw. His friend, hearing the screams, rushes over to him and asks him what he did. The wood cutter explained what happened with a gesture of his hand towards the saw. He screams in agony again as a second finger is removed by the blades. The shop manager comes over to investigate the commotion and asks what happened; the wood cutter demonstrates again.

The 'away from' message is to change behaviour rather than persisting with a behaviour which leads to disastrous consequences.

Stories which are particularly powerful are those which carry both 'away from' and 'toward' messages.

People tend to be very aware of at least one end of the direction of a goal, in terms of either the target they seek or consequences they wish to avoid. However, if they have not created change with this degree of motivation, a story which includes both the 'towards' and the 'away from' aspects may serve to enhance the motivation of the recipients.

For instance, in using the Abdul story above, a sub-story about the mother's fears about the consequences for her son's future would serve to enhance the motivation to change, over and above the 'toward' goals of better behaviour, etc. A possible embellishment may be to describe how the mother was so concerned that Abdul did not grow up like her cousin, who had suffered a difficult relationship with his mother, and subsequently had turned out to have many problems. The description of this sub-story should also focus on features which would have particular relevance to the recipient. This would provide a significant additional 'away from' element to the story. Stories in this format are referred to as 'stacked stories': a story within a story, which will be considered in more detail later.

3. Unexpected qualities

A further enhancement to a story in addition to the 'away from' and 'toward' directions is the introduction of hidden qualities. This involves the key character's recognition of qualities they have, but had not realised before.

This gives the recipient the opportunity to access their own hidden qualities which they can bring to bear in their own situation, enhancing the opportunity for change.

The second of the two axioms presented at the start of the text was to the effect that people have all the resources they need, though frequently they do not manage to recognise them, or their value, in situations where they could be useful. This parallels the assumptions made in context reframes, considered in Chapter 11, where alternative contexts are suggested where a behaviour would be seen as an asset rather than a problem.

With unexpected qualities it is assumed that people deal with many situations and have a large variety of behaviours across a range of situations. However, in some situations they seem lost for the personal qualities or behaviours which would be helpful, even though they are able to provide just those qualities and behaviours in other situations.

Weaving into the story the recognition that a person initially shows those unexpected qualities, and only afterwards recognises that they had them all the time, and that they were not exceptional, can be a powerful message for the recognition of the individual's ability to change.

In terms of the above example of Abdul, the story may be extended to include the mother's recognition that she could eventually begin to feel affection for her child, something that she never thought she would be able to do. After some considerable time she recognised that she was beginning to think of Abdul in a similar way to how she thought and felt about her younger son, and as time went by she began to realise that she was a loving mother for all her family.

Therapeutic stories offer analogies. They may be completely, or partially, based on real experiences, or be quite fictitious. They are valuable tools to bring about change.

4. Stacked stories

Stacking stories is where one story is put inside another. The example given above of adding an 'away from' component to Abdul's story by inserting a sub-story about the mother's cousin illustrates this. Stacking stories in this way is useful to increase the therapeutic effect, making the story more appealing, or more clearly elucidating the principle which is being conveyed. Below is a further case example based on Abdul's story.

Case example: David

David, aged 16 years, was brought to the Child and Family Consultation Service by his mother. She initially expressed concerns that he was not very co-operative with her; he spent a lot of time outside the house in the evening, and generally did not show much of an interest in anything except sitting around watching television. David seemed lethargic and sad about what his mother was saying about him.

He had been placed in a residential special school for children with emotional and behavioural problems from about the age of 8 years to 14 years, with his mother's agreement. It seemed that there was a degree of ambivalence in the mother's attitude towards David.

About a week after the first meeting, David's mother arrived at the centre unexpectedly without an appointment. She stated that she was at her wit's end with David; she had him outside the building in her car with his suitcase packed. She wanted to know where she could go with David to have him taken away from her.

Initially the mother's request was responded to directly (particularly with the intention of establishing a level of rapport) by realistically describing that she could take David to Social Services and asking them if they would take David into care in a children's home. It was noted that children's homes are not the best places for children, and this would underlie the social worker's likely reluctance to receive David into care. His mother accepted this point and consideration was given as to what residential education may be available. The mother was also reluctant to consider this as she had reservations about his previous residential placement.

Following these discussions, it was possible to begin to consider her relationship with David. This eventually led to his mother being told the story of the case of Abdul described earlier. At the end of the story David's mother said, in a tone of amazement, 'It's amazing what the power of love can do.' After a brief 'thank you' she left with an appointment to return in two weeks' time.

Two weeks later David and his mother returned, both with smiling faces, David much more animated, and both clearly enjoying their mother/son relationship.

This change lasted quite a considerable period, but it was not the resolution of all the issues, many of which were unknown at the time. However, the change did provide the basis for beginning to work on the other, more difficult issues.

The case example has not been presented here as a stacked story, to avoid repetition of Abdul's story. However, David's story as a therapeutic story can be told with the full description of Abdul's story included within it at the point where it is told to David's mother. The story of David with Abdul's story inserted has been used successfully in several cases where it conveys a message (and intervention) very effectively.

5. Simple stories

Simple stories are easy to use therapeutically. Everyday cases from the psychologist's own experience can be used as a basis for a story. The story need not be completely true, as it is the intention behind the message that is important. For example, when using the spelling strategy as an intervention with children who have spelling difficulties, it is not only necessary to teach them the strategy, giving them the experience to challenge their beliefs, but also enable the system to hold the belief that the intervention can be effective. The story of Chloe described in Chapter 15 has been used very effectively in communicating the message that a strategy can be the key issue, and not some intrinsic ability, in the effectiveness of learning to spell.

Another story useful with this same intervention is to indicate where the ideas come from. For the spelling strategy the basic story is of some researchers who worked to find out how 'good spellers' learned and remembered words. They did this by getting together a whole group of people who were good at spelling and spent time working with them to establish how they remembered the words. They found that all of them used more or less the same strategy. That is, they had a picture in their mind's eye of what the word looked like and used this to read off the spelling. They then got a group of people who were not very good at spelling and they found out what it was that they did when they tried to remember words for spelling. They found that the people in this second group did all sorts of things, except use the picture of the word in their mind's eye.

The researchers decided that it was quite likely that the strategy of picturing the word was the important issue about whether someone was a good speller or not. They decided that, if the strategy was the key issue, and they taught it to the 'poor spellers', then they should improve as they began to learn to spell words using this strategy. They did this, and found that the people who previously had difficulty with spelling were now beginning to learn to spell words more effectively.

As another example, Allen's work in Chapter 15 on attribution and declaration in developing literacy skills can be used as a foundation to a powerful story where the research can be described to give the key message that successful people are those who recognise their success or failure as a consequence of the effort they make, rather than their ability. This is a very useful message when helping a student struggling with learning, and despondent about the value of engaging with a well-targeted learning programme.

Stories of previous cases where interventions have been successful can be very helpful in motivating people in the system to carry out the interventions suggested. Most of the case examples which have been quoted as examples throughout this text have also been used in some form or another to convey a message in an interview, be it with the individual child or the system, or both.

The stories are the convincer to either the individual or the system about the value of an intervention, helping to ensure that the intervention is carried out. They can also be used as an intervention without necessarily implying that those present are being asked to do the intervention. The David/Abdul story has often been used like this with the result that the parents will frequently decide to do something along the same lines of their own accord.

Embedded commands

Embedded commands are messages included in phrases and sentences which can be slightly highlighted by voice tone or volume. This serves to set the message off from the rest of the sentence, but not to the extent that the recipient of the message is consciously aware that the message has been made to stand out excessively. It is difficult to give examples where embedded commands have in themselves been the source of change; they are used as the opportunities arise, to promote change in the desired direction.

For instance, in working with an individual using the spelling strategy, it is useful to indicate that none of us *always remember all the words we learn* rather than saying that we all 'forget some of the things we learn'. The italic is intended to represent a slight vocal shift.

Another example, again without any concrete validity in its use but which seems to have some effect in the counselling sort of interviews with teenagers, where you may be discussing the possibilities of changing behaviour, is to use phrases such as 'it's obviously up to you to *make the decision to change*, and when the time is right you can *decide to change*. I don't know when the time to *change* will be, but you might *decide to change tonight*, or it might be some other time.' Eventually they may get the message, but will be less resistant than if told overtly to change.

Embedded commands can be included in comments in meetings both with children and adults. The phrases to use are important, as are how we say them, but these seemingly small things may be the features which make quite important differences, and certainly are the skills we can develop and use as skilled communicators.

Changes in the system

Information gathering, hypothesising, agreeing outcomes, engaging with the adults and bringing credibility to a purposeful intervention, as described in the last chapter, is important to gain commitment to the intervention. However, no matter how viable the intervention plan is, if it is not carried out change is unlikely. The techniques described above can be very helpful in convincing the adults to gain their commitment to change.

However, if there are systemic issues which are maintaining the current situation, or are barriers to the child and adult's commitment and engagement, then sustained change is unlikely to be achieved without creating change in the system. This may be apparent in the early stages of involvement and can be addressed in trying to bring a helpful working relationship to the system. There may also be times when it is possible to create some changes without the full engagement of the system. This may be feasible with older young people where they have greater personal locus of control. However, situations where there are inherent systemic issues which are not addressed are likely to reduce the probability of sustained change significantly.

A further opportunity to explore systemic issues is if little progress is identified at the review of a well-planned intervention. The key area of exploration may be *if* the intervention has been carried out or *how* it was carried out. Unpicking the process in detail is likely to highlight where there are systemic barriers to effective intervention.

The systemic perspectives described in Chapter 6 will have relevance even though the school/family system is larger and more diffuse than the family system. The principles discussed, namely circular causality, myths, boundaries, life events and secondary gain, could all be relevant areas for exploration, while maintaining a stance of neutrality.

The psychologist may work with overt and covert hypotheses, based on individual and systemic frameworks. A specific form of intervention, based on an overt hypothesis from an individual perspective, may be offered as a basis for changing or developing new behaviours in the child. There may be covert hypotheses from a systemic perspective which also inform the intervention, and focus on promoting new behaviours, and ways of interacting, from all the members of the system.

This suggests two types of hypothesis, the covert, which is 'meta' to the system, and the overt, which is more likely to be shared and accepted by the system. The latter may serve as the justification for the intervention, based on an individual child level hypothesis, while the former systemic hypothesis focuses on the elements of the system which maintain the child's current behaviour or difficulty.

Tasks from a systemic perspective

Exploration of issues with the adults in the system may offer insights and understanding to how their interactions impact on the child's behaviour, attitude and emotion. Tasks, as a form of intervention, can provide a very concrete way of creating systemic change in interactions to be more positive and coherent.

Many family therapists frequently use tasks, directives or prescriptive rituals for families to follow. In this way tasks are seen as working to resolve symptomatic behaviour, but also provoke a reorganisation of the relationship pattern within the family. This can be paralleled in the school/ family system.

From the systemic perspective symptomatic behaviour is seen as a part of the functioning of the system of interaction and relationships as a whole. The symptoms are seen as an essential part of the system and maintain its functioning. Tasks, as a form of intervention, serve a number of functions from a systemic perspective.

- They provide useful information about the system, the relationships within it, and the function of the symptomatic behaviour, particularly if the task is not carried out.

- They limit guilt and defensiveness by emphasising an action and avoiding a verbal rationalisation (of the hypothesis), which could be inferred as attaching blame. In this respect tasks set may be proposed as based upon an individual hypothesis.

- There is a demand on the system to accommodate to the requirements of the task, which in itself creates a change in the functioning of the system so the symptomatic behaviour may no longer be necessary.

Direct task presentation

When direct tasks are presented to the system this needs to be done congruently, with a commitment to the value of the task on the part of the psychologist. Tasks need to recognise the functioning of the system and reorganise this where necessary, but major change may not occur all at once. This parallels the principle of pacing and leading where one acknowledges the functioning of the system (pacing) and proposes an adjustment or small change (leading).

Ideally it is best to involve all members of the immediate system, and get everyone's agreement to carry out the task.

It is likely that a foundation of agreement can be reached about achieving some beneficial outcome for the child. Negotiating this might be a question of finding common ground that the adults are all prepared to agree. For example, if the school perceives a behaviour problem and the perception isn't shared by parents, there might be a common ground in considering that the child is not happy and all may be prepared to agree to work to an outcome of the child being happier in school, which may be identified through better relationships with teachers.

Tasks can be agreed to work to this outcome which would address some of the systemic issues as an important element of the intervention. The rationalisation presented for the task may have less emphasis on the systemic hypothesis, but be based on an individual hypothesis, which the system may more readily accept.

Reviews as previously mentioned are crucial to providing a time context for the intervention, and give a sense of containment to sustain the system to continue. The review also gives an opportunity to assess the system's resistance to change, particularly in providing an opportunity for considering what may have stopped the system from carrying out the task. It also provides an opportunity to gain feedback on the feelings and commitment of the members of the system to change. The review is the point to gain direct feedback about the task. This may necessitate a change in the working hypothesis. If the task is reinterpreted, not attempted or the system has clearly promoted the failure of the task, it may be appropriate to indicate that too much has been attempted too early, and consider paradoxical approaches.

Paradox

There is a dilemma, or paradox, which an intransigent system presents in the wish to change the symptomatic behaviour, but maintaining the functioning of the system unchanged. Assuming the symptom is a consequence of the functioning of the system, these two aims are mutually exclusive. Where direct tasks fail to create change, perhaps because the system has found some way of avoiding or failing to carry out the task, then the use of paradox may be useful. Paradoxical tasks arise where the system has been unable to sustain a direct task. Paradox is dependent on the need for the symptom to maintain the system.

Paradoxical interventions stress the need for the symptomatic behaviour to continue and prescribe the symptom, indicating the importance of the behaviour to the functioning of the system, and suggesting the system refrains from attempts to change. Paradoxical interventions overtly present a systemic hypothesis linking the symptomatic behaviour directly with the functioning, or needs, of the system.

A paradoxical-type task may be for members of the system to observe and record when the symptomatic behaviour occurs, and discuss the findings, but on no account at this stage attempt to do anything about it, until we have gained much more information from the observation and analysis.

Direction and outcome

When working with the parent/school system it is important to have a clear sense of the direction of change the psychologist is trying to support in the system. This direction is derived from the joint agreement of the participants in determining the outcomes they are seeking to achieve and, from the psychologist's point of view, the hypotheses about what has prevented the system from achieving these outcomes already.

It was suggested in Chapter 1 that the role of the psychologist is to attempt to bring about the possibility of change within the system around the child in what is believed to be the child's best interests. The psychologist in supporting and managing this process needs to engage with the participants in the system without becoming part of the system itself. It is difficult to understand how a system functions or supports change and achieves its goals from within. The hypotheses, sense of direction and identified outcomes help to maintain this 'meta' perspective.

The hypotheses as they relate to the identified outcomes should direct the psychologist towards the most beneficial changes in the system for the child, and will derive from the particular perspective they have of the child, and the functioning of the child in the system.

In any particular meeting, it is useful to have a sense of direction for the specific meeting. This may be to achieve as much as is feasible in the PDR process: clarifying concerns; developing a shared intended outcome; and developing and agreeing an intervention. The degree to which this is achieved will be determined by the information available and the level of rapport established between the participants and with the psychologist.

As an example, in a meeting including the head teacher, parents and psychologist, the psychologist may have had an intention to support the development of an effective communication system, between the parents and school, to support the child's efforts to respond to targeted behaviour, and ideally to negotiate how this might be done in relatively practical and concrete terms. However, in arriving at the meeting it may be that the underlying issues between the parents and school are such that a more realistic outcome for the meeting is merely to enable each to express their views with relative calmness, and get an agreement to meet again in the near future to discuss in more detail some way in which the parents could find out more of what is going on in school, and enable the school to be more able to understand and appreciate the parents' concerns. (The case of Jack described in Chapter 12 is an example of such a situation.)

The original aim of the meeting may not be achieved, although there is movement in the general direction.

Gaining satisfactory outcomes and interventions

There are a number of useful principles that are helpful to bear in mind to ensure that interventions and outcomes are well constructed, and therefore more likely to be taken forward by those involved. These are intended as a guide to help make the difference between the motivation to change, or not.

1. The form of the outcome is stated in the positive; that is, the agreements made in the meeting are about things that people want to achieve and *will* do rather than things they will not do. It is easier for people to change their behaviour by seeking a positive goal and agreeing to do something rather than to stop something happening or stop doing something. If you want someone to stop doing something it is probably easier to get them to agree to do something different which is incompatible with the thing you want them to stop.

2. The outcomes can be achieved, and the interventions can be put into practice, by those who are making the agreement. An exception to this may be where a head teacher is speaking on behalf of the class teacher, where the former has the authority to ensure that the latter will carry out the agreement.

   Frequently agreements made by one parent on behalf of the other can scapegoat the absent parent, who will find it impossible to carry out an intervention, and thereby present a situation where blame is allotted but in which change may be impossible.

   Similarly if the child is not present, agreements about what the child will do cannot be made, as in the same way the child can then be made the scapegoat for a failure of the system to change. The adults in the system can make agreements about what they will do in order to influence the child's behaviour. Even with the child present they are not necessarily in a position to make free and considered choices or represent themselves. That is not to say that a child cannot take part in an intervention, but the adults must be the ones to take the responsibility for ensuring the child's role is clear, and carried out, rather than leaving the responsibility with the child to change.

Frequently home/school liaison books as interventions fail because the responsibility is placed on the child to ensure that the communication is made. The adults are not taking the responsibility. (In this case it may well be useful to look at the functioning of the system in order to understand the functional value, or secondary gain, of the system's effective support for the failure of the intervention.)

3. The intended outcome needs to be clear and specific, so that everyone is clear and understands what they are seeking to achieve, and will be able to identify that it has been achieved. Similarly the intervention needs to be clear and specific so all involved are clear what they have agreed to do, and what the others in the system have agreed to do. This will enhance the potential for success of the intervention and also prevent arguments at a later stage if the intervention has not produced the expected effects. If the agreed actions are specific, then those involved will know if they have failed to do what they had agreed; frequently they will acknowledge this and thereby avoid a disagreement. Going through the agreed actions in precise terms is helpful to ensure that everyone can carry out what they have agreed, and check that it is realistic.

4. The intervention needs to be organised for a fixed period with subsequent review. The review is particularly useful in providing containment for those who are carrying out the actions as specified, and consequently they are much more likely to carry out the intervention thoroughly. It is also useful in case the intervention subsequently is found to be unmanageable by those involved; people are much more apt to persist with an intervention if they know there is an end point. In this respect the review can also prevent premature giving up by those involved, if they are hoping for immediate results. The reviews set stages in the overall timeframe for the management of the case.

5. The outcome and intervention need to be congruent with the beliefs of those involved. A merely superficial agreement to an outcome and intervention without commitment will result in no subsequent action. The importance of noticing that agreements are made congruently (i.e. no evidence of incongruity in the communication) is important. If there is an incongruity in the communication from one or more of those involved it is important to identify their reservations about the proposed outcomes.

6. Any system or behaviour which continues to be maintained is likely to produce secondary gains for at least parts of the system. Such gains if not recognised and addressed will serve to sabotage any intervention and outcome. It needs to be ensured that any necessary secondary gains arising from the difficulties are maintained through some contingency other than the difficulty. Secondary gains may not be too readily apparent initially, but may arise more clearly in review meetings. If an intervention has not been successful, attempting to ascertain what prevented it from working, or being carried out, may identify some secondary gains in maintaining the problem.

7. The outcome needs to be worthwhile to those who are agreeing to be involved, both in terms of their valuing the outcome, and have an investment in addressing the problem. In other words it needs to be established that it is worthwhile for those involved to make the effort to perform the actions agreed in the intervention, through some ownership of the concerns and commitment to the intended outcome. If it is suspected that there is a lack of ownership, perhaps through incongruent messages, it may be most appropriate to attempt to address this openly.

If these general points are considered in relation to particular outcomes from meeting with the system, then it is quite likely that the agreed actions specified in the intervention will be carried out with a degree of commitment. The key skill for a psychologist in working with the system is not in terms of trying to build a hypothesis around the behaviour which is causing concern, but, more often than not, is about motivating the members of the system to behave differently in order to promote change in the functioning of the system.

Generally if the intervention actions have been clearly specified, and congruently agreed, there is rarely any confusion. If a reasonable degree of rapport has been achieved it is likely they will be carried out with enthusiasm.

This set of outcome and intervention rules has been described in terms of its use with members of the parent/school system. The outcome rules can also be very useful in individual work in exploring the basis for change. They provide a set of conditions which help to establish a well-formed outcome as a basis for intervention.

These conditions are useful in individual work where an individual is contemplating a potential change. They not only clarify and specify the outcome so that it is well formed, but also serve to highlight issues which could jeopardise the success of attaining the desired outcome. The following is a case example of the outcome conditions used in a piece of individual work.

Case example: Kerry

Kerry, a 15-year-old secondary school pupil, had been a cause for concern in school because of her difficult manner with staff, but more so because of her bullying of other girls and the consequent fear she created. Kerry was not achieving particularly well academically and it was known that her mother, with whom she lived, also seemed to have little interest in school. Discussions with teachers suggested that there was perhaps little that Kerry gained from her school experience. As an initial step it was decided that meeting with Kerry's mother and Kerry in school may be useful in attempting to engage the mother to show an active interest in Kerry's school life, to attempt to facilitate a more positive appreciation of school. In the meeting it was very apparent that Kerry's mother had little interest in Kerry's school life, indicating that as far as she was concerned it was up to Kerry if she was deciding to waste her education, and there was nothing she could (or would) do about it.

During the meeting both Kerry and her mother agreed to Kerry meeting the psychologist. The purpose of the proposed meeting, from the psychologist's point of view, was to see if there was any opportunity through meeting Kerry of exploring her beliefs and values about school and herself with the hope of enabling her to gain some positive views of herself in relation to the school. Given her age and independence from her mother (in terms of school), it was recognised that she had a high level of personal locus of control and an individual approach could be feasible.

In the interview Kerry initially seemed reluctant to become involved, so questions were asked in a conversational manner rather than as pencil and paper exercises. Among other techniques similar to those described in earlier chapters, Kerry was invited to explore how she would be if things were going well in school, and what she would be doing, thinking and feeling differently. The seven outcome issues outlined above were then used to explore with Kerry the feasibility of her changing her attitude to school peers and teachers, from her point of view. Generally all the outcome conditions were satisfactory except the secondary gain where she was able to acknowledge that her misbehaviour paid off by brightening up the day with a bit of excitement and fun. This enabled her to focus on what other ways she could gain excitement and fun from school in more creative and constructive ways. Although in the session she was unable to think of any alternatives, she seemed quite clearly to be mulling this over in her mind at the end of the meeting. It was agreed that there should be a brief review meeting in about two weeks.

Prior to the review meeting, Kerry's teachers were reporting a noticeable improvement in her behaviour. In the meeting Kerry presented as considerably happier than she had done on the previous occasion and was pleased to acknowledge the improvements she had made. To indicate that it had been her decision to change, she was asked how she had made the decision to change. She replied that she had been thinking about how worthwhile it would be for her to change, that it was possible, and therefore she could make the change which would be in her best interests from her point of view.

Very brief meetings were arranged each half term for Kerry with the psychologist, and attempts were made by the school to try to contact the mother on a regular basis to let her know of Kerry's improvements; however, there were no replies. Nevertheless these messages to the home by the school were the attempts to change things for Kerry at a systemic level to support the changes she had made at a personal level. The continued meetings with the psychologist were intended to also attempt to support and recognise the changes.

The outcome conditions can be very useful, as in this example, in clarifying why change had not previously happened, and also isolating the issues which are effectively militating against change. Once these particular issues have been identified it is easier to consider them more thoroughly, and perhaps create solutions as Kerry did.

Final comment

It has been the intention throughout this text to provide a skeleton for psychological casework practice. It is hoped that some of the theoretical perspectives set out and the implications for practice will be of use to psychologists. The material, however, is only a starting point for further development and refinement in both personal theory and practice. The psychological theories we use are the tools to help us make sense of the world, and specifically the children and circumstances we meet in schools. A notion from PCP is of man the scientist, conducting experiments to find out how the world works, confirming, or disconfirming, personal predictions. As psychologists working with children we need to not only be creative in generating hypotheses from information and theory, but we also need to develop the skills which will enable us to make a difference and create change.

Appendices

Appendix 1 contains exercises and ideas in developing the behavioural and sensory skills referred to in Chapter 3 for the development of rapport.

Appendix 2 is a handout frequently offered to parents as a reference to the spelling strategy. This has been used by parents teaching their child two words per day (provided by the school) in a precision teaching format. The handout has been devised to help parents remember the strategy once this has been agreed as an intervention. This is referred to in Chapter 17.

Appendix 3 is a report of a study of the correlates of behavioural changes in secondary pupils which was referred to in Chapter 19.

Appendix 4 contains a sample of therapeutic stories developed by Eric Harvey, which he has used very successfully in working with the parents of children with behaviour difficulties. They provide a very effective means to conveying a message about the behavioural paradigm in which the child lives. They offer a sense of how the world may be from the child's perspective in a way which the adults can appreciate. These are referred to in Chapter 19.

Appendix 1: Skills for Rapport

This appendix provides a series of exercises designed to develop rapport skills through the process of pacing and leading. Explanation of the concepts can be found in Chapter 3.

Pacing is the process of matching over time. Matching requires two basic skills: attending to the other person's behaviour, frequently referred to as sensory acuity, and the ability to adapt one's own behaviour styles to those of the other person, frequently referred to as behavioural flexibility.

Given that these are skills to practise, the next sections include exercises which can be practised with colleagues or friends.

Behavioural flexibility

We are all familiar with the verbal aspects of communication, but may be less familiar with the subtleties of non-verbal communication, as this generally operates at a less conscious level. In NLP we bring these processes into consciousness in order to be able to make decisions about our behaviour. Basically at the non-verbal level we are attempting to give a communication which implies a sharing or commonality; to this extent we attempt to demonstrate a similar form of non-verbal behaviour to that of the person we are communicating with.

This requires that we have a flexibility in the behaviours that we can adopt. Each of us will have our own individual patterns of behaviour and it is important not to be constrained by this if we are to become effective communicators.

With a friend or colleague, as an exercise, practise mirroring their behaviour during a conversation (i.e. doing exactly what they are doing).

Matching is distinct from mirroring or mimicry, as you will probably notice if you do this exercise. Mirroring behaviour is usually quite obvious to the other person and this usually causes the communication to break down, generally into laughter if done in an exercise where everyone knows what is going on. However, if it is obvious to others, it can seem to be insulting, which could lead to a more serious form of breakdown. In the following exercise attempt to mirror as many of the gestures, postures, voice tone and tempo breathing patterns, etc. as you can. Basically, mirror as much of what the other person does as is possible.

Exercise 1

Work in a group of four people.

Sit as shown:

          Operator 1   Operator 2

          Subject 1   Subject 2

Operator 1 and Subject 1 have a conversation.

Operator 2 and Subject 2 have a conversation.

Operator 1 attempts to mirror exactly Subject 2's postures and gestures.

Operator 2 attempts to mirror exactly Subject 1's postures and gestures.

Do two minutes in each role as operator and subject.

A slightly more progressive exercise follows, in experimenting with how far to go in following someone else's behaviour without breaking the communication flow. Consider the other person's behaviour and how best to respond to it with your own non-verbal (and verbal) behaviour.

Exercise 2

Some flashcards need to be prepared prior to this exercise. These have behavioural instructions on them. Examples of instructions could be:

    stand up

    lean forward

    sigh loudly

    scratch your back

    look out of the window

    put your head in your hands

    take off your shoe.

Work in a group of three as shown and follow the instructions:

          A

              C

          B

A and B have a conversation. B attempts to match A's postures and gestures.

C shows A the flashcards; say one every 20 seconds.

A does as instructed in the flashcards.

B attempts to pace A's behaviour (or not?), but note the behavioural feedback from A.

Take turns in each role.

Exercise 3

This next exercise has the same format as the last one, but focuses on the vocal shifts in communication.

Examples of flashcards for this exercise may be:

talk faster

talk louder

talk slower

use higher pitch

use lower pitch

talk rhythmically

talk quietly.

Four particularly useful means of avoiding mirroring, but gaining a good match, are using the following tactics.

USE OF TIME DELAY

A time delay of around 30 seconds between an aspect of their behaviour and your matching will help to make the matching more covert.

MINIMISING THE BEHAVIOUR

Particularly if their behaviour is quite gross, then some minimal form of the same behaviour will serve to provide a match for the pattern, if not the degree.

CROSSOVER MATCHING

Matching the form of the other person's behaviour in some other way can be quite effective. For instance, pacing their chest movement during breathing with an up and down motion of your hand.

CONGRUENT (RATHER THAN MIRRORED) MATCHING

This is matching behaviour, not as an opposite or mirror image, but as a more exact and congruent replication. This is more covert than mirroring, presumably because we are generally quite used to seeing our behaviours in mirrors, and mirroring is therefore more recognisable.

Sensory acuity

Although rapport building through non-verbal matching requires a degree of sensory acuity, particularly in order to detect if behavioural 'leads' have been followed, sensory acuity is a key skill for a good communicator. Both verbal and non-verbal communications give important cues to subjective experience. As most subtle non-verbal communication operates at an unconscious level, this information can be particularly useful.

An important point is that each person's non-verbal communications can be different, so general rules about what each communication means are not useful. This means that for each individual their particular non-verbal communications will have their particular meaning. We can assume there will be a consistency within individuals, but not necessarily between them as to what particular communications mean.

In NLP this leads to the notion of 'calibration'. Calibration is the observation of the characteristics of an individual's particular external behaviour in certain circumstances, so as to be able to infer its likely meaning and interpret the behaviour as a meaningful interpretation.

The following exercises are to introduce and begin to practise sensory acuity and calibration. Each exercise asks you to detect and note some non-verbal correlates of a person's particular experience, and then use these to attempt to guess what they subsequently experience.

Exercise 4

Again work in a group of three.

A, when asked, thinks of someone they really like. Remember what they look like, sound like, and how you feel when you are with them.

B and C really push A to get the memories of what it is like to be with this person, and observe A closely, that is, they try to gain a picture of, or calibrate to, the non-verbal behaviours of A when thinking of this person.

B and C then distract A to think of something quite different.

Once A has been distracted from thinking about the person they liked, ask them to think of someone they really dislike. Again push them into the memory, and observe closely; again calibrate to the look of A when thinking of this person.

Distract A again.

A then thinks of one or other of these people. B and C, by observing A, try to decide which person they are thinking of, the one they like or dislike.

If B and C cannot tell the difference, repeat the exercise until they are able to observe a difference in A between thinking of each person. It is important, if there are to be noticeable differences, that A does think of people they do like and dislike rather than people they feel indifferent to.

The exercise could be repeated using liked and disliked foods.

The previous exercise concentrated on visual acuity; the next exercise uses the same format using auditory acuity.

Exercise 5

Again work in groups of three.

B and C close their eyes.

A, when asked, thinks about a favourite food. Remember the sight, taste, smell and any sounds or feelings that might be associated with the food. Re-live the experience of having the meal. While doing this count backwards from 10 to 1. B and C calibrate to the tone, tempo, volume and rhythm of A's voice.

B and C distract A.

B and C close their eyes again.

A then thinks of the worst-tasting thing they have ever had in their life, again remembering all modalities relevant to the memory, and then counts backwards from 10 to 1.

Again B and C calibrate to A's voice.

B and C distract A.

A then chooses one or other of the foods to think of and re-lives the experience in memory, counting backwards from 10 to 1.

B and C attempt to decide which one A is thinking of,

BREATHING PATTERNS

An effective focus for non-verbal matching are breathing patterns. Changes in breathing pattern can be a particularly useful focus for calibration. Being quite subtle, a degree of sensory acuity is often required. Some useful cues to detect breathing patterns are:

> folds and creases in clothing
>
> defocusing your eyes to detect movement
>
> shoulder movements
>
> noting breathing in upper chest/mid chest/stomach
>
> arm movements
>
> auditory cues
>
> nostril movement
>
> pauses in speech
>
> breathing sound.

Breathing can frequently be matched best using a crossover strategy.

Pacing and leading in behavioural rapport, and the sensory acuity and calibration skills to make effective use of non-verbal communications, are skills which take practice. In the next exercise try to use as many aspects of the non-verbal communication as you can.

Exercise 6

> Again work in a group of three.
>
> A talks about something they believe in.
>
> B paces A at all levels they can for about one minute.
>
> B then paces in all non-verbal means they can, but disagrees with what A is saying verbally, for about one more minute.
>
> B then mismatches A non-verbally, but agrees with the verbal content for about one minute.
>
> Finally pace at all levels, for about one minute.
>
> C observes and feeds back to A and B afterwards.

Congruity and incongruity

We have noted that there are numerous channels of communication a person uses. Often the messages that are given are not congruent. For instance, the verbal language message may be 'yes' but aspects of the non-verbal message may be calibrated as a 'no'. There are a number of strategies for dealing with this; to address the issue directly may not be the most useful.

Possible strategies could be:

> Pace both messages but in the opposite form to that presented.
>
> Ask for more information.
>
> Use direct comment but attribute it to someone else.
>
> Use 'but', i.e. at the end of their verbal 'yes' message say 'but' as if expecting them to continue.

As the non-verbal communication is more likely to be unconscious (compared with a verbal communication), it is more likely to be acted upon, as the non-verbal communication is less easy for them to manipulate consciously. Clearly if you want an agreement from someone which you hope they will adhere to, it is important to ensure that the agreement is given congruently in all channels.

Exercise 7

> Work in groups of three.
>
> A imagines themselves in the situations below and responds to B as the person involved in the situation.
>
> B attempts to deal with the incongruity.
>
> C observes and offers feedback.

The situations are:

1. A really good friend has given you an awful present.

2. A person you really dislike has invited you to dinner.

3. You have to tell someone you are happy to go along with their request but you resent it.

4. You have to tell someone you are absolutely sure of something even though you have doubts about it.

Finally we have really only considered communications based on visual and auditory modalities. To the extent that there is a kinaesthetic channel of communication the same principles can apply. As an everyday exercise match handshakes with people you meet, noticing how different people's handshakes differ. This may be quite a useful way of developing rapport from the beginning of any meeting.

Appendix 2: Teaching Words for Reading and Spelling

This method of teaching children to remember words does not teach 'spelling out', which is a useful way of working out unknown words, but teaches them to recognise, and spell, by sight rather than sound. Remembering words by sight has been found to be used by most people who are good at spelling and reading, even though it is only a method for remembering, rather than working out words.

The teaching gets your child to make a mental picture of a word and associates this with the name of the word.

Once your child has made the correct mental picture of the word, your praise is used to make them feel good, and this becomes linked with the correct spelling of the word, so that in future your child can check his or her own spelling by sensing if the word 'feels' right.

The mental picture can then be used for recognition of the word in reading, and to read off the letters for spelling.

The learning process is quite quick, and there is no failure in getting a mental picture of the word, only more practice until it is correct. Some children find making mental pictures more difficult than others, but all get faster with practice. Often children who can picture the words quickly tend to lose them more quickly and need more day to day repetition – again with practice, remembering should get better.

The teaching steps: Creating the picture
At all possible stages give the name of the word being taught.

1. Write the word to be learned clearly on a piece of plain paper. Figure A2.1 provides an example.

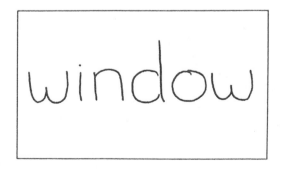

Figure A2.1 'Window' written on card

2. Show this so your child has to look up to see it. (Generally people look up when they think in pictures.)

3. Say the word.

4. Tell your child to make a picture, in their 'mind's eye', of the piece of paper with the word written on it (Figure A2.2). (Like having a photograph in their mind.) Often talking about a 'mental camera' inside their head to take photographs of words is helpful in getting this idea across to children.

Figure A2.2 Visualising the word 'window'

5. Say the word again.

6. When your child has the picture in mind, take the paper away and ask them to spell the word by reading letters off from the picture in their mind (Figure A2.3). (If they don't know the names of letters ask them to copy it from their picture onto a sheet of paper.)

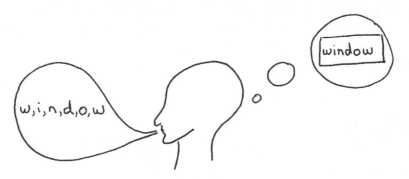

Figure A2.3 Spelling 'window' from the visual image

7a. If the spelling is correct, give praise immediately and repeat the word. (Be enthusiastic here; the more praise the better, but be genuine.)

7b. If incorrect just say, 'You haven't got the picture quite right yet', re-present the picture as before and say, 'Change your picture so it looks just like this.' Then go back to Step 4 as before.

8. For more practice, get your child to write the word out from his or her picture, and spell it out. Praise each time it is correct (as Step 7a); if incorrect, go back to Step 7b.

9. Now as a check that it is a picture, ask them to spell the word backwards by reading the letters from the other side, that is, right to left from the mind picture. Again if incorrect do as Step 7b; if correct comment how well they have learned the word if they can do that.

10. If you are teaching two words in the session, review both words at the end.

Remembering: Stopping the picture fading

Children will often forget, or lose the pictures they have learned, very quickly if they do not use them soon and frequently. So this is an additional task each day.

1a. Take all the words you have taught so far and present each one at a time. Ask, 'What does this say?' If correct praise as before. If incorrect make a note to teach it again at some point (although it may be remembered another day with further teaching).

1b. An alternative is to just say the word without presenting the picture and ask how it is spelt (this is much harder).

2. Keep a record of how many words your child remembers each day and plot this on a graph with him or her (Table A2.1)

Table A2.1 Keeping a record of spellings learned

Monday	Tuesday	Wednesday	Thursday	Friday
				plant
				apple
			people	people
			toilet	toilet
		giant	giant	giant
		shoe	shoe	shoe
	pencil	pencil	pencil	pencil
	window	window	window	window
car	car	car	car	car
table	table	table	table	table

Note that progress will probably deteriorate after a period without practice; however, starting practice again will probably recover lost ground.

General points to bear in mind

1. The teaching and reviews should be fun and have an atmosphere of success, however little progress is being made. If it isn't successful it's more likely this programme or your teaching is at fault rather than your child. Children learn much more when they enjoy themselves.

2. Keep the teaching and review period to a minimum – no more than 15 minutes and no more than two new words at once.

3. Don't do too much, however quickly your child is learning the words – or however enthusiastic to begin with. Too many words at once will lead to future forgetting and, if your child leaves the session keen for more, there is always tomorrow.

4. Help your child to be proud of their achievements.

Appendix 3: Correlates of Behaviour Changes for Secondary School Students

Summary

Statistically significant points of behaviour change were identified, using a Finite Integer Analysis (Theios 1969), in the classroom behaviour of students in a secondary school. The school's student records were then used to investigate the correlates of these changes in terms of the school-initiated interventions, and the subsequent agency involvement.

Introduction

Theios (1969) has described a Finite Integer Analysis to detect changes in the strings of single learned task response data by a probabilistic method and derived the best fitting models by likelihood functions.

This study uses Theios's analysis to detect changes in similarly structured data relating to the classroom behaviour of students in school. From this the correlates of change may be investigated by recourse to the individual student's school records.

Although the Finite Integer Analysis assumes that change occurs as a discrete event, Bower (1962) has demonstrated that mathematically the 'all or none' and 'gradual' learning models amount to the same thing.

Psychologically and therapeutically there are numerous theoretical models which offer a view of discrete change in relation to human behaviour, as well as the theoretical models of learning from which the analysis derives.

Kelly (1955), in elucidating PCP theory, has as a central tenet constructive alternativism, a notion which yields the possibility of creating discrete changes in the individual's construction of the world, and thereby having implications for discrete changes in the individual's behaviour.

Therapeutically Watzlawick, Beavin and Jackson (1967) have shown the value of interventions which initiate, or even force, discrete changes in behaviour.

Many other therapeutic techniques assume interventions such as reframing which serve to change the meanings of situations and behaviours resulting in different reactions from those habitually used by the client.

Further models such as NLP (Bandler and Grinder 1979) also demonstrate changes in beliefs and behaviour through relatively brief discrete interventions.

Although the theoretical basis of the study is not dependent upon the assumption of discrete change, the notion of discrete change points does seem to fit in with established educational psychologists' practice, in terms of both their consultation work and casework with children, parents and families.

Method

Overview
The study used detailed records of classroom behaviour in an attempt to identify times of change for individual students. Their school records were then used to link these changes in the recorded classroom behaviour to school-related events and actions.

Collection of data on classroom behaviour
Class behaviour reports were obtained from a large secondary school. These had been developed by the school and had been in operation for some time before the study.

Each class in the first three years (National Curriculum Years 7, 8, 9) of the school carried a behaviour sheet to all lessons, which was given to a member of the class by the form tutor. This log sheet was to be presented at each lesson to the subject teacher who could make comments as they wished. Subject teachers would be able to comment on individual students' positive as well as negative behaviour. Obviously not all subject teachers commented on each lesson and there were a number of omissions in the records for the year.

From the records, strings of data were derived for students by attributing a value of '1' when they were named specifically in a negative comment and a value of '0' when a comment had been made by a teacher but did not include the student's name in any negative sense.

Individual records of this sort were obtained for all students in the first three years who had at least one negative comment in the year records.

Identification of points of change
THE FINITE INTEGER ANALYSIS
Theios (1969) developed the Finite Integer Analysis from applications in mathematical modelling of learning.

In simple terms the analysis assumes that there is a discrete change in the probability of an event occurring within a string of data describing the occurrence of the event at intervals in time. There are distinct states, before the change point, and after the change point. The states are identified, and defined, by the probability of the event occurring.

In terms of the behaviour data collected in this study, the probability of a '1' occurring (i.e. a negative comment) in a string of data will be given by the number of occurrences in the data divided by the total number of data points.

Any transition point can be selected where it is assumed a discrete change in probability occurs. The probability of a '1' occurring can be obtained as above for the periods before and after the transition point.

Clearly transition points can be selected at all points in the string of data. To compare the goodness of fit of models with different transition points a likelihood function can be derived. From this the model with the transition point which yields the maximum likelihood can be selected.

Different levels of model can be considered from the simplest single state model with no transition points through to those having several transitions. The number of calculations increases enormously as the number of transition points included increases.

Theios describes a formula to compare the likelihood of two different levels of model based on an approximation to the chi-squared function. With this it is possible to determine the significance of the improvement in goodness of fit provided by a more complex model having more transition points over a less complex model having less transition points. This takes into account the increasing number of variables involved in the more complex models.

To summarise, the strings of individual student data derived from the class records were analysed in terms of a single-state model (i.e. no transition point) and a two-state model (i.e. one transition point). Comparisons were then made to determine the best-fitting model, with an indication of the significance of the improvement in goodness of fit gained in assuming the more complex model.

Where the best-fitting model is a two-state model, this will provide the most likely transition point (in time), the probabilities of receipt of a negative comment in each state, and an indication of the significant improvement in fit to the data over the single-state model in terms of the chi-squared statistic.

PRACTICAL DETAILS

The Finite Integer Analysis was written into a computer program using Basic. The program was tested using small strings of data for which derived values could be calculated by hand.

It soon became apparent that for the length of data strings (up to 190 data points) only a single-state (no transition point) and a two-state (one transition point) model could be handled adequately.

The program yielded:

1. The likelihood of the single-state model.

2. Probability of '1' for the single-state model.

3. The likelihood of the two-state model.

4. Probability of '1' in state 1 (prior to transition).

5. Probability of '1' in state 2 (after transition).

6. Transition integer (the data point at which the transition occurred).

7. The proportionate improvement in likelihood.

8. The chi-squared value.

For comparison between a one-state model and a two-state model, the 5 per cent level of significance chi-squared value is 5.991.

The transition point could be translated to a specific date by recourse to the individual student's data string.

Collection of individual data

The school's individual student records for the academic year of the study were investigated, and details of the records summarised for all children where the two-state model provided a significantly better fit to the data than the one-state model.

Particular attention was given to details of the individual student's record around the time of the transition point.

Results

Initially 45 children were identified from the classroom records as having caused teachers to note their names in a negative comment. This represents a quite small percentage of the school population for the school years under study.

The analysis yielded 27 strings of data for which the two-state model provided a significantly better fit to the data than the one-state model.

Of these 27, 16 showed a transition to a lower probability, implying classroom behaviour had improved. The remaining 11 showed a transition to a higher probability, implying their behaviour had deteriorated.

Two terms had elapsed by the time the data had been analysed to identify these individuals. This led to some loss of information subsequently and prevented a successful analysis of some individual student records.

Specifically:

1. Two individuals could not subsequently be identified.

2. Four individuals had left school during the year and school records had been transferred. All these demonstrated improved behaviour to a highly significant degree and the change point seemed to be associated with the time of leaving school. This factor served to further validate the program in correctly identifying change points in addition to the previously mentioned test data.

    Student A   Chi-squared = 40.37

    Student B   Chi-squared = 41.24

    Student C   Chi-squared = 25.15

    Student D   Chi-squared = 9.28

    A further student left the school after the academic year under study (student 14), and although individual school records were unavailable, full records from the EPS were still available.

3. Of the remaining students, a further five had individual records which contained little information. While this is unfortunate, it is noted that there are other aspects to a child's life which have a profound impact upon them other than the influences of school. Specifically:

Student E	Chi-squared = 13.64	Only three entries, all related to attendance.
Student F	Chi-squared = 9.19	Only two entries.
Student G	Chi-squared = 12.7	Only two entries.
Student H	Chi-squared = 9.28	Few entries, which hint at intensive social services involvement with the family.

Student I   Chi-squared = 6.15   Few entries, comment-
                                          -ing on hospitalisation
                                          and issues of personal
                                          hygiene.

Of the remaining 15 students, nine made transitions to lower probabilities (behavioural improvements) and six students made transitions to higher probabilities (behavioural deterioration).

Discussion of results

Using the information provided from the student's individual records in the school file the following were considered: (a) the nearest recorded event or action to the transition date; (b) differences between students showing improvements and deterioration in the nearest recorded event; (c) other concomitant changes; and (d) agency involvement.

(a) The nearest recorded event or action to the transition date

In Table A3.1, students 1–6 are those whose classroom behaviour showed a significant deterioration; students 7–15 are those whose behaviour showed a significant improvement.

Table A3.1 Recorded event or action and transition date

Student	Days between	Letter to parents	Parental interview	Student on report
1	0	✓		
2	+22			✓
3	−35	✓		
4	−32	✓		
5	−8		✓	
6	−6	✓		
7	0		✓	
8	+2	✓		
9	+2		✓ (F)	✓
10	+1		✓ (F)	
11	−3			✓
12	+15	✓		
13	+16	✓		
14				
15	−10	✓		

F = interview failed by parents.

Student 14 – No records, but discussions with parents about EPS referral likely about this time.

Table A3.1 clearly shows a link between parental involvement (either by letter or interview) with the transition point. This includes interviews arranged which parents then failed to attend.

Clearly school records of students will selectively include items involving parents; however, overall only 42.3 per cent of recorded items on these students' files involved parents. This contrasts with the 11 cases from 14 (78%) having parental involvement as the nearest event to the point of transition, which suggests the link is not artefactual.

It is perhaps surprising that there is no immediately apparent difference in this respect between students in the deteriorating and improved groups. This could suggest that while parental involvement may be powerful it is not necessarily exclusively beneficial. This could clearly be linked to parental perceptions of the form of the communication.

(b) Differences in the nearest recorded event between students showing improvements and deterioration

A couple of aspects seem worthy of consideration in order to explain differences between the groups:

1. The students showing improvements in behaviour generally seemed to have more recorded incidences of parental involvement prior to the transition point, compared with those whose behaviour showed a deterioration.

   The Randomisation Test for two independent samples described by Siegal (1956, p.152) shows this level of recorded parental involvement is higher for the students showing improvements ($p = 0.0078$, two-tailed test).

   It needs to be recognised that students whose behaviour has shown an improvement will generally have been a cause for concern in school prior to the transition point, so it is not unexpected that the school would have attempted to initiate more contact with the parents. A further look at the table may suggest a trend to higher levels of parental involvement for those showing improvements, in that four changes in this group are associated with parental interviews and only three with letters to parents. This contrasts with one parental interview and three letters to parents associated with the transition points for those showing a deterioration in behaviour.

   Although care needs to be taken in drawing conclusions, particularly from such a small sample, this could suggest the gradually increasing escalation of parental involvement precedes the improvement, whereas the deterioration can occur with a relatively more superficial level of contact. This could reflect a difference in the level of rapport developed between the school and parents.

2. In looking specifically at those students whose transition seems to be linked with parental involvement (i.e. excluding students 2 and 11), the contact tends to take place before the transition for the students showing a deterioration, and after the transition for students showing an improvement, as indicated in Table A3.2. The

Randomisation Test for two independent samples indicates there is a significant difference between these two means (p = 0.0328).

These findings could be interpreted to suggest that the students showing improved behaviour appear to change in anticipation of parental involvement, whereas those showing a deterioration seem to change in response to parental involvement. Although the data are minimal and the conclusion simplistic, it does present an interesting hypothesis.

Table A3.2 Duration between parental contact and transition point

Deterioration		Improvement	
Student	Transition to event	Student	Transition to event
1	0 days	7	0 days
3	−35 days	8	+2 days
4	−32 days	9	+2 days
5	−8 days	10	+1 day
6	−6 days	12	+15 days
		13	+16 days
		15	−10 days
Mean = −16.2		Mean = +3.71	

(c) Possible concomitant changes in student records

While investigating the individual student records it was noted that many comments after the transitions did seem to reflect behaviours and incidences which had not previously been noted.

Star ratings have been given to attempt to rate the newness of behaviours, where one star represents a new behaviour, although related to the previous problem areas, for example student 1 whose lateness appeared to change to absences. Two stars indicate behaviours of which no hint was apparent in the previous record prior to transition.

Table A3.3 gives these data and also notes the involvement of agencies outside school.

The table shows that 8 of the 14 students show quite pronounced changes in their behaviour outside the classroom, in addition to the changes they have made in classroom behaviour. Notably students 7, 8, 10 and 11 show improvements in their classroom behaviour, but a significant degeneration in their out of class/school behaviour. Conversely student 4, whose classroom behaviour deteriorates, appears to show improvements in out of class/school behaviour.

Table A3.3 Concomitant changes from student records

Student/ change	Subsequent problems noted	Star rating	Agency involve-ment A – After B – Before
1 (−)	Absence – previous lateness	*	None
2 (−)	Some behaviour problems	*	None
3 (−)	Depression (doctor's comment)	**	None
4 (−)	None (although previous out of school problems on file)	**	None
5 (−)	Stealing, misconduct, threats and harassment out of school	**	None
6 (−)	None (no change)		EPS (A)
7 (+)	Running away from home, into care, victimisation and nervous problems	**	Social services (A)
8 (+)	Stealing and harassment (out of school)	**	None
9 (+)	Withdrawn (head of year comment)	**	EPS (A)
10 (+)	Fighting, threatening and harassment out of school	**	EPS (A)
11 (+)	Fighting and harassment out of school	**	None
12 (+)	No change		None
13 (+)	Continued truancy		EPS/ CAMHS (A)
14 (+)	No record		EPS (A)
15 (+)	No change		EPS (A)

This does not make any comparison with the developmental changes which may be occurring for students whose classroom behaviour remains much more constant, so the finding is not really anything other than an interesting coincidence at this stage.

It is notable that students 7, 8, 9, 10 and 11, whose classroom behaviour improves, show quite significant changes in out of class behaviours. These students are those with relatively close links in time between the transition point and the nearest recorded event. This contrasts with students 3, 4 and 5 whose classroom behaviour degenerates, where there is a greater time interval between the transition point and nearest recorded event.

(d) Agency involvement

Clearly students who are a cause of concern in school are the most likely to be involved with outside agencies, and it is not surprising that the EPS is the most frequently involved.

Of the nine students whose behaviour showed improvements, other agencies were engaged or considered for involvements in six cases, and it is apparent that this occurred after the time of transition.

In the case of student 13, there was a parental request for EPS involvement; however, this was not taken up as it was considered that the presenting home difficulties would be better dealt with through a referral to the Child and Adolescent Mental Health Service. This option was not subsequently taken up by the family. However, the meeting in which this option was discussed with the student's mother was the nearest recorded event to the transition point.

It is clear from the data that all outside agency involvement seems to occur after the transition point. For students 9 and 10, the nearest recorded event to the transition point was the meeting arranged for parents with the psychologist to discuss the possibility of referral (although in both cases the parents failed to attend). It also seems that discussions with parents about referral seem to link with transition for student 14, who had the first interview with the psychologist four weeks after the transition. Without records to confirm it seems likely that discussions about referral between the parent and school were taking place around the time of transition.

Student 15's involvement with the psychologist was some four months after the transition. Student 6, whose behaviour deteriorated, was subsequently referred to the psychologist some two months after the transition.

Table A3.4 gives the duration from transition to referral. In all cases the transition point preceded the referral.

Given the relatively rapid involvement of the EPS after the transition date in three of the four cases of students whose classroom behaviour improved it could be inferred that this involvement may be quite important in supporting and helping to maintain change. Additionally the school's discussions with parents considering the involvement of outside agencies may reflect the establishment of a satisfactory level of rapport between the school and parents, serving as a spur to change.

Table A3.4 Duration between transition point and referral

Student	Duration from transition to referral
6 (−)	Approx. 2.5 months
9 (+)	Approx. 30 days
10 (+)	Approx. 15 days
14 (+)	Approx. 25 days
15 (+)	Approx. 3.5 months

Conclusions

This study has been an initial attempt using a Finite Integer Analysis to identify students who show significant changes in their classroom behaviour and identify the correlates of these changes.

In the study a relatively small proportion of the students showed significant changes in classroom behaviour.

These changes in behaviour seem to be most strongly related to the school involving parents; however, parental involvement did not necessarily lead to change nor did it always result in change for the better.

Improvements in behaviour seem to have some association with a series of communications between the school and parents. There is some indication that these changes seem to occur in anticipation of a particular contact. Some anecdotal evidence from students' files suggests that the significance of the particular meeting associated with the transition is when parents and school begin to appreciate each other's point of view. This is perhaps related to the link with the subsequent involvement of an outside agency, requiring the school to obtain parents' consent and thereby necessitating some level of rapport and mutual understanding.

Interestingly, where behaviour deteriorated, there was much less prior involvement, and again some anecdotal evidence suggests that a poorer quality of contact, for example via an unexpected letter, may have had some significance. This perhaps also links with the behavioural change point being after the time of contact.

Behaviour changes noted on students' files concerning events outside the classroom indicate the importance of the students' wider environment, and perhaps the systemic nature of their interaction with the environment.

Although the study does not provide conclusive evidence of the factors which modify students' classroom behaviour, it does show a very close association between behaviour and parental involvement with the school, and is suggestive of the need for a level of rapport to be developed.

Further work is currently attempting to focus on qualitative aspects of parent/school communication and the links with classroom behaviour. Matched groups, based on pre-transition probabilities, where controls show relatively static probabilities throughout the string length, would enable a comparison of the parent/school communication.

Appendix 4: Stories Used to Give Insight to Parents

With great thanks to Eric Harvey, former Senior Social Worker from the Sunderland Psychological Service.

Relieving parent guilt

Training for Every Job but Parenthood

Being a parent is the most important job in the world. It is the longest (if you murdered somebody you would be out in 10 or 12 years). It is probably the most difficult because we are so close to the problem. Even the simplest job will have some training; when a baby is born, however, it is dumped in your lap and you have to 'get on with it'. It is not surprising we run into difficulties.

The parents, the ones who are trying the hardest, are the ones who are most vulnerable. The more she misbehaves, the more you want to stop her – so you 'fall right into her trap'.

Car on a Hill

This illustrates how problems gradually get out of control.

Difficulties start off very small and we make allowances and put up with things little by little. Gradually, however, matters escalate until we wake up one day to find that things are out of control and we wonder how we got to this situation. It's rather like a car on a hill. When it first starts to roll you could stop it with one finger. Once it has picked up a bit of steam, however, it will roll right over you.

Worrying about the Bills

This illustrates how children can concentrate all their efforts but adults can't.

It often seems strange that small children can 'win' against their parents. One of the reasons is that parents have got a lot on their minds – paying the bills for the house, arranging the holiday, buying new shoes for Johnny, worrying about Sarah's birthday party, etc. Children have none of this. They only need to concentrate on 'number one'. It is not that they are selfish, they just don't have your responsibilities, so, over the weeks, the months and the years, they gradually come out 'on top' because they have little else to concentrate their minds on other than what is right for them. It is not that the children have to sit down and plan this, they just stumble over it.

Going to the Doctor with Spots

Parents often feel embarrassed, guilty and inadequate about asking for help.

You might wonder, 'Where have I failed?' If, however, your child came out in spots you wouldn't hesitate to go and seek professional advice from a doctor; in fact you would be silly not to. When children 'come out in behaviour problems', rather than come out in spots, it is important again to get the right kind of advice.

Misbehaviour brings attention

'Knockey Nine Doors'

This is a game we have all played as children; it has different names in different parts of the country. We can all remember the way to play it – you knock on some poor soul's door and run away. The adult comes out and shouts and screams. The adult thinks that will put the children off, but that of course is looking at matters through the adult's eyes. Looking through the child's eyes, that is exactly what is wanted. The more the adult shouts and screams the more they come back; they have the adult on a string.

So when we respond to children's misbehaviour they see this rather like a game of Knockey Nine Doors – the more we respond, the more they do it.

1001 Ways of Getting Attention

Consider the average child coming in from school. First of all he slams the door; Mum or Dad shouts, 'Don't slam the door, you'll have it off its hinges, look at the plaster, you'll break the glass...' There's one lump of attention. Then he drops his coat in the corridor. 'Look at that coat, you're treating it like an old rag, pick it up, you've walked past the peg, how many times have I told you...?' There's two lumps of attention. Then his muddy boots are all down the carpet. 'Look at the mess, how many times have I told you to clean your shoes before you come in, I've been all day cleaning up...' There's three lumps of attention and he's hardly in the door yet.

Then he goes into the front room and starts arguing with his sister. Mum and Dad go in – 'Who started that?' 'It was him/It was her...' You never get to the bottom of it and in the meantime the children get masses of attention.

Then it's teatime – a favourite time for getting attention – 'I'm not eating that.' 'I hate that.' So Mum and Dad try to persuade him to eat and end up feeding him – not food, but masses of attention.

Then he sits fidgeting. 'Will you stop?' 'For heaven's sake, have you got ants in your pants...?'

Then he's biting his nails. 'How many times have I told you?' 'You'll have no fingers left...'

The child can go on the whole evening and never repeat himself. Each one of these looks very different, and they are, *but* they have one thing in common: they get Mum or Dad talking, arguing, reasoning, threatening, shouting, asking, etc. In other words, they all get masses of attention.

The value of praise
The Loaf of Bread Story
This of course can be adjusted for males or females.

Imagine you have got a new neighbour and you hear on the grapevine that she is not very well. You are going to the shops and on the way you decide to call in and ask her what she wants. She asks you to get her a loaf of bread. Imagine on the way back that you knock on the door and offer her the bread and she takes it off you and slams the door in your face. Would you go back? Probably not, you'd feel hurt and upset.

Let's imagine, however, you came back and she said, 'I'm ever so pleased I've got alongside a good neighbour like you, I was worried to death about getting the children's sandwiches, etc.' Then probably you would say, 'I'm going along to the shops again tomorrow, I'll give you another knock.'

Thus, your behaviour has switched right round, from refusing to go to volunteering to go. The only difference was a little bit of praise, a pat on the back. We all respond to praise, we all enjoy it, it's very powerful, it can change our behaviour. Think how much more powerful it could be with children, yet we don't use it often enough.

Baby Learning to Walk
When a child learns to walk we automatically make a big fuss. Praise it, cuddle it and tell Granny. Praise seems to come easily with a baby. We even make a big fuss when a baby gets a tooth – and that happens naturally! Then, however, we get out of the habit and somehow expect 'good behaviour' just to carry on without encouragement. We also find praise difficult to do and feel embarrassed about it as the children grow up.

The Anniversary Meal

This illustrates the need to praise first and leave criticism until later as early criticism strikes home very powerfully. This can easily be directed to either Mum or Dad.

Imagine it is your anniversary and you decide to cook your wife a smashing meal – steak and all the trimmings, a bottle of wine, etc. She comes in from work, sits down, takes a mouthful and says, 'The peas are hard as cannonballs.' You'd be hurt and upset and probably want to throw the whole meal in the bin. Even if she tries to make up afterwards and says, 'Oh yes, but the steak is lovely, etc.', it's too late; the damage has been done.

If, however, she says, 'That's great, just the way I like it, lovely steak, smashing bottle of wine, new potatoes in the skins just the way I like them; mind you, the peas were a bit on the hard side', then you would probably agree and say, 'Yes, I felt they could have done with a bit longer.' In other words the criticism is a lot easier to take when it comes *after* praise.

This kind of approach is very important, for instance in dealing with a child's behaviour or a report from school which has mixed comments on it. Praise first, then the criticism.

Marks & Spencer's

This illustrates the need for consequences. Parents are often very reluctant to ensure that children feel the consequences of their behaviour.

Imagine you go down to Marks & Spencer's and stuff a jersey in your bag. On the way out, the store detective stops you but says, 'That's okay, we don't mind, help yourself.' After a while you wouldn't be able to get into Marks & Spencer's, the queue would be round the block. We need to know that there will be appropriate consequences to our behaviour or life can't go on.

Children need this certainty just the same.

Threats are Promises

If you promised your child a present on the weekend, you would do your best to keep your promise. Threats are like a promise. Children need to know that when we make a promise we will carry it out and when we make a threat we will also carry it out.

Insight into a child's feelings

Torn in Two

The child cries because she is 'torn in two'. Many of the children we deal with cry easily. This story explains why!

Think of a child coming out of her house. She can either go up the street or down the street. Imagine that going up the street is what she is allowed to do and down the street isn't. So, going up the street is doing what Mum and Dad want – the problem is the child doesn't get any attention for this. Going down the street is what Mum and Dad don't want – this, however, brings lots of attention. So, the child coming out of the house is torn in two. She wants to go one way but she really wants to go the other way. She is pulled this way and then that way. This causes the rapid shifts of mood and also leads to the child crying easily because she is 'torn in two'.

Breaking Windows

This explains why the child seems to get 'picked on' at school (this is not intended to exonerate staff but to help parents share their difficulties in dealing with the child).

Imagine there is a child in your street who is always up to mischief. As you are going out you can see him in the road throwing stones around dangerously. You know he has caused a lot of trouble before and has broken lots of windows, so you warn him to be careful near your windows.

When you come home your windows are broken. Who do you blame? Well, little Jimmy of course. Unfortunately you have no proof it was him – that's just your automatic natural reaction, as it was always him in the past. It is not that we are unreasonable as adults – we are just human.

A similar situation happens at school. A child can be told off, quite appropriately, by a teacher many times for 'messing about'. Then one day she is writing on the board and turns round because of some misbehaviour at the back of the class right near where your child is. Who is she going to single out? Naturally, the child who was always in trouble in the past. It's not fair, but it happens because teachers are human also, just the way you would tell little Jimmy off for breaking your windows.

(In addition, it can be useful to ask the parents if they 'pick on' their child. They will deny this hotly and say he is only punished when necessary. It is useful then, at times, to reflect back to parents the child's feeling of being 'picked on' at home also.)

Start 8 O'clock Sharp
In other words, clear rules relieve anxiety.

Imagine you are starting a new job next week. The boss says, 'Come in at a reasonable time.' You lie awake at night worrying. Does he mean 6 o'clock or is that too early? Nine o'clock, is that too late? Your anxiety is very high. If, however, he says 'Start 8 o'clock sharp' then you know where you stand. Having a clear set of rules around you helps to relieve anxiety.

Children actually can visibly relax once they start to see parents are 'setting the rules down'. They will always fight against the rules (that's what children are in business for) but deep down they like to know that the rules are there.

We were dealing some time ago with a boy who was in a great deal of trouble. We talked to him about home. He said that at home he could do as he pleased. He could come and go as he wanted. Stay up late, not go to school, drink, do whatever he wanted. Strangely his comment about this state of affairs was, 'Mum and Dad don't give a damn what I do.' In other words he *did not* see this as freedom. He saw it as neglect!

General points
Soft Foreman / Hard Foreman
This illustrates the need for a team approach. (Ask the parent for their job or previous job if they are not working now.)

Have you ever worked for two bosses, two foremen? Imagine the situation where one is easy going and one is very, very strict. You are coming to the end of your shift and you want to get away early. The soft foreman is on duty and he says, 'It's okay, leave it, you can finish it off tomorrow.' You are just putting your coat on, about to walk out of the door, when who turns up? That's right, the strict one. He gives you hell! You feel angry and upset. You're 'piggy-in-the-middle'. You'd like to say to them, 'You two sort yourselves out, then I'll know what to do.' You're angry and you still don't know whether you're allowed off early or not.

Where are children if we set two sets of rules: Mum's rules at one level and Dad's rules at another? That's right, the children are 'piggy-in-the-middle'. It's hard enough to learn one set of rules, never mind two. That's why it is much better if possible to adopt a common standard. One parent may need to ease off a little, one parent may need to tighten up a little. This allows us to present a consistent approach to the child and to leave less room for argument. There is enough to argue about in a marriage without arguing about how to handle the children.

The Liver and Bacon Story

This illustrates the need for clear communication. (Again this one can be adapted for either Mum or Dad.)

Imagine the first week after your honeymoon; you make your husband liver and bacon on his first night back at work. He actually hates liver and bacon but doesn't like to say so in case it hurts your feelings. So, having said nothing, you think he likes it – so you make it again, every week for ten years.

One night you serve up liver and bacon and he screams, 'I can't stand the damn stuff.' You're hurt and upset – quite naturally. The problem is he hasn't communicated clearly, so the issue which was put off simply became worse.

When dealing with children it's no good moaning about what they are up to yet not saying clearly, 'I don't want this!'

The Cash Register

This illustrates the need to trust – particularly important for teenagers.

Many parents nag at their children when they are going out and check up when they come back about what they have been up to. Basically what they are showing to the children is that they don't trust them.

Imagine you started a new job in a shop and you are in charge of the till. Suppose the manager is constantly checking up on what you're doing, asking if you have counted the change, making sure that you've made the money balance, etc. After a while the message would get through that he doesn't trust you. Your confidence would be undermined and you would be tempted to leave.

Children unfortunately can't leave, and yet we undermine their confidence by showing lack of trust.

Child Locked in the House

This illustrates the dangers of over-protection. Many parents want to wrap their children up to prevent harm coming to them!

Imagine you have a child who seems very vulnerable. You keep her in the house all the time, never let her go out and she plays happily in her own room. You feel she is very immature and can't be trusted out on the roads and mixing with the ordinary children. She never learns to cross a road. One day you go out and are involved in an accident and taken to hospital. The child eventually finds her way out of the house and walks straight onto the road.

So, in a strange way, by protecting children too much from harm, we actually end up as 'worse parents' as the children haven't learned to cope with difficult situations.

Visiting Friends

This illustrates how children read your reactions very easily.

Imagine you are visiting friends. They have just had a row. Even though they aren't rowing when you walk in, you can tell, you can 'cut the air with a knife'. It's not what they say, it's the way they say it. We can read emotions – children are a hundred times better. They have to be able to read every flicker of emotion on your face from day one. It's survival value for them! So, if you think you are ignoring your child, think again – he can read you like a book.

Final Warning – Things Can Get Worse Before They Get Better

When you start this approach the child's first reaction is usually to notice that things have changed – in particular she is not getting the attention she used to get. Her automatic response then is usually to try to pile on the pressure to make you respond as this has always worked in the past. If you stick to your guns, however, and continue to ignore the irritating behaviour while increasing your attention for acceptable behaviour, then eventually she will start to come round. So don't worry if things start to get worse, that means the approach is working! You just have to live through this initial difficult time.

References

Allen, A. (2009) *Evaluating Declaration and Attribution Retraining with Regards to Improvements in Reading.* Doctoral research thesis, University of Exeter.

Bandler, R. and Grinder, J. (1975) *The Structure of Magic I.* Palo Alto, CA: Science and Behavior Books Inc.

Bandler, R. and Grinder, J. (1979) *Frogs into Princes.* Moab, UT: Real People Press.

Bandler, R. and Grinder, J. (1982) *Reframing: Neuro-Linguistic Programming and the Transformation of Meaning.* Moab, UT: Real People Press.

Bandura, A. and Walters, R.H. (1963) *Social Learning and Personality Development.* London: Holt, Rinehart and Winston.

Baxter, J. and Frederickson, N. (2005) 'Every Child Matters: Can educational psychology contribute to radical reform?' *Educational Psychology in Practice 21*, 2, 87–102.

Bower, G. (1962) 'Applications of a model to Paired Associate Learning.' *Psychometric 20*, 225–280.

Burns, R. (1982) *Self Growth in Families: KFD Research and Application.* New York: Brunner Mazel Inc.

Burns, R.C. and Kaufman, S.H. (1970) *Kinetic Family Drawings: An Introduction to Understanding Children through Kinetic Drawings.* New York: Brunner Mazel Inc.

Burns, R.C. and Kaufman, S.H. (1972) *Actions, Styles and Symbols in Kinetic Family Drawings.* New York: Brunner Mazel Inc.

Department for Education and Skills (2003) *Every Child Matters.* London: DfES

Dilts, R., Grinder, J., Bandler, R. and DeLozier, J. (1980) *Neuro-Linguistic Programming 1: The Study of Subjective Experience.* Cupertino, CA: Meta Publications.

Dunsmuir, S., Brown, E., Iyadurai, S. and Monsen, J. (2009) 'Evidence-based practice and evaluation: From insight to impact.' *Educational Psychology in Practice 25*, 1, 53–70.

Festinger, L. (1957) *A Theory of Cognitive Dissonance.* Evanston, IL: Row Peterson.

Feuerstein, R., Rand, Y. and Hoffman, M. (1979) *Learning Potential Assessment Device.* Baltimore, MD: University Park Press.

Feuerstein, R., Rand, Y., Hoffman, M. and Miller, R. (1980) *Instrumental Enrichment.* Baltimore, MD: University Park Press.

Friedman, M. (2005) *Trying Hard is not Good Enough.* Victoria, Canada: Trafford Press.

Haley, J. (1973) *Uncommon Therapy: The Psychiatric Techniques of Milton H. Erickson M.D.* New York: W.W. Norton.

Imich, A. and Roberts, A. (1990) 'Promoting Positive Behaviour: An evaluation of a behaviour support project.' *Educational Psychology in Practice: Theory, Research and Practice in Educational Psychology 5*, 4, 201–209.

Kelly, G.A. (1955) *The Psychology of Personal Constructs.* New York: Norton.

Kiresuk, T.J. and Sherman, R.E. (1968) 'Goal attainment scaling: A general method for evaluating comprehensive community mental health programs.' *Community Mental Health Journal 4*, 6, 443–453.

MacKay, T. (2007) *Achieving the Vision: The Final Research Report of the West Dunbartonshire Literacy Initiative.* Dumbarton: West Dunbartonshire Council.

Mallon, F. (2006) *Goal Attainment Scaling: Evaluating EPS Service Delivery*. Available from http://www.bps.org.uk/downloadfile.cfm?file_uuid=835C9B9F-1143-DFD0-7E35-1D705F9 3A87D&ext=ppt, accessed on 18 February 2011.

Maslow, A. (1954) *Motivation and Personality*. New York: Harper and Row.

McGoldrick, M. and Gerson, R. (1985) *Genograms in Family Assessment*. New York: Norton.

Mehrabian, A. (1972) *Nonverbal Communication*. Chicago, IL: Aldine-Atherton.

Monsen, J.J. and Frederickson, N. (2008) 'The Monsen *et al.* Problem Solving Model Ten Years On. The Problem Analysis Framework: A Guide to Decision Making, Problem Solving and Action within Applied Psychological Practice.' In B. Kelly, L. Wolfson and J. Boyle (eds) *Frameworks for Practice in Educational Psychology: A Textbook for Trainees and Practitioners*. London: Jessica Kingsley Publishers.

Ravenette, A.T. (1980) 'The Exploration of Consciousness: Personal Construct Intervention with Children.' In A.W. Landfield and L.M. Lietner (eds) *Personal Construct Psychology: Psychotherapy and Personality*. New York: Wiley.

Ravenette, A.T. (1992) (unpublished) *Asking Questions within a P.C.P. Framework*. Paper to the Institute of Education, University of London.

Robbie, E. (1987) (unpublished) *The NLP Training Programme*. London.

Rogers, C. (1965) *Client Centered Therapy*. New York: Houghton Mifflin.

Salmon, P. (1988) *Psychology for Teachers*. London: Hutchison.

Siegal, G. (1956) *Non Parametric Statistics for the Behavioral Sciences*. New York: McGraw Hill.

Solity, J., Deavers, R., Kerfoot, S., Crane, G. and Cannon, K. (2000) 'The early reading research: The impact of instructional psychology.' *Educational Psychology in Practice 16*, 2, 109–129.

Strupp, H.H., Fox, R.E. and Lessler, K. (1969) *Patients View Their Psychotherapy*. Baltimore, MD: Johns Hopkins University Press.

Theios, J. (1969) 'Finite integer models for learning in individual subjects.' *Psychological Review 73*, 4, 292–307.

Watzlawick, P., Beavin, J. and Jackson, D.D. (1967) *Pragmatics of Human Communication*. New York: Norton.

Index

Printed in Great Britain
by Amazon

16510301R00159